COMPUTER GRAPHICS AND ENVIRONMENTAL PLANNING

COMPUTER GRAPHICS AND ENVIRONMENTAL PLANNING

Eric Teicholz
Harvard University

Brian J.L. Berry
Carnegie-Mellon University

Prentice-Hall, Inc.
Englewood Cliffs, NJ 07632

Library of Congress Cataloging in Publication Data

TEICHOLZ, ERIC
   Computer graphics and environmental planning.

   Bibliography: p.
   Includes index.
   1. Computer graphics. 2. Environmental
engineering. I. Berry, Brian Joe Lobley, 1934-
II. Title.
T385.T44 1983   333.7′068   82-12203
ISBN 0-13-164830-6

T
385
.C568
1983

Editorial/production supervision
  and interior design by Kathryn Gollin Marshak
Jacket design by Diane Saxe
Manufacturing buyer: Gordon Osbourne

Printed in the United States of America
10 9 8 7 6 5 4 3 2 1

ISBN 0-13-164830-6

Prentice-Hall International, Inc., *London*
Prentice-Hall of Australia Pty. Limited, *Sydney*
Editora Prentice-Hall do Brasil, Ltda., *Rio de Janeiro*
Prentice-Hall Canada, Inc., *Toronto*
Prentice-Hall of India Private Limited, *New Delhi*
Prentice-Hall of Japan, Inc., *Tokyo*
Prentice-Hall of Southeast Asia Pte. Ltd., *Singapore*
Whitehall Books Limited, *Wellington, New Zealand*

Contributing Authors

ROBERT R. BELL
Tennessee Technological University
Cookeville, TN

STEPHEN H. BERWICK
School of Forestry
and Environmental Studies
Yale University
New Haven, CT

TIMOTHY L. CHAPMAN
Computer Consultant
Sacramento, CA

DAVID J. COWEN
Social and Behavioral Sciences Lab
and Department of Geography
University of South Carolina
Columbia, SC

JACK DANGERMOND
Environmental Systems Research
Institute
Redlands, CA

C.J. EMERSON
Environmental Sciences Division
Oak Ridge National Laboratory
Oak Ridge, TN

RANDI FERRARI
Henningson, Durham & Richardson
White Plains, NY

T.K. GARDENIER
T.K.G. Consultants, Ltd.
Washington, DC

H.V. GIDDINGS
Honeywell
Minneapolis, MN

JOHN MICHAEL HADALSKI, JR.
City of Philadelphia
Philadelphia, PA

YEHONATHAN HAZONY
Princeton University
Princeton, NJ

MARK HORNUNG
Princeton University
Princeton, NJ

KAY H. JONES
Roy F. Weston, Inc.
West Chester, PA

J.M. KLOPATEK
Environmental Sciences Division
Oak Ridge National Laboratory
Oak Ridge, TN

ALAIN L. KORNHAUSER
Princeton University
Princeton, NJ

JEROME M. LUTIN
Princeton University
Princeton, NJ

ROBERT F. MILLS
Bureau of Planning and Automated
Systems, Department of
Environmental Protection
Trenton, NJ

R.J. OLSON
Environmental Sciences Division
Oak Ridge National Laboratory
Oak Ridge, TN

ALAN PALLER
ISSCO Graphics
Washington, DC

GARY C. PICKETT
Tennessee Technological University
Cookeville, TN

JOHN H. ROBINSON
Dames & Moore
Los Angeles, CA

JOSEPH T. SCARDINA
Tennessee Technological University
Cookeville, TN

J.B. SCHNEIDER
University of Washington
Seattle, WA

DENNIS R. SMITH
Dames & Moore
Los Angeles, CA

C. DANA TOMLIN
School of Forestry
and Environmental Studies
Yale University
New Haven, CT

SANDRA M. TOMLIN
College of Agriculture and Natural
Resources
University of Connecticut
Storrs, CT

SENATOR JAMES M. WADDELL, JR.
Columbia, SC

Contributing Authors

Contents

Contributing Authors   v

Preface   xvi

PART I   COMPUTER GRAPHICS IN ENVIRONMENTAL DECISION
          MAKING   1

Chapter 1   The CEQ Air Pollution Exposure Risk Model
             Kay H. Jones, Timothy L. Chapman, Randi Ferrari   3

             ABSTRACT   *3*
             THE AIR POLLUTION PROBLEM   *4*
             METHODOLOGY FOR
                THE AIR POLLUTION-HEALTH RISK MODEL   *3*
             THE ROLE OF COMPUTER GRAPHICS   *7*
             THE CO HEALTH RISK MODEL   *7*
             CONCLUSIONS   *11*
             REFERENCES   *13*

Chapter 2   A Statewide Mapping System for Generalized
Planning Analysis

Robert F. Mills   **15**

ABSTRACT   *15*
BACKGROUND   *16*
 Policy Issues and Institutional Setting, 16
 Response, 16
METHODOLOGY   *17*
 Landsat Data Base—"A Picture Is Worth 8.4 x 10⁶
  Words,"17
 Cartographic Data Bases, 18
SOFTWARE   *18*
 Landsat, 18
 Cartographic Relational Interface, 20
 Cookie-Cutter, 20
APPLICATION AND EXAMPLES   *20*
 Use in 208 Water Quality Planning, 20
CONCLUSION   *24*
 In Retrospect, 24
 The Role of Graphics, 24
STATE MAPPING SYSTEMS—THE NEXT STEPS   *27*
ACKNOWLEDGEMENTS   *28*
REFERENCES   *28*

Chapter 3   Beyond Hardware and Software:
Implementing a State-Level
Geographical Information System

David J. Cowen, Alfred H. Vang, Senator James M. Waddell, Jr.   **30**

THE DEMAND FOR A GEOGRAPHICAL INFORMATION
 SYSTEM   *30*
 The Impetus: The Coastal Zone Management Act, 31
CREATING A GEOGRAPHICAL INFORMATION SYSTEM: THE IDEAL
 VERSUS REALITY   *32*
 The First Stage: Coastal Mapping Program, 34
 Second-Stage Development: Information System, 35
 The Role of Computer Graphics and Automated
  Geographical Data Handling, 37
 Examples of Outputs from the Geographical Information
  System, 38
STATE-LEVEL APPROACHES TO GEOGRAPHICAL INFORMATION
 SYSTEMS   *44*
 The Next Step, 49
REFERENCES   *50*

Chapter 4   Program Evaluation and Policy Analysis
             with Computer Mapping

             Robert R. Bell, Gary C. Pickett, Joseph T. Scardina   52

             MAPPING AND PROGRAM ANALYSIS   *53*
             REQUIREMENTS FOR MAPPING   *53*
                 Data Files, 54
                 Address-Matching Software, 56
                 Computer Mapping Tools, 57
                 Combining Features and Data, 57
                 Selecting and Specifying the Data, 58
             DESCRIPTION OF THE TENNESSEE TECH MAPPING SYSTEM   *58*
             METHOD DESCRIPTION   *59*
             RESOURCES REQUIRED   *61*
             AVAILABLE MAPPING OPTIONS   *61*
                 Choice of Mapping Reference Areas, 61
                 Data Selection, 63
                 Overlay Mapping, 63
                 Window (or "Zoom") Mapping, 63
                 Plotter or CRT Copy Maps, 63
                 Multicolor Mapping, 63
                 Modification of Density Functions, 63
                 Histogram Support Charts, 63
             PROBLEMS ENCOUNTERED   *64*
             IMPLICATIONS OF THE MAPPING PROJECT   *64*
                 Further Applications, 64
                 A Final Note of System Effectiveness, 65
             REFERENCES   *65*

Chapter 5   A Graphics-Oriented Computer System To Support
             Environmental Decision Making

             H. V. Giddings   66

             ABSTRACT   *66*
             PROGRAM DEFINITION   *67*
             THE REAP COMPUTER SYSTEM   *69*
             FUNCTIONAL DEFINITION   *70*
             THE DATA BASE   *71*
             BROWSE   *73*
             QUERY   *76*
             MAP   *77*
             GAP   *78*
             INTEGRATED SOFTWARE   *78*
             THE MASTER MONITOR   *79*
             A SET OF TOOLS   *79*

A TYPICAL EXAMPLE   *79*
CONCLUSION   *81*
REFERENCES   *83*

PART II   COMPUTER GRAPHICS FOR REGIONAL POLICY
            ANALYSIS   85

Chapter 6   Use of Computer Graphics In Policymaking
              Alan Paller   87

ABSTRACT   *87*
THE GROWTH OF COMPUTER GRAPHICS   *88*
    Barrier 1: The High Cost of Equipment, 88
    Barrier 2: Low-Quality Output, 88
    Barrier 3: Dependence on Programmers, 90
    Barrier 4: Lack of Demand from Management, 90
EXAMPLES OF COMPUTER USE BY POLICYMAKERS   *91*
    The Special Action Office for Drug Abuse Prevention, 92
    The Equal Employment Opportunity Commission Action
        Against AT&T, 93
THE PRINCIPAL ROLE OF GRAPHIC DISPLAY IN
    POLICYMAKING   *95*
    Chart Books for Program Managers, 96
    Choosing the Right Chart, 96
ACTION PLAN FOR THE FIRST COMPUTER GRAPHICS
    PROJECT   *97*

Chapter 7   Regional Environmental Analysis and Assessment
              Utilizing the Geoecology Data Base
              R. J. Olson, J. M. Klopatek, C. J. Emerson   102

ABSTRACT   *102*
GEOECOLOGY DATA BASE   *103*
    Data-Base Design and Contents, 104
    Computer System, 106
    Data Resources, 107
APPLICATIONS OF THE GEOECOLOGY DATA BASE   *108*
    Natural Vegetation and Land Use, 112
    Wilderness-Area Evaluation, 113
DISCUSSION   *116*
REFERENCES   *116*

Chapter 8   Selecting New Town Sites in the United States Using
             Regional Data Bases
             Jack Dangermond   119

THE PROBLEM   *119*
THE METHODOLOGY   *120*
      The Process for Selecting the Region Studied, 121
      General Outline of the Process of Regional Analysis for
        New Town Sites, 122
      The Study Area, 122
      Data Collection, Image Acquisition,
        and Base-Map Creation, 122
      Image Interpretation, 124
      Data Integration and Mapping, 124
      Map and Data Automation, 124
      Data Conversion to Grid-Cell Format, 124
      Computer Modeling, 125
      Computer Mapping, 125
      Further Analysis of Candidate Areas for New Towns, 126
      Detailed Site Analyses, 127
      Resources Required, 127
THE ROLE OF COMPUTER GRAPHICS IN SOLVING THE
   PROBLEM   *132*
      Some Special Characteristics of the Methodology, 132
      Special Benefits of the Methodology, 133
EXAMPLES OF COMPUTER GRAPHICS PRODUCED   *134*
      Project Example, 134
      Color Graphics, 134
      Plotter Maps, 134
      Electrostatic Plotter Maps, 134
      Printer Maps, 135
SOME NEXT STEPS IN USING THIS METHODOLOGY   *137*
REFERENCES   *137*
APPENDIX   *138*

Chapter 9   Cartographic Analysis of Deer Habitat Utilization
             C. Dana Tomlin, Stephen H. Berwick, Sandra M. Tomlin   141

PROBLEM   *141*
METHODOLOGY AND RESULTS   *142*
USE OF COMPUTER GRAPHICS   *145*
EXAMPLES   *146*
RETROSPECT   *148*
REFERENCE   *150*

PART III   TWO COMPUTER GRAPHIC CASE STUDIES: FEDERAL
                AND LOCAL GOVERNMENT   151

Chapter 10   Graphical Display Maps Foster Regulation Policy
                T. K. Gardenier   153

                ABSTRACT   153
                RELATED QUANTITATIVE METHODOLOGY   154
                COMPUTER GRAPHICS IN IDENTIFYING STATISTICAL
                   ASSOCIATION   155
                ILLUSTRATIONS OF GRAPHICAL MAPS FOR ENVIRONMENT AND
                   HEALTH   157
                     Exploration of Interrelationships
                       through Bivariate Maps, 162
                     Advantages of Cross and Diamond Defaults, 164
                     Possibilities for Future Refinements
                       in Mapping Graphics, 165
                REFERENCES   167

Chapter 11   The Influence of Computer Graphics on Local
                Government Productivity
                John Michael Hadalski, Jr.   171

                ABSTRACT   171
                MAPPING AND LAND-DATA SYSTEMS IN LOCAL GOVERNMENT, AS
                   PORTRAYED BY THE CITY OF PHILADELPHIA   173
                THE INFLUENCE OF COMPUTER GRAPHICS ON LOCAL
                   GOVERNMENT PRODUCTIVTY   174
                TECHNOLOGICAL ISSUES IN A LOCAL GRAPHICS
                   PROGRAM   176
                POLICY AND ORGANIZATION ISSUES IN LOCAL GOVERNMENT
                   COMPUTER GRAPHICS PROJECTS   179
                CONCLUSION: THE FUTURE OF COMPUTER GRAPHICS IN LOCAL
                   GOVERNMENT   183
                REFERENCES   184

PART IV   ANALYTICAL CAPABILITIES OF GEOGRAPHIC
           INFORMATION SYSTEMS   185

Chapter 12 Computer-Aided Siting of Coal-Fired Power Plants:
            A Case Study
            Dennis R. Smith, John H. Robinson   187

            ABSTRACT   *187*
                Computer-Aided Siting, 187
                Case Study Background, 188
            SITING METHODOLOGY AND TECHNIQUE   *189*
                Site Suitability Model, 189
                GIMS—Geographic Information Management System, 189
            SITE-SELECTION CRITERIA   *190*
                Environmental Sensitivity, 190
                Cost of Construction and Operation, 192
                Power Plant Derating, 194
            SITE-SELECTION ANALYSIS   *194*
                Information Flow, 194
                Spatial Analysis, 196
                Composite Overlay, 199
            CONCLUSIONS   *199*
                Case Study Results, 199
                Summary of the Siting Method, 201

Chapter 13 Mapping Congestion Patterns on Urban Highway
            Networks
            J. B. Schneider   202

            DESCRIPTION OF THE PROBLEM   *202*
            METHODOLOGICAL APPROACH   *205*
            ROLE OF COMPUTER GRAPHICS   *206*
            EXAMPLES OF DISPLAYS FROM THE CDS   *214*
            NEXT STEPS   *219*
            ACKNOWLEDGEMENTS   *221*
            REFERENCES   *221*

Chapter 14 The Princeton Railroad Network Model: Application of
Computer Graphics in the Analysis of a Changing
Railroad Industry
*Alain L. Kornhauser, Mark Hornung, Yehonathan Hazony,
Jerome M. Lutin*   224

ABSTRACT   *224*
MAJOR ELEMENTS OF THE PRINCETON RAILROAD NETWORK
    MODEL   *225*
THE LINK-NODE NETWORK OF U.S. RAILROADS   *226*
DEMAND DATA-CARLOAD WAYBILL STATISTICS   *226*
FRA ACCIDENT/INCIDENT FILE   *228*
MODELS OF SHIPPER AND RAILROAD ROUTING BEHAVIOR   *230*
INTRACARRIER ROUTE-GENERATION
    MODEL   *230*
INTERCARRIER (QUANTA-NET) ROUTE-GENERATION
    MODEL   *232*
TRAFFIC ASSIGNMENT   *232*
PARTICIPATORY VALUE   *236*
OPPORTUNITY COST   *236*
ELEMENTARY TRAFFIC DIVERSION   *238*
ADVANTAGES OF GRAPHICS   *238*
REFERENCES   *241*

Index   243

Preface

The 1960s have been characterized as the era of computer numbers, the 70s as the era of computer words, and the 80s as the era of computer graphics. Computer graphics has extended traditional data processing methods by providing ways of communicating information pictorially.

What makes graphics the most rapidly growing segment of computer technology? What appeal does this technology hold for decision makers of all kinds? For one, computer graphics saves a most valuable and coveted resource—time. Since many types of data are already available in digital form, often with geographic location identifiers, it is relatively simple to use graphic systems to convert these numbers into charts, graphs, and maps. Time is saved not only in the production of the charts but, more important, in the interpretation and communication of complex sets of data.

The proliferation of computer graphics products has been nurtured by service bureaus and time-sharing companies, which offer customized graphic products for decision makers as well as access to specialized data bases.

A more significant reason for its growth is the role of computer graphics in the decision-making process. Information can be both digested and understood more readily when it appears visually. Trends and anomalies in data often are more readily discerned when information is rendered in graphic as opposed to numeric or tabular form. Decision makers need this ability to spot deviations in the data both for trend validation and for exception reporting. Computer graphics also provides decision makers with the ability to ask "what if" questions in order to test alternatives scenarios and depict the results quickly and efficiently.

Finally, there is the technology itself, which, given the proliferation of general-purpose software systems and color computer graphic hardware, is making computer graphics available to decision makers at all levels.

Thus computer graphics and graphic communication are now being recognized by decision makers as a powerful and convenient mechanism for exchanging information between people in a wide variety of situations. Beyond the simple depiction of the graphic image itself, these images can be used in the context of a comprehensive information system to achieve expanded analytic and representational capabilities. A geographic information system (GIS) allows a user not only to display results pictorially but also to perform a number of analytic operations on the data, interface other existent data bases, and enjoy a general-purpose data-creation capability. New geographic information systems are emerging daily. A primary reason for the recent rapid growth of computer graphics in regional planning, for example, has been the significant expansion in availability of environmental data. This has come about principally because of satellite and airborne sensors, such as Landsat, and the increasing need on the past of federal, state, and local government agencies to use these data if they are to discharge their administrative responsibilities. The magnitude of the data has called for digital computers to store, analyze, and display them and for the development of sophisticated geographic information systems.

As information systems become more general, and the human/machine interfaces more facile through the use of higher-level languages, color display devices, and the like, an increasing number of users are turning to such systems. These new users include corporate managers wanting to generate demographic data for estimating a new product's market penetration, resource-exploiting companies wanting to compare LANDSAT coverage of an area of interest with data required by traditional on-the-ground surveys, utility companies wanting to see what types of infrastructure already are underground before excavating for new sewer lines, and a myriad of other applications.

This book provides an introduction to those and similar uses. It is divided into four parts. The first gives examples of how computer graphics has been used for decision-making related to the environment. Examples include general statewide applications and specific case studies, together with comparisons of implementation scales. The second part discusses the use of computer graphics for regional policy analysis. Part III provides two case studies, and Part IV includes chapters on specific GIS analytic capabilities.

At a statewide level, Robert Mills discusses his graphic project in New Jersey related to generalized planning analysis. Cowen, Vang, and Senator James Waddell, Jr., discuss the implementation of a statewide GIS in South Carolina; and Bell, Picket, and Scardina discuss the role of computer mapping for program evaluation and policy analysis in Tennessee. Finally, Richard Giddings relates computer graphics to policy and environmental decision making for the North Dakota Regional Environmental Assessment Program (NDREA).

Chapters on environmental and management information systems include one by Alan Paller that talks about graphics in policy making by federal analysts and corporate executives. Olsen, Klopatek, and Emerson discuss environmental analysis and assessments using a geo-ecology data base; Jack Dangermond describes new-town site selection using graphics; and C. Dana and Sondra Tomlin discuss the use of graphics for deer habitat utilization.

Two chapters compare scales of implementation. The first, by T. K. Gardenier, discusses the federal government's Domestic Information Display System (DIDS) and how it is used within the federal regulatory process for prioritizing budgetary allocations by relating health benefits to changes in environmental quality. The second, by John Hadalski, describes a graphic system used for a variety of purposes by the City of Philadelphia.

Three chapters examine analytical capabilities associated with geographic information systems. Dennis Smith and James Robinson show how graphics have been used in the siting of coal-fired power plants. Jerry Schneider discusses the use of mapping to increase understanding of congestion of urban highway networks. Finally, Kornhauser, Hornung, Hazony, and Lutin describe a model developed at Princeton University for analyzing the railroad industry.

A number of approaches have been developed for designing and evaluating geographic information systems. Tomlinson and others (1976) suggest a three-stage process (Figure P-1). It includes the determination of the system's objectives (stage 1), the generation and evaluation of various system designs (stage 2), and their evaluation in terms of meeting systems specifications determined during stage 1 (stage 3).

Clearly, the array of such systems is proliferating, and a variety of investigators have attempted to develop schemes designed to categorize and codify the array. Some recent attempts include Power's "Computerized Geographic Information Systems" (1975), the International Geographic Union's "Inventory of Computer Software for Spatial Data Handling" (1976), Tomlinson and others' "Computer Handling of Geographical Data" (1976), Salmen and others' "Comparison of Selected Capabilities of Fifty-Four Geographic Information Systems" (1977), Cowen's "Coastal Plains Regional Resource Information System Study" (1978), and Knapp and Rider's "Automated Geographic Information System and Landsat Data: A Survey" (1979).

We offer our own basis of comparison, a matrix that lists and facilitates speedy comparison of the papers in this book on the basis of four sets of characteristics: subject matter; data base for the GIS; hardware environment of the GIS; and scale of the data in question.

We could, of course, have opted for a normative as opposed to a descriptive characterization of each effort.

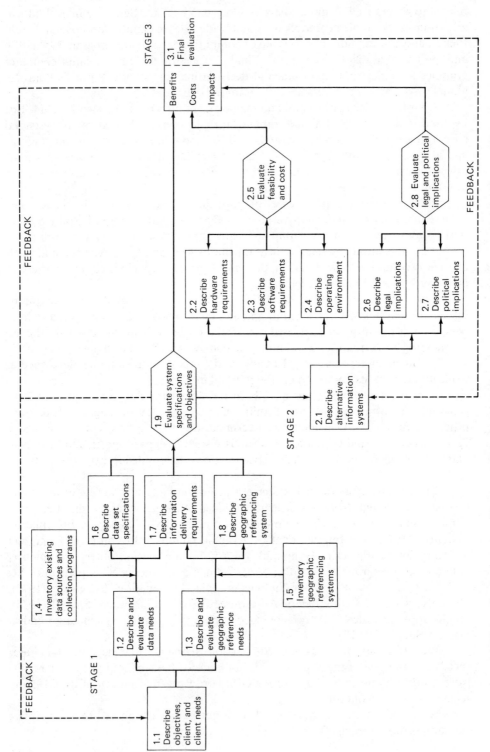

Figure P-1 Information system design and evaluation model (from Tomlinson and others, 1976, p. 16)

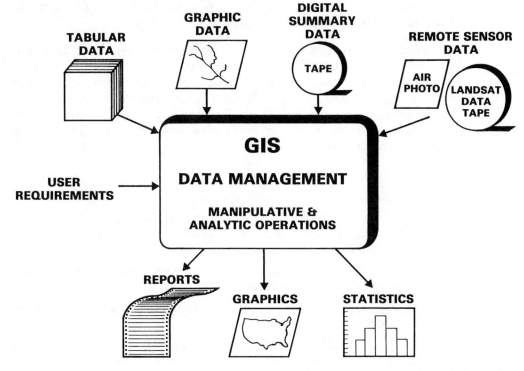

Figure P-2   Graphic representation of GIS (from Knapp and Rider, 1979, p. 58)

A geographic information system, as opposed to a management information system, has as its input geographic or location specific data (*X, Y* coordinates, a street address, latitude/longitude, and the like). Figure P-2, from Knapp and Rider (1979), graphically depicts the essential components of an idealized geographic information system.

An ideal GIS has four subsystems:

1. *Data acquisition* concerns itself with graphic and statistical data encoding and input processing. Supporting structures must encompass points, lines, and surfaces, and polygons. Encoding structures include grids and polygonal types (see Peucker and Chrisman, 1975). The merits of each type are discussed in detail by Kennedy and Meyers (1977).

2. *Data management* applies to both graphic and attribute data and deals with capabilities such as report generation, security, data integrity, and a variety of statistical reporting functions.

3. *Data manipulation and analysis* applies to both the graphic data base and the statistics that relate to the geographic areas of interest. Operations here might include projections, transformations, combination of different types of data, polygon overlay, statistical analysis on the data, and so on.

4. *Data display* relates to the ability to output maps, graphs, and tabular information on a variety of output media.

Ultimately, the test must be whether any given GIS includes each of these components, and what quality and sophistication it achieves in each. As the state of the art develops, we would expect the base to switch from mere categorical comparison to more normative assessment of purposes and capabilities. We have no doubt that in a short span of years this transition will take place. Meanwhile, we offer the essays in this book as an example of the exciting work that is taking place at the frontier of a vital new field.

REFERENCES

COWEN, DAVID J., "Coastal Plains Regional Resource Information System Study: Recent Geographic Information Systems," paper presented at the Third International Symposium on Computer Assisted Cartography, January 1978.

IGU COMMISSION ON GEOGRAPHICAL DATA SENSING AND PROCESSING, *Inventory of Computer Software for Spatial Data Handling*, 1976.

KENNEDY, MICHAEL, and CHARLES R. MEYERS, *Spatial Information Systems: An Introduction*. Louisville: Urban Studies Center, 1977.

KNAPP, ELLEN M., and DEBORAH RIDER, "Automated Geographic Information Systems and Landsat Data: A Survey." Cambridge, Mass.: Harvard Library of Computer Graphics, 1979 Mapping Collection, pp. 57–69.

PEUCKER, THOMAS K., and NICHOLAS CHRISMAN, "Cartographic Data Structures," *The American Cartographer*, April 1975, pp. 55–69.

POWER, MARGARET A., "Computerized Geographic Information Systems: An Assessment of Important Factors in Their Design, Operation and Success." St. Louis: Center for Development Technology, Washington University, 1975.

SALMEN, LARRY, JAMES GROPPER, JOHN HAMILL, and CARL REED, "Comparison of Selected Operational Capabilities of Fifty-Four Geographic Information Systems." Ft. Collins: Western Governors Policy Office, 1977.

TOMLINSON, R. F., H. W. CALKINS, and D. F. MARBLE, "Computer Handling of Geographical Data. Geneva: UNESCO Press, 1976.

CHARACTERISTICS	CHAPTER													
	2	1	10	4	3	13	9	5	12	7	8	14	11	6
Subject														
Natural Resources (Environmental)	X	X	X		X		X	X	X	X				
General Statistical Mapping	X													
Facility Location	X				X				X		X		X	
Network Analysis						X			X			X		
Health Systems		X	X											
Transportation						X						X		
Land (Parcel) Data Systems								X					X	
General Government Administration														
Modelling		X				X		X	X			X	X	
Business Applications														X
Data Type														
Line or Polygon	X	X		X	X	X	X	X	X	X	X	X	X	
Grid	X		X				X	X			X		X	
Landsat Interface	X										X			
Hardware Characteristics														
Large Processor	X		X		X	X	X		X	X		X	X	
Mini- or Micro- Processor				X				X			X			
Interactive	X		X	X	X	X	X	X	X	X	X	X		
Color Output	X		X			X					X	X		
Scale														
Local		X		X	X	X	X				X		X	
State	X		X	X	X			X	X	X	X			
Regional			X		X					X	X	X		

Part I

COMPUTER GRAPHICS IN ENVIRONMENTAL DECISION MAKING

Chapter 1

The CEQ Air Pollution Exposure Risk Model

Kay H. Jones

Timothy L. Chapman

Randi Ferrari

ABSTRACT

An Air Pollution–Health Risk Model for relating ambient air quality data, population statistics, and health impacts has been developed by the Council on Environmental Quality. The model was designed to quantify the health risks of air pollution in metropolitan areas. The concept and mechanics of the model were demonstrated by an analysis of the relationship between carbon dioxide exposure and the related increase in angina attacks for stable angina pectoris patients. This analysis demonstrated that the risk of CO exposure to stable angina pectoris patients appears to be quite low, although the authors have not necessarily concluded that the risk is low for other cardiovascular disease categories. Rather, they are advocating a method of analysis that provides greater insight into the actual risk associated with various levels of pollution. Such modeling results should facilitate sound regulatory judgments.

THE AIR POLLUTION PROBLEM

It is probably not possible to have air quality in our urban environment that is absolutely free from health risk. The nation would have to achieve zero emissions to reach such a goal. We must, therefore, accept a certain amount of marginal air quality—but how much and at what cost? The Environmental Protection Agency is presently dealing with the air pollution problem by establishing National Ambient Air Quality Standards (NAAQS) for known health-related pollutants and then applying rigid emissions-control policies with which states must comply. National emissions standards for both stationary (i.e., power plants) and mobile sources (i.e., automobiles) have been established to achieve the NAAQS by 1982 or, in some cases, 1987. By 1987 most regions of the country will experience pollution levels at or below the standards with only a handful of cities above the standards for ozone. The NAAQS are presently established by reviewing the literature to determine what pollutant levels cause significant health effects. The standard is then set below this level, thus creating a "margin of safety."

This approach of dealing with air pollution seems quite simple, until one realizes that the recognized health-effect levels and the current margins of safety are extremely controversial. There is no specific threshold at which health effects occur and below which none occur. Because of the uncertainties involved, we need to estimate the health risk or minimally the population exposure in order to make sound policy decisions on air pollution control. Costs of pollution abatement can be then compared to the benefits in reduced health risk or population exposure risk.

Analysis of exposure risk will also help focus health research on pollutant concentrations and frequencies similar to those found in the ambient environment. This approach is more useful than analyzing the effects of exposure to extreme levels of pollutants and then attempting to extrapolate downward to ambient conditions. Studies that lend themselves to the generation of continuous damage curves should emerge.

METHODOLOGY FOR THE AIR POLLUTION–HEALTH RISK MODEL

The Council on Environmental Quality developed the Air Pollution–Health Risk Model, which is illustrated in Figure 1-1, to generate health risk and/or exposure data. This model can be used to analyze either one pollutant relative to its one or more known health effects or an aggregate of pollutants and their health effects. Exposure data are generated when health-effects information is insufficient to be integrated into the model.

It is difficult to quantify directly the *in situ* health risk experienced by a population that is attributable to a single pollutant. However, one can extrapolate from clinical studies of single-pollutant effects on subsets of the population. One can also extrapolate from epidemiological studies of site-specific populations to

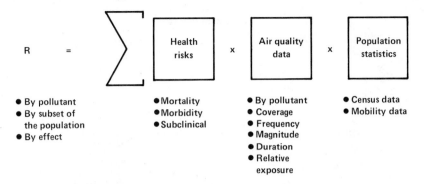

FIGURE 1-1   CEQ air pollution-health risk model.

estimate the health risk for the entire population. The functional relationship between the health risk and a particular exposure to a given pollution concentration is called a *damage function*. The most desirable form of this function is continuous; however, step functions can also be used. Most continuous functions are assumed to be linear because of the uncertainties in their derivation. Once the damage function is approximated, it can be integrated with ambient exposure information.

Risk rates for each monitoring station can be calculated by integrating the frequency distribution of pollutant concentrations (the number of days per year at each concentration) with the damage function. Integration is performed by simply multiplying, interval by interval, the number of days by the damage rate at that concentration, then summing the products. In this study it has been assumed that health risks at pollutant levels below the National Ambient Air Quality Standards (NAAQS) are either highly uncertain or relatively insignificant; therefore, the authors show the health damage function beginning at the standard (see Figure 1-2). This assumption is valid if the standard-setting protocol established by the Environmental Protection Agency is followed in a rigorous fashion. Standards are to be set with a reasonable margin of safety below those levels that are known to affect the more sensitive segments of the total population. Hence, when such standards are met, the risk to the sensitive population is assumed to be of very low probability, hence risk at levels below the standards is considered insignificant.

The frequency distribution of ambient pollution observations probably should be adjusted before use, because such measurements do not represent the actual population exposure to air pollution. Variables such as monitoring-site configuration, indoor/outdoor relationships, and near source/far source factors must be considered. Despite all these confounding factors, fixed-monitoring-station data can be used as a surrogate for population exposure if the influence of these factors on actual exposure can be reasonably accounted. The indoor/outdoor and near source/far source relationships have been examined in a separate CEQ paper by Jones and Ferrari, (1978).

The public health risk of ambient air pollution is generally a problem in urban areas, because population densities are high and most pollution impacts occur there. Therefore, the appropriate geographical unit to analyze is the Standard Metro-

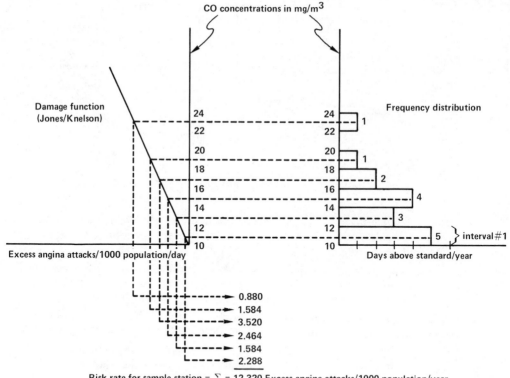

CO concentrations in mg/m^3

Damage function
(Jones/Knelson)

24	24	1
22	22	
20	20	1
18	18	2
16	16	4
14	14	3
12	12	5 } interval #1
10	10	

Frequency distribution

Excess angina attacks/1000 population/day

Days above standard/year

0.880
1.584
3.520
2.464
1.584
2.288

Risk rate for sample station = Σ = 12.320 Excess angina attacks/1000 population/year

$- - - \blacktriangleright$ Dotted arrows signify integration process

Formula used: $0.176 \times \left(\begin{array}{c} \text{concentration in mg/m}^3 \quad - \quad \text{CO standard in mg/m}^3 \\ \text{of interval midpoint} \qquad\quad \text{[or the Y intercept]} \end{array} \right) \times \text{frequency} = \text{Risk rate}$

For example, interval #1: $0.176 \times (11-10) \times 5 = 0.880$

FIGURE 1-2 Methodology for risk calculations.

politan Statistical Area (SMSA). Population statistics are available for SMSAs down to the census tract level. The total population at risk within the SMSA is derived in the following way: The risk rates are integrated with (simply multiplied by) the population data at the census tract level and then summed over all census tracts. Subsets of the total population, representing those individuals susceptible to the health effect being evaluated, can be used in lieu of the total census tract population. For example, these subsets can isolate age, sex, race, income, and disease categories or any combinations thereof.

Air pollution levels in central business districts tend to be quite different than in the surrounding suburban areas. For example, high carbon monoxide (CO) levels tend to be localized, occurring in downtown street canyons with high traffic volumes; the transport and transformation of hydrocarbons tend to cause higher levels of ozone in suburban areas downwind of the urban centers that produced the high hydrocarbon emissions. Therefore, mobility of the population should be considered when estimating population exposure. In order to estimate the change in population exposure that results from the influx of people into the center city during the day, two sets of population figures can be derived: census-tract resident population (Census Bureau data) and census-tract population during working hours derived by subtracting the census-tract residents employed from the resident population and adding the number of workers in the census tract.

The Census Bureau's 1970 Urban Transportation Planning Package analyzed the number of workers in census tracts, but only a small percentage of the population in a few urban areas was sampled. Better data will be available from the 1980 Census. If population exposure occurs during working hours, the risk rates should be integrated with "at work" population figures. Population exposure occurring throughout the day may require a segmented approach in which different risk rates are used for the same population but at various times and locations—for example, four hours at work downtown, one hour commuting, and three hours at home.

THE ROLE OF COMPUTER GRAPHICS

This model uses computer mapping for creating isopleth lines of risk rates derived from ambient air monitoring data and for plotting the populations at risk by census tract. Machine-readable files of the two maps are integrated, and the resultant cross-product may in turn be mapped. Harvard's SYMAP package was chosen for this application largely because it produces both isopleth and choropleth maps in the same output format—a line printer file—thus facilitating integration.

In this article the risk data are visually presented by an overlay of the isopleth lines of risk on population-density maps from the Census Bureau's Urban Atlas, which are also created by computer graphics. The data could also be presented by plotting the total risk calculated for each census tract. These figures are calculated by multiplying the population census-tract data times the interpolated risk rates within each census tract.

THE CO HEALTH-RISK MODEL

Carbon monoxide is emitted almost exclusively by cars and other gasoline-powered vehicles. Variation of CO levels is caused by changes in the emission rates and traffic densities normally associated with the morning and evening rush hours. High CO concentrations can stress persons with cardiovascular disease because it combines more easily with the oxygen-carrying hemoglobin in the blood than oxygen, forming carboxyhemoglobin (COHb) and thus constraining oxygen transport to the heart muscle. The Air Pollution–Health Risk Model has been used to assess CO exposure effects on stable angina pectoris patients. The model quantifies the health risk by estimating the annual number of excess angina attacks associated with daily CO exposure. It is estimated that 2.1 percent of the national population suffers from stable angina pectoris. Most stable angina patients suffer from one to five involuntary attacks per day from all causal factors (Knelson, 1975).

The 1975 CO data used in this study were from UPGRADE's Pollutant Standards Index (PSI) data base, which contains daily maximum eight-hour average values retrieved from the Environmental Protection Agency National Aerometric Data Bank. Hard-copy summary data for the entire nation were reviewed to locate those SMSA's that had at least three stations showing violations of the National Ambient CO Standard. The SMSA's were screened in this manner because three data points were considered the minimum necessary for mapping purposes. In this review, 26 SMSA's qualified. The data were then screened to eliminate any stations that monitored less than approximately half the year and/or had fewer than 100 days of monitoring. After this screening twenty SMSA's had at least three stations with violations (see Table 1-1); nine SMSA's were analyzed for this report. Philadelphia had the highest number of stations monitoring CO but had the worst yearly coverage of the twenty SMSA's that met the screening criteria.

The CO risk rates were derived from integration of the frequency distributions of days above the NAAQS for CO (10 mg/m^3) produced by the UPGRADE system with the damage function developed by Jones and Knelson (1979), as shown in Figure 1-2. The Jones/Knelson damage function illustrates the relationship between eight-hour CO exposure and the number of additional angina attacks expected per 1000 population. The Jones/Knelson function is based on three clinical studies (Anderson, 1973; Aronow, 1972; Aronow, 1973) that related the decreased time to onset of angina attacks to CO exposure. This decrease in time to onset of an attack was translated into risk of additional attacks. Because the relationship between blood carboxyhemoglobin levels and CO exposure is known, the risk of additional

TABLE 1-1   SMSA's with Three or More Stations Having Violations
and Sufficiently Monitoring CO in 1975

SMSA Name	Number of Stations	Number of Stations Having Violations
*Boston	6	4
Chicago	12	7
Dayton	3	3
*Denver	6	6
Detroit	5	3
Los Angeles	13	13
*Louisville	9	9
Milwaukee	9	4
Minneapolis	4	3
Newark	4	4
New York	16	10
Oakland	10	4
*Philadelphia	17	12
*Phoenix	8	7
*Portland	5	5
Riverside	14	8
*St. Louis	9	8
*Seattle	4	4
*Washington, D.C.	11	9
Wichita	4	4

* SMSA's included in this study

attacks can be equated to eight-hour CO exposure using the formula: percent COHb = 0.144 × mg/m³ CO (NATO/CCMS, 1972). It is assumed that an eight-hour daily maximum value will achieve saturation of COHb in the blood. Saturation means that a maximum level of COHb has been reached for the level of CO exposure. Any further exposure to that CO level will not increase the COHb in the blood.

The calculations in Figure 1-2 produces a risk rate in attacks per 1000 population per year for the station analyzed. As discussed previously, any stations with all values below 10 mg/m³, the national standard, were assigned risk rates of zero. In this analysis, the frequency distributions were not adjusted for indoor/outdoor variation. It was assumed that the entire population was being exposed to monitored levels. This obviously yields conservative estimates.

The isopleth lines of risk rates are overlaid on the population density map in Figure 1-3 for Denver. The numbers on the isopleth lines represent the annual number of excess angina attacks experienced per 1000 population as a result of CO exposure. The number in the center of the isopleths is the highest calculated risk rate in the SMSA. For illustration purposes, only part of the SMSA was used, because

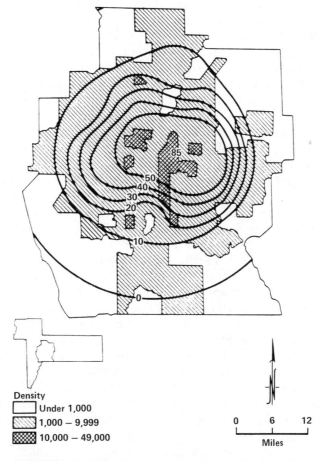

Density
Under 1,000
1,000 – 9,999
10,000 – 49,000

0   6   12
Miles

FIGURE 1-3   CO-related angina attacks, Denver 1975.

TABLE 1-2   Per Patient CO Related Angina Attack Rates for 9 SMSA's

SMSA name	Average number of attacks/SMSA	Average number of attacks at worst location	Average number of attacks at worst location/worst day
Philadelphia	0.0004	0.0012	0.042
Washington, D.C.	0.0006	0.0031	0.092
Boston	0.0008	0.0030	0.059
St. Louis	0.0005	0.0038	0.260
Seattle	0.0002	0.0034	0.092
Denver	0.0037	0.0011	0.159
Portland	0.0015	0.0048	0.025
Phoenix	0.0013	0.0065	0.126
Louisville	0.0024	0.0170	0.159

risk occurred primarily near the center city. The census tracts surrounding the center-city area had much lower population, low or no CO violations, and hence negligible or no angina risk as a result of CO exposure.

There are several ways to analyze these data. One can analyze the risk experienced by individual patients in reference to their locations, or one can analyze the total risk experienced by stable angina pectoris patients resulting from their CO exposure in the SMSA. Cardiologists try to minimize the number of attacks that their patients experience, either by reducing environmental factors such as stress and exercise or by prescribing drug therapy or both (Haak, 1978). Risk is therefore best expressed in terms of excess attacks per patient. The annual attack rate by SMSA allows one to compute the average daily risk of attack per angina patient. Further, the site-specific risk numbers provide for calculating average daily and maximum daily risk by location within each SMSA. These data for the nine SMSA's studied are shown in Table 1-2, where the average daily and maximum daily risks by location are calculated only for the area having the highest risk within each SMSA. These rates are conservative, because they are related to outdoor CO measurements that are near the source. It appears that the SMSA average daily risk is quite low, 0.0002 to 0.0037 attacks per patient. The average daily per patient risk in the highest exposure areas of each SMSA appears low as well, 0.0011 to 0.0170 attacks. The day with the highest level of CO at the site that most frequently violates the standard represents a maximum risk of approximately 0.025 to 0.260 attacks per patient for that one day. Recall that all these risks are for the base year 1975.

In terms of relative risk, it does not appear that CO exposure contributes significantly to the stable angina attack risk attributable to all causes. If we assume that the average stable angina patient currently suffers from one to five attacks per day, CO exposure appears to contribute a maximum of 0.122 percent of the total angina attack risk in the worst SMSA analyzed (see Table 1-3). SMSA's other than Denver have estimated CO risk levels of 0.007 to 0.079 percent of the total angina attack risk. Denver's CO risk level is 0.122 percent of the total attack risk, causing 34.1 thousand attacks. Although this analysis has yet to be done for Los Angeles and New York City, one would expect their rates to be similar to that in Denver because of similar air quality profiles.

TABLE 1-3   Annual Angina Patient Risk Data for 9 SMSA's
(thousands)

SMSAS	Population	Total Attacks	CO-Related Attacks	CO-Related Attacks as Percent of Total
Philadelphia	4,816	111,000	16.0	0.014
Washington, D.C.	2,860	65,800	13.7	0.021
Boston	2,753	63,300	15.7	0.025
St. Louis	2,362	54,300	8.3	0.015
Seattle	1,421	32,700	2.2	0.007
Denver	1,227	28,200	34.3	0.122
Portland	1,006	23,100	11.9	0.052
Phoenix	936	21,500	9.2	0.043
Louisville	826	19,000	15.1	0.079

The predicted risk in Denver, assuming the expected 50 percent reduction in emissions by 1985 and using a proportional rollback model, is illustrated in Figure 1-4. Because the reduction in violations is disproportional to the reduction in emissions (Jones, 1977), an 85 percent decrease in the number of predicted excess angina attacks per year as a result of CO exposure is forecast, which calculates to 5.1 thousand attacks. This statistical phenomenon is illustrated in Figure 1-5, in which the areas under the curves and to the right of the air quality standard line represent the number of violations in days above the standard. The upper end of the predicted distribution, the maximum daily concentration, is 50 percent less than the present maximum daily concentration, and the shaded area of the predicted distribution is 85 percent less than the present distribution.

CONCLUSIONS

The CEQ Air Pollution–Health Risk Model has provided greater insight into actual air pollution health impacts by producing visual and quantitative estimates of health risk and damage. The model is currently being used to analyze those pollutants for which SMSA specific data appear to be adequate vis-à-vis the health-related criteria pollutants. Although the current monitoring coverage for these pollutants is controversial, we find that most of the more polluted cities meet monitoring guidelines.

In analyzing the risk rates due to CO exposure for angina pectoris patients, they appear quite low, although the authors are not rendering a judgment as to the medical significance of the results. Rather, the authors are providing a methodology for translating clinical findings into estimates of the relative contributions of air pollution to all causes of a particular disease. The medical experts can then, with appropriate recognition of the uncertainties involved, render opinions as to the significance of the air pollution insult.

Besides making this specific risk analysis, the model can make a general exposure analysis simply by calculating person-day exposures to a particular pollutant. There is a maximum total number of exposure days for an SMSA (above a determined pollution level) of 365 multiplied by the total population of the SMSA.

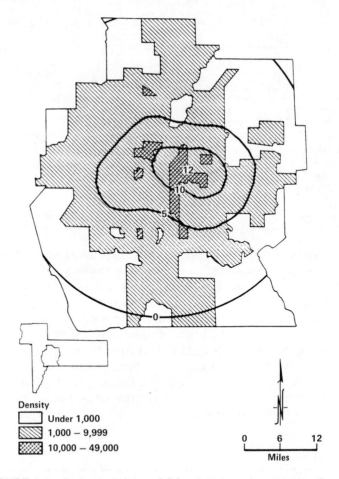

FIGURE 1-4 Projected risks of CO-related angina attacks, Denver 1985. Note: a figure on an isopleth is the number of attacks per thousand per year. (Source: based on U.S. Environmental Protection Agency SAROAD data system and U.S. Bureau of the Census data).

This analysis is useful for determining total exposure and making case-study comparisons of residual pollution problems associated with various pollution-control scenarios. It is hoped that such analysis will replace emissions residuals, percent deviation from a single-pollutant concentration, and other vague indicators of public health impacts that appear in most current air quality planning documents.

Further applications of the model can be made by substituting emissions data for ambient air data. This flexibility is useful for making risk analyses when no ambient data exist. When data on emissions and ambient air quality are both available, the mapping package in the risk model will give insight into the spatial relationships of the two.

When they become less cumbersome computer graphics will become more effective in solving air pollution problems.

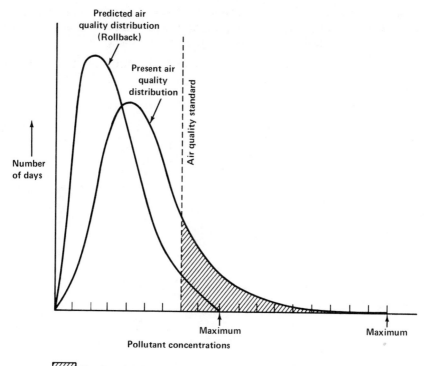

FIGURE 1-5 Observed and predicted air quality before and after controls are applied.

REFERENCES

ANDERSON, E., R. J. ANDELMAN, J. STRAUGH, N. FORTVIN, and J. H. KNELSON, *Ann. Intern. Med.,* **79,** 46–50 (1973).

ARONOW, W. S., C. N. HARRIS, M. ISBELL, S. N. ROKAW, and B. IMPARTO, *Ann. Intern. Med.,* **77,** 669–676 (1972).

_____, and M. W. ISBELL, *Ann. Intern. Med.,* **79,** 392–395 (1973).

HAAK, E., Health Effects Research Laboratory, Office of Research and Development, Environmental Protection Agency, 1978.

JONES, K. H., *CEQ Projections of Ozone Air Quality in 1990.* Springfield, Va.: National Technical Information Service, 1977.

_____ and R. L. FERRARI, "Development of a Relative Exposure Factor for the CEQ Health Risk Model." Council on Environmental Quality, 1978.

_____ and J. H. KNELSON, "A Continuous Stress Function Relating Ambient Carbon Monoxide Exposure and Angina Pectoris Attacks," *Council on Environmental Quality Annual Report,* June 1979.

KNELSON, J. H., "General Population Morbidity Estimates from Exacerbation of Angina Pectoris Related to Low-Level Monoxide Exposure." Environmental Protection Agency, Health Effects Research Laboratory, August 1975.

NATO/COMMITTEE ON THE CHALLENGES OF MODERN SOCIETY, *Air Quality Criteria for Carbon Monoxide*. Washington, D.C.: Government Printing Office, 1972, p. 7–13.

Chapter 2

A Statewide Mapping System for Generalized Planning Analysis

Robert F. Mills

ABSTRACT

Geographic base files of municipal boundaries and watersheds have been congruenced with Landsat data for the entire State of New Jersey. The three data sets have been geometrically adjusted and related to the New Jersey State Plane Coordinate System. A statewide computer mapping system using these data has been operating for two years and has evolved into an integrated system for graphic and statistical analysis. A color graphics CRT is the principal display device, with a light-pen allowing the user to take full advantage of the interactive nature of the system. Analytic maps can be produced based on a variety of information, ranging from population, housing, and employment to Landsat interpretations by watershed or political jurisdiction. The completion of a 208 Water Quality Management project for one-third of the state, and initiation of new applications such as DOE-sponsored Coastal Energy Impact Planning and a HUD Technical Assistance Grant to federate with the data of other agencies, indicate the increasing role of computer geographics as a cost-effective tool. The future of computer mapping in New Jersey will witness involvement by many state agencies. While technical improvements will continue, the development of a more comprehensive state information system is dependent upon institutional problems and interagency cooperation.

BACKGROUND

Policy Issues and Institutional Setting

The U.S. District Court decision mandating state responsibility for 208 Water Quality Management Planning in areas that had not been initially designated to receive 208 funding generated a fair degree of chaos in New Jersey, as in other states. Since the huge initial round of funding had been almost entirely expended on the "designated areas," planning in "nondesignated" areas, or 31 percent of the state, had to be carried out by state agencies that were simultaneously facing severe cutbacks from traditional sources of planning funds, and a general "Proposition 13" mentality. At the same time, public pressure for good planning, particularly with regard to the environment, was increasing.

New Jersey was far from unique in responding to this problem by employing computer graphic techniques and Landsat satellite data for land use requirements of the 208 program. In this case, the Division of State and Regional Planning, an arm of the Department of Community Affairs, proposed the idea to the Department of Environmental Protection, which had direct responsibility for the 208 program. Long experience with manual mapping techniques indicated that an automated technique was necessary to stay within the remaining 208 budget. We also had several years of experience-testing our own computer graphic software and felt that it offered a means of achieving the 208 needs at minimum cost.

Response

Early in proposal preparation for the 208 effort, it was realized that the large proportion of the state to be analyzed offered an opportunity to pole-vault from what was then an architecture for a statewide information system (Jones, 1975) into an operational system with implications broader than 208. The amount of effort required for a county-by-county automated approach was in some ways more imposing than the technical problems to be solved in creating a monolithic system to handle all counties, and it would have left us with a typical "case-study" system; the history of pilot projects indicates that they have relatively little success when applied to the larger problems they intended to anticipate.

A further impetus to go for all the marbles was an ongoing project with Princeton University to digitize the state's municipal boundaries and watersheds. We realized that completion of this project should be expedited owing to its crucial role in 208 of disaggregating land-cover acreages from Landsat by watershed, municipal, and county jurisdiction.

The Division therefore ambitiously committed itself to:

1. Achieve a statewide Landsat data base that could be used directly and flexibly by planners.

2. Complete the editing of the statewide cartographic data base of 567 municipalities and 21 counties begun a year earlier.

3. Digitize a statewide map of 145 watersheds (first, second, and third-order basins).

4. Merge the three data sets by relating them to the New Jersey State Plane Coordinate System.

5. Develop interactive software for their joint use, and

6. Use all of the above in a project to map one-third of the state's area for 208 needs.

METHODOLOGY

Landsat Data Base—"A Picture Is Worth 8.4 × 10⁶ Words"

Staff examined Landsat images in the NASA/Goddard browse facility and selected a group of three successive scenes taken on July 18, 1976. Before using the data, however, it was desirable to convert them to a form more amenable to analysis. The Landsat data are distributed in four computer tape files per scene, with each file comprising a vertical strip of the data. Since it took three scenes to cover the state, twelve tape files had to be merged into one comprehensive tape of the data for New Jersey.

In addition, the data came in a complicated scrambled format, which would have to be unscrambled each time they were used. Therefore, a program was developed that simultaneously extracted the appropriate data for New Jersey from the individual quarter-scene strips, unscrambled the format, remerged the data, and stored the result on another tape. The new image created was a rectangle of 3891 by 2157 pixels, or 8,392,887 pixels (picture elements). Since each pixel required one word of computer storage, a picture of New Jersey is worth considerably more than a thousand words.

The final preprocessing phase was to geometrically correct the Landsat data. This had to be done quite accurately over the entire area of the state, so that the Landsat data could be related to the cartographic data bases (described below), thereby yielding land-cover maps and statistics aggregated by municipality or watershed.

Software obtained from H. K. Ramapriyan of Computer Science Corporation was used to "rubber-sheet," or geometrically adjust, the raw Landsat data for the entire state. The importance of applying the geometric correction to the raw data, rather than a categorized map data set, cannot be overemphasized. One advantage of this approach is that it permits a variety of maps to be generated from the same raw data base, without the necessity of correcting each output map separately.

Secondly, training analysis to categorize the raw data (described below) is incomparably easier given a geometrically correct raw data plot that can be compared directly with ground truth. Finally, only by having the raw data corrected can we construct a fully automated system for an entire state that can be related to municipal and watershed boundaries in a flexible and convenient way for planners. Using this approach, staff can simply type a place name and obtain the corresponding raw data or a categorized map according to their preference, or they can make some unsuspected use of the data.

Cartographic Data Bases

In cooperation with Princeton University, the boundaries of the state's 145 first-, second-, and third-order watersheds and its 567 muncipalities (including shoreline features as well as political jurisdiction) have been digitized. The resulting data have been transformed to a link-listed random-access chain file structure, as described previously (Mills, 1979). All component polygons of the municipal file and most of the watershed file have been utilized operationally, and the files are now quite reliable.

SOFTWARE

Landsat

The conventional technique of using sample areas of known land cover to develop spectral signatures for land types from Landsat data was employed to calibrate the raw digital data to map categories useful for planning. Interactive software written by the author enabled this to be carried out easily by student interns with backgrounds in natural resources, rather than by computer technicians with no training in natural processes. This system, known as ARGOS, has been in use since 1973 and has evolved to meet the needs of a large spectrum of users. The students found that they could conduct useful analyses of the digital data with two or three hours of experience on the system. "Bulletproofing" the dialogue ensured that they would not receive intimidating system messages and codes. Cues and instruction on system use were built into the dialogue.

The ease of use of the software is hinted at in Figure 2-1, which illustrates the naive user's approach to the system. The user's commands are in lower-case letters, computer responses in capitals.

The mapping process may be capsulized as follows. Starting with a small area (window), the user correlates "training sites" with specific types of land cover with corresponding areas in the Landsat data. The user then uses the interactive software to obtain signatures for each of the ground-cover conditions to be mapped, and a small area is classified according to those spectral responses. This map of the window is reviewed and, if necessary, further training sites are analyzed. Once a window has been mapped accurately, the signatures used for the area may be used as mapping coefficients for a county or watershed. These maps are then analyzed, and if warranted, further training is done. Since most analyses of the Landsat data are

```
argos
WELCOME ABOARD LANDSAT...
YOU ARE NOW 514 NAUTICAL MILES ABOVE THE SURFACE OF THE EARTH
COURTESY NASA, THE DEPARTMENT OF ENVIRONMENTAL PROTECTION,
AND THE DEPARTMENT OF COMMUNITY AFFAIRS, STATE OF NEW JERSEY

THE FOLLOWING WINDOWS ON NEW JERSEY AND VICINITY ARE
AVAILABLE FOR YOUR IMMEDIATE ANALYSIS:

BRIDGETN ERTS        A4

WHAT IS THE FIRST NAME OF THE WINDOW YOU WOULD LIKE TO USE?
.bridgetn
EXECUTION BEGINS...

14:24:15    OCTOBER 5, 1981

PLEASE TYPE A COMMAND OR HELP
.help

THIS IS A MENU OF POSSIBLE TYPES OF ANALYSIS
YOU CAN PERFORM ON THE LANDSAT DATA USING THIS PACKAGE:

    PIXEL           DISPLAYS THE RAW LANDSAT BRIGHTNESS VALUES
                    FOR INDIVIDUAL PIXELS

    HISTOGRAM       DISPLAYS THE FREQUENCY DISTRIBUTION HISTO-
                    GRAM OF THE BRIGHTNESS LEVELS OF ANY BAND
                    THE NORM OF ALL BANDS, OR THE UNIFORMITY MEASURE

    LEVEL-SLICE     PRODUCES A LEVEL-SLICED (SEGMENTED) CHARACTER MAP
                    OF ANY SINGLE LANDSAT MSS BAND
                    THE NORM OF ALL BANDS OR THE UNIFORMITY MEASURE
                    WITH USER-DEFINED DATA LEVELS AND MAPPING CHARACTERS

    EDIT            ALLOWS YOU TO DISPLAY, EDIT, MERGE
                    DELETE AND ENTER NEW TRAINING STATISTICS

    TRAINING        PERFORMS SUPERVISED STATISTICAL ANALYSIS
                    WHICH TRAINS THE COMPUTER TO RECOGNIZE LAND-COVER TYPES

    CLASSIFICATION  PRODUCES A CHARACTER MAP USING
                    THE EUCLIDEAN-DISTANCE METHOD

    MAXIMUM         PRODUCES A CHARACTER MAP USING THE
                    MAXIMUM-LIKELIHOOD ALGORITHM

    WINDOW          ALLOWS YOU TO CHANGE THE VIRTUAL WINDOW
                    SIZE AND COVERAGE FOR CONVENIENCE OR FOREIGN TERMINALS

    MASK            ALLOWS YOU TO RESTRICT THE WINDOW BY LEVEL-
                    SLICING CRITERIA. THIS IS USEFUL IN WATER-QUALITY ANALYSIS

    STOP            PERMITS YOU TO CHOOSE A NEW
                    WINDOW OR QUIT

PLEASE TYPE A COMMAND OR HELP
```

Figure 2-1   Novice's use of Landsat software

conducted in an interactive processing mode, training and mapping of windows can
be repeated quickly as needed, which greatly expedites the mapping process.

Extensive analysis of Landsat data generated vast amounts of statistical data
relating to the spectral characteristics of land cover. All training signatures were
cataloged on disk by land-cover type and geographic area. This library of information, in conjunction with more sophisticated hardware received after 208 project
completion, eliminated much of the intermediate mapping. Since it is now feasible
to use previous training results to map new areas, more emphasis can be placed on

updating maps via graphic editing on the CRT, as described below. This increased efficiency of producing large-area land-cover maps has lowered the cost to approximately $3 per square mile, including staff time and computer costs.

Cartographic Relational Interface

The next problem encountered was how to relate the Landsat data and the cartographic data bases in an efficient and convenient way for the planner, for surely there can be no quicker way to discourage potential system users than to require them to learn computer jargon, abstract coordinate systems, or complicated numerical coding schemes for municipalities they know easily by name.

A program was therefore developed that enables the user to select by name a municipality, group of municipalities, county, or watershed to be analyzed. The computer then performs a simple table look-up to find the appropriate polygon code and corresponding geographic data. The program can then call the "cookie-cutter" programs that control processing of the Landsat data.

Cookie-Cutter

The cookie-cutter software was so named because its function (in a somewhat more esoteric domain) is the same as that of its kitchen counterpart: to extract the material appropriate to a polygon (cookie) from a monolithic mass of gridded data (dough). Readers with experience in computer graphics will recognize that doing this with Landsat data is a somewhat complicated case of the classic region-infilling problem. The solution employed here was a combination of artificial intelligence (line following) and brute force (sorting). The combination of the algorithms to do this with those for efficient data management and image classification of the huge mass of Landsat pixels in a statewide system, and the simultaneous segmenting of the results for line-printer output, present interesting programming problems.

APPLICATION AND EXAMPLES

Use in 208 Water Quality Planning

Staff selected "test municipalities," one per county in the 208 area, for intensive training analysis on the Landsat data, developing spectral signatures which were then extended to surrounding areas. This concept proved generally successful.

However, as larger and physiographically diverse regions were analyzed, each class of land cover showed a broader range of spectral response. This necessitated the use of numerous spectral signatures in order to accurately classify the variations within each category. For example, the variety of crops planted within a county is wider than those planted in a municipality. Also, the styles of development change from one area to another. Bare soil varies considerably in its reflectance. Thus, a land-cover category consists of numerous subsets or components, each requiring a unique spectral signature. Without exception, the first test map of each county contained several misidentified areas. Consequently, further training outside the test municipality was necessary. Training statistics were generated from the misidenti-

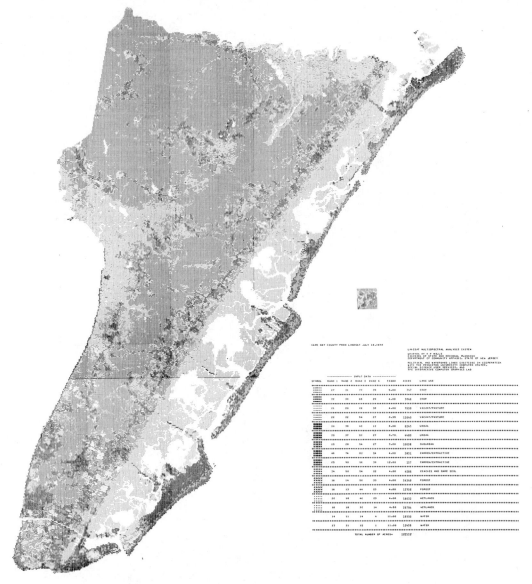

Figure 2-2 Line printer map of land cover by county.

fied areas, analyzed for their utility, and incorporated into countywide maps (Figure 2-2), and watershed maps (Figure 2-3).

In order to establish some measure of accuracy for the Landsat maps, sample areas containing significant geographic features were compared with aerial photographs and first-hand knowledge of the staff. The maps have shown a maximum of 15 percent misclassification, with most samples containing less than 10 percent (Dwyer, 1978).

However, despite a campaign to educate the Public Advisory Committees of

Figure 2-3 Line printer map of land cover by watershed.

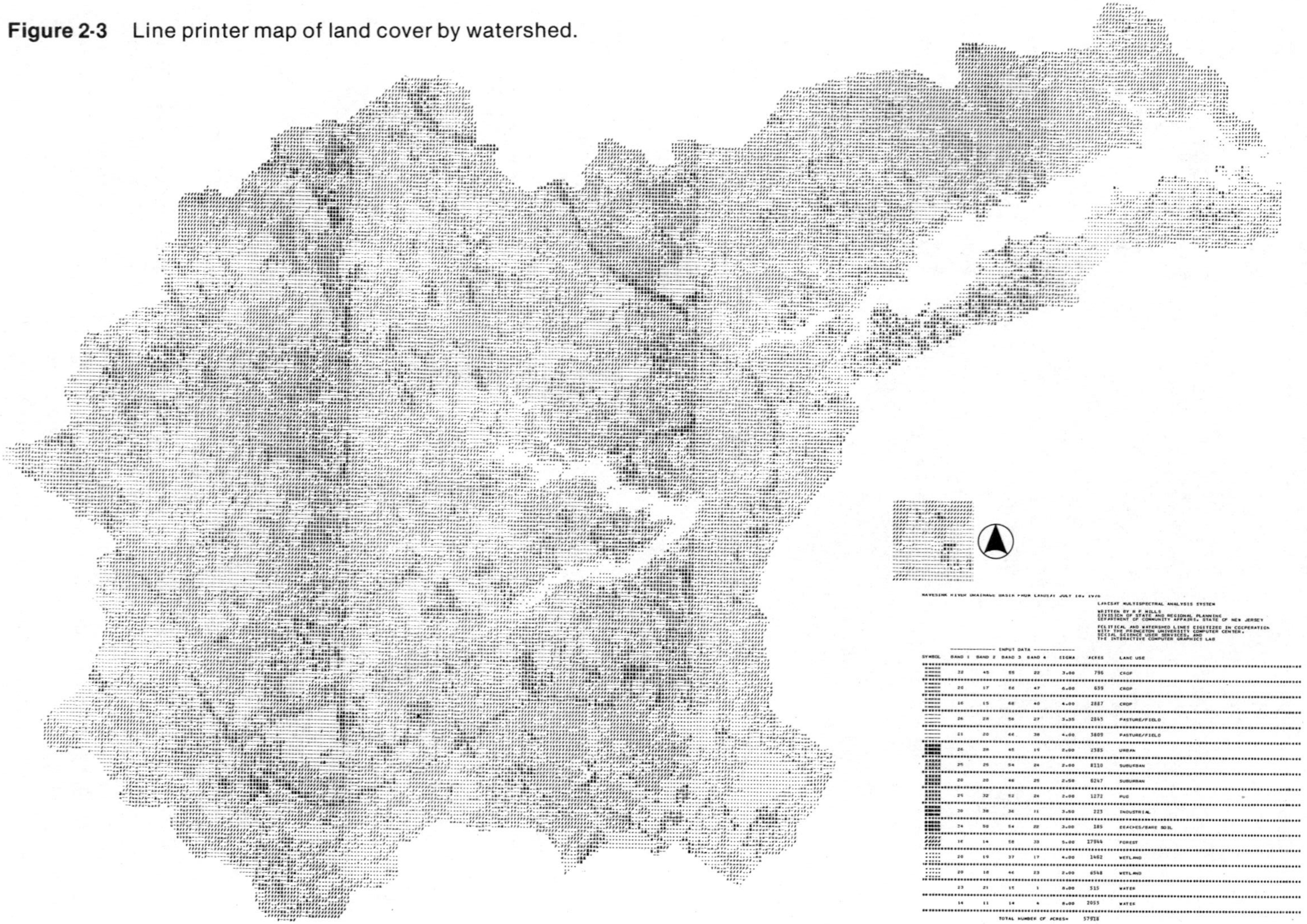

22

the various 208 areas, we found considerable resistance to the gray-scale maps used to portray land-cover types. We also discovered that it was essential to emphasize that land-cover patterns were being depicted, not land use. The emphasis on terminology was necessary to ensure that individuals using the data would interpret them properly. Areas of different land use may be similar in terms of their land cover. This can result in areas of pure land use being mapped as a mixture of land cover. For example, many suburban areas are actually a mixture of houses, roads, and vegetation (lawn, shrubs, trees). Although the land use is homogeneous, the actual land cover is not.

Additional difficulties arose in evaluating county and watershed land-cover acreages with respect to conventional sources. First, conventional data could not account for 100 percent of the land cover for any geographic province. As much as 20% of total acreage was unaccounted for in conventional inventories; our mapping system classified all acreages into one of eight categories. Second, most conventional sources could only (at best) be used for comparison with county-level acreages, and only for certain types of land cover or land use. For example, all crops statistics from conventional sources deal with *harvested* cropland, or agricultural pasture. We used Landsat to interpret planted cropland, agricultural and non-agricultural pasture, fields, and lawns (open space). There were similar ambiguities with open water, because the Bureau of Lake Management included shoreline acreage in their data. Although some data were useful, most could not be disaggregated to meet our needs. Subsequently, most of the training using our summer 1976 Landsat data was done with spring 1972 aerial photography as a guideline. The difference of four years and one season allowed for significant alteration of land cover.

Problems also occurred with the type of graphic display used in-house. A color raster graphics CRT with light-pen had been ordered near the beginning of the project, with the following objectives:

1. quicker, more accurate training
2. some type of color output (even photographic) for public meetings
3. staff massaging of the land-cover data with the light-pen to correct residual classification errors

When delivery of the terminal was postponed by the vendor, these goals were temporarily scuttled. As a result:

1. Training analysis was slower and less accurate than expected, owing to the use of a typewriter terminal.
2. We had to train for categories that existed only in isolated areas of certain counties, instead of merely changing them graphically with the light-pen and software.
3. Public suggestions for improving the maps could not be incorporated.

A final negative aspect of the project was the particular set of Landsat images chosen. The time of year presented extensive problems with bare soil, owing to mid-summer replanting, that could have been avoided with earlier or later imagery.

CONCLUSION

In Retrospect

The positive aspects of the 208 project outweighed the difficulties encountered. In addition to accomplishing its immediate goal of mapping the land cover of 31 percent of the State of New Jersey for water quality management purposes, the program significantly advanced our ability to apply automated graphic techniques to planning problems.

The most important stride was in making what was theoretically a statewide capability for landcover analysis an operational system, conveniently used by planners rather than intermediate computer technicians. We now have a data base consisting of Landsat data in 1.14-acre cells for the entire state. Another giant step was the completion of the geographic base files of all watersheds and municipal boundaries in the state. We also have the software for using these data, and updating them if desired, firmly established and tested in a full-blown statewide project, as opposed to test cases.

The availability of these three data files, referenced to the New Jersey State Plane Coordinate System, will be an important planning resource for years to come. Further, their development provides the basis for a new generation of mapping products that will increase with accuracy over time, rather than degrade with constant manual redrafting.

The Role of Graphics

Another important phase in the development of the geographic information system commenced after completion of the 208 project, when a color raster graphics CRT was obtained. Although we had been utilizing cartographic data bases and Landsat data for some time, this was the first piece of specifically graphic equipment obtained. The important points realized with this device were:

1. It could display and overlay hierarchical cartographic data bases using lines of different colors, greatly clarifying topological relationships.
2. It could display dense pictorial information in color, easing the analysis and display of Landsat and other gridded data.
3. It permitted direct graphic interaction with the data, making possible the maintaining, editing, and updating of the data bases.

The first two of these points were operationally critical; we had been laboring for some time with effective display for neither the cartographic data bases nor the Landsat data. We had remote access to line printers for gray-scale overprint maps (i.e., we could drive four miles to pick up output the day following analysis), and local display was limited to a ten-character-per-second hard-copy terminal.

The third point is more subtle, but in our estimation equally crucial, because it enabled us to more actively pursue a long-term goal of hybrid human-machine intelligence applied to graphic problems, linking human spatial pattern recognition and nonquantitative decision making with the computer's capacities for data reduction, statistical pattern recognition, and drafting. Operating in an interactive mode, the user is now able to edit Landsat displays and to input personal knowledge of an area; edited versions can be stored and retrieved for future use; maps are fully annotated with political or watershed lines, legends, acreage summaries, scale, north arrow, and so on; and images can be copied onto tape in a format compatible with color or black-and-white hard-copy facilities at NASA Goddard Space Flight Center (Figure 2-4).

We quickly discovered that even environmentally concerned citizens of long-term residence could not orient themselves well to maps solely of land cover by watershed outline, sans the accustomed features of USGS quadrangles. However, the ability to overlay such simple cartographic references as municipal bounds in contrasting colors or as blinking lines on the land-cover base clarifies the situation immensely. (Since even the detailed one-acre grid of Landsat confuses those unaccustomed to seeing the earth's surface as discrete samples, simple annotations such as a square-mile scale are also of great help.) For staff use, tests of overlaying experimental soils data produced by SCS' Advanced Mapping System on land-cover maps have also been made, and they indicate the enormous potential that comprehensive synthesis of these data will provide.

The ability to interactively produce choropleth maps in color is also proving to be of great use. Software links between the municipal geography file, demographic data, and the "cookie-cutter" have enabled us to produce eight-color maps that would be difficult to produce manually. For example, a simple linear regression model was used to produce maps of year-2000 population density by minor civil division (MCD) for 208 water quality planning. The process is quite cheap; a map of MCD's for a particular county costs about five dollars to produce.

The importance of this graphic technique lies more in its ease of application than in its sophistication. The planner who has this approach available can conduct exploratory data analysis in a spatial fashion, which cannot be done casually when relying on manual cartography. One immediate result in our analysis of data that would otherwise have been presented in tabular form was the detection of errors in data that had been considered sacrosanct. A confusion in coding data for several towns with similar names, which had existed for several years undetected, became immediately apparent when a township was plotted with a color indicating higher population density than the boro it surrounded. While this is not an impossible situation, it is an unusual one; however, it only appeared unusual by virtue of its presentation to the eye in a form that was amenable to human spatial pattern recognition: a *color* transformation of population *density*.

All of the above, of course, requires software as well as hardware. In the rapidly changing world of computer graphics peripherals, however, it is often difficult to define where and how the software should be applied. Operations previously performed on the host computer are being replaced with terminal firmware. To add to the confusion, still other functions will of necessity be required both in firmware (for strictly graphic display) and in host software (for data-base manipulations). A

Figure 2-4 Black and white map of Union County land cover.

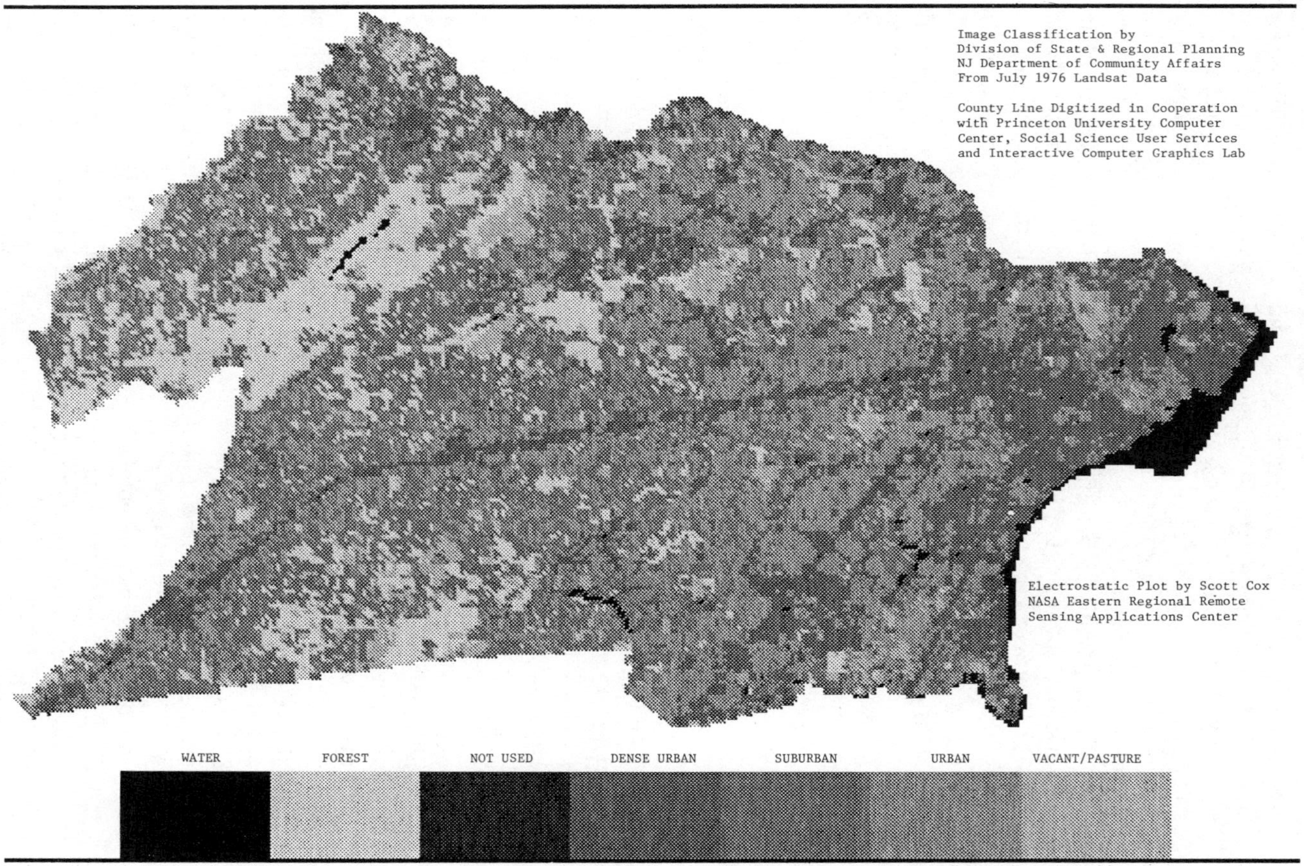

Image Classification by
Division of State & Regional Planning
NJ Department of Community Affairs
From July 1976 Landsat Data

County Line Digitized in Cooperation
with Princeton University Computer
Center, Social Science User Services
and Interactive Computer Graphics Lab

Electrostatic Plot by Scott Cox
NASA Eastern Regional Remote
Sensing Applications Center

WATER   FOREST   NOT USED   DENSE URBAN   SUBURBAN   URBAN   VACANT/PASTURE good example of this is the cookie-cutter, or region-infilling requirement, which can validly be applied both for data analysis and as a graphic display tool.

STATE MAPPING SYSTEMS—THE NEXT STEPS

Many agencies in the state have taken interest in the potential applications of computer cartographic techniques. In December 1978 the Division of State and Regional Planning cosponsored a symposium on satellite remote sensing and computer graphics. This conference was attended by professionals from various state, county, and private agencies and universities. The purpose was to illustrate how computer graphic and remote sensing technologies can be used in various areas of planning. As a result, three Landsat pilot projects involving the state's Department of Environmental Protection have been initiated with NASA, and interest has been shown in exploring the development of other digital cartographic data bases.

There is currently no formal effort in the state, however, to develop an interdepartmental system to service common cartographic needs. To some extent this may be attributed to lack of foresight, but a real question remaining for states, corporations, and other large consumers of computer graphics is the organizational location of capabilities. The trend seems to be toward a centralized, service-bureau type of system, similar to centralized traditional DP services. This is generally seen as a step up from the natural evolutionary path of in-house capabilities in several agencies, which results in parallel systems functioning independently—but we wonder whether it is not instead a step to the side. While centralization enables the multiple users to apply more combined financial leverage to equipment, personnel, and maintenance costs, if taken to an extreme, it inserts intermediary staff and can create logistical problems for users.

One logical solution would be a distributed approach, with centralization of certain expensive hardware (e.g., mainframe, if needed, array processor, digitizer, and bulk storage devices) and specialized skills (computer cartographers, systems programmers). Appropriate software would then allow applications skills, soft-copy graphic peripherals, and certain data bases to reside with the agencies requiring them.

Whatever physical approach is implemented, however, the major problems facing an incipient state system are institutional rather than technical. The Department of Environmental Protection has the largest volume of cartographic needs together with significant funding sources for those needs, and therefore it feels it has a major claim to jurisdiction over mapping activities. The Division of State and Regional Planning believes its previous financial leadership and technical expertise in automated mapping indicate a major role in the evolving system. The Department of Transportation is officially designated to service DP needs of both agencies, and it has its own mapping needs. The Treasury's Division of Data Processing and Telecommunications supervises acquisition and operation of equipment by all of the above, seeking to protect and maximize the state's overall investment. Lack of inter- (and intra-) agency coordination, and even outright bureaucratic paranoia in some cases, makes a cooperative endeavor difficult to initiate.

One thing we have learned in the application of computer graphic techniques is that the common conception that automation will make mapping cheaper is a misconception. When one had to make paper, grind inks, construct a drafting pen, and so on in order to make a map, they were expensive, one-of-a-kind things. With the development of printing techniques, the per-map cost declined, but since it was possible to mass-produce maps, the overall expenditure on them increased enormously. Today, technology makes it possible to conduct exploratory analysis of spatial data, and ironically, brings us full circle back to one-of-a-kind maps; the ability to quickly draft new maps, rather than simply reproduce existing ones, will be exploited fully, leading eventually to the concept of personalized maps, custom-crafted by automated means, and even greater total expenditure on maps. These personalized maps may eventually supplant, to a large extent, mass-produced maps made for the average person. We all know that the clothes made for the average person never quite fit us; similarly, maps can't convey their full information content when limited by a "one size fits all" approach.

Finally, owing to the current mismatch between soft-copy and hard-copy raster mapping technologies, we are currently dealing largely with "fugitive maps," analogous to the fugitive literature on the frontier of scientific research. It remains sufficiently difficult and expensive to reproduce maps made with soft-copy raster technology that only maps of great interest are copied before the screen is erased. Further, there is no adequate way to distribute dynamic maps that are produced by computer, such as the Harvard Lab for Computer Graphics' *American Graph Fleeting,* or CRT equivalents. With the declining cost of computer graphic peripherals, however, distribution of phsyical map copies may prove unnecessary.

By definition, we exist in conflict between the maps of the past and the maps of the future. The maps of the past have a long history of use that has inured us to their quirks and enables us to use them with relative ease. We have had no such period to become accustomed to the vagaries of the maps of the future, if they may be so called, but they make feasible certain cartographic operations that are otherwise expensive or impossible.

ACKNOWLEDGEMENTS

The work described herein was conducted under the aegis of the Division of State and Regional Planning, New Jersey Department of Community Affairs. The author wishes especially to acknowledge the contributions of Dennis Jones, who was the seminal thinker in computer graphics in New Jersey, and John Dwyer, source of several of the more coherent passages of this paper.

REFERENCES

DWYER, J. L., "An Evaluation of Satellite Mapping for Water Quality Management Planning." Division of State and Regional Planning, 329 West State Street, Trenton, N.J., 08625 (1978).

JONES, D. K., and others, *A Coastal Area Information System for the New Jersey Department of Environmental Protection: A Feasibility Study.* Bureau of Regional Planning,

Division of State and Regional Planning, N.J. Department of Community Affairs, 329 West State Street, Trenton, N.J. 08625, 102 pp. (1975).

MILLS, R. F., "An Operational English Dialogue System for Statewide Integration of Polygon and Landsat Data." Harvard Library of Computer Mapping, 1979 Collection, Vol. 4, Center for Management Research, 850 Boyleston Street, Chestnut Hill, Mass. 02167 (1979).

Beyond Hardware and Software: Implementing a State-Level Geographical Information System

David J. Cowen
Alfred H. Vang
Senator James M. Waddell, Jr.

THE DEMAND FOR A GEOGRAPHICAL INFORMATION SYSTEM

The involvement of the federal government in areas of environmental concern during the past two decades has imposed an enormous burden on state governments to develop mechanisms for complying with the mass of technical and administrative requirements accompanying each new program. As one recent account suggests, "The primary task of state agencies in natural resource management is to move rapidly and efficiently to identify the resources that require management to see that they are protected. Information gathering is always subservient to these goals" (American Society of Planning Officials, 1975). In order to meet these goals, new technical and administrative programs for gathering, organizing, and analyzing pertinent information in a meaningful fashion have been created. "This process is rather complicated, as it involves assembling a vast array of natural resources, the development pressures acting upon it, and the actions necessary to protect it'' (American Society of Planning Officials, 1975). Furthermore, collection and integration of these data must be achieved within limited budgets, as well as personnel and time constraints.

When one recognizes that presently the federal government has more than 130 programs requiring some form of analysis of land- and water-related data, the inevitable confusion and inefficiency that result become understandable. States frequently react with frustration, since they believe that they have been dealt administrative and technical problems for which they are neither adequately compensated nor prepared. Subsequently, in order to receive their state's fair share of the taxpayers' money, they find themselves reluctant customers of federal programs.

This chapter discusses the process through which the State of South Carolina implemented an automated geographical information system to meet some of these requirements. Although the original system was designed to meet the needs of the Coastal Zone Management Act, the evolutionary process discussed should be representative of the experiences that other states involved in automated geographical data handling would encounter. The chapter essentially presents a case history of an incremental approach to the conceptualization, design, construction, and operationalization of a system in which a state university played a major role.

The Impetus: The Coastal Zone Management Act

The passage of the federal Coastal Zone Management Act of 1972 (PL 92-583) singled out the fragile ecological system of the coastal zone for special environmental attention. As finally passed, the Act relied upon the states to develop and establish administrative procedures to enforce a coastal zone management plan. Specifically, the act mandated that the states involved designate

1. coastal zone boundaries
2. permissible uses
3. areas of particular concern
4. areas of preservation
5. areas of priority uses
6. organizational structures

The determination of the first five of these items requires the detailed analysis of a diverse set of related geographical data. As one of the states covered by the Act, South Carolina was forced to formulate a program for handling such information.

The requirements of the 1977 South Carolina Coastal Zone Management Act indicate considerable faith in the technical ability of the newly established Coastal Council to inventory and model data relating to the coastal zone. Specifically, the Act charged the Coastal Council with

1. Undertaking the related programs necessary to develop and recommend a comprehensive management plan
2. Examining, modifying, improving, or denying applications for permits for activities

3. Managing estuaries and marine sanctuaries and regulating all activities therein

4. Establishing, controlling, and administering pipeline corridors and location of pipelines used for the transmission of any form in a critical area

5. Directing and coordinating the beach and coastal shore erosion control activities (Code of Laws of South Carolina, 1976)

Further, as part of the development of the Coastal Management Program the Council was responsible for the following specific tasks:

1. The identification of present land uses and coastal resources

2. The evaluation of these resources in terms of their quality and quantity and capability for use both now and in the future

3. The determination of the present and potential use and the present and potential conflicts in use of coastal resources

4. The inventory and designation of areas of critical state concern in the coastal zone, such as port areas, significant natural and environmental, industrial and recreational areas (Code of Laws of South Carolina, 1976)

These functions imposed an immediate need for the South Carolina Coastal Council to develop certain analytical tools, as well as a sophisticated geographical data handling system in which display was simply one component.

CREATING A GEOGRAPHICAL INFORMATION SYSTEM: THE IDEAL VERSUS REALITY

Ideally, an information system should be developed only after all the potential users have met, discussed, and agreed upon specific objectives and the operational environment. Calkins and Tomlinson have documented the difficulty of this task at the state level. They provide a useful inventory of the critical decisions that must be made during the design stage. These relate to questions concerning data acquisition, scale, classification systems, storage, file structure, centralization of the system, user access, institutional arrangements, authority to operate, and data confidentiality. They suggest that the number of combinations of alternatives available could easily reach more than 700 million (Calkins and Tomlinson, 1977). Furthermore, the literature in the field now provides the basis for the development of a model of proper steps to follow in designing, building, and operating a successful geographical system.

According to this model the initial stage in the evolution of any system should involve a statement of need on the part of a group of users. Typically, the initiation of a natural resource information system has emanated in response to a specific planning function. Dueker (1975) suggests that there are six such functions:

1. Policy planning
2. Program planning
3. Land inventory
4. Impact analysis
5. Land capability analysis
6. Regulatory activities

Intuitively, many believe that automation will accomplish any one or all of these functions better, quicker, or cheaper than manual procedures. Once the user group has begun to outline a conception of the system, it usually produces a broadly defined, grandiose goal, such as "to provide better information for wise decision making." Armed with such a vague goal statement, the users attempt to attract a sponsoring group. In light of the considerable number of federal, state, and local programs requiring analyses of geographical data, sponsors willing to support an innovative approach to data handling have not been too difficult to acquire in recent years.

Once the financial commitment has been assured, the users, in conjunction with designers, data collectors, and administrators, must begin to develop specific objectives for the system. These objectives usually address one or more of the following six tasks outlined by Dueker (1975):

1. Measurement, association, and display
2. Record keeping and monitoring
3. Locational analysis
4. Diffusion studies
5. Spatial interaction
6. Trend projection

According to Marble and Calkins (1976), in order to accomplish any of these tasks several components must be designed. In fact, they maintain that separate subsystems must be developed to handle problems relating to

1. Management
2. Data acquisition
3. Data input
4. Retrieval and analysis
5. Information output
6. Information use

At the design stage the various components and parameters of the system should also be precisely defined. After a thorough search of existing methodological approaches, several alternatives should be selected for detailed evaluation in terms of their individual benefits and costs. Only after a detailed benchmark test has been conducted can the system be prepared. During a pilot study the users, sponsors, designers, data collectors, and administrators should work closely together in order to establish the proper feedback channels that will promote each individual's understanding of his role within the system and an empathy for the problems encountered by the others.

The idealized system, of course, can never become operational until the subsystems have been tested and it has been demonstrated that they can perform together efficiently. In order for this to occur, all of the appropriate training sessions must have been conducted; documentation of each aspect must be available in a looseleaf notebook; a well-managed public relations plan must have been implemented, both to inform users of the benefits and to ensure that the sponsor can demonstrate the value of the new systems; and marketing and distribution policies that will maximize the utilization of the system over the first five years must be well-formulated. Additionally, data collectors in various agencies must have been convinced that only through the collection of accurate, timely, and relevant data will wise decisions be made. The public, too, must be assured that only through the use of the modern system can a perfect balance between economic development and environmental protection possibly be achieved. Finally, the designers and implementers must have been allotted at least ten years and several million dollars to bring the system into full production (Kennedy and Meyers, 1975).

Such idealized models serve as valuable reminders of the enormous gaps that exist between expectations and reality. During its evolution, the South Carolina system faced severe constraints in terms of forced deadlines, limited financial and personnel resources, faulty understanding and communication of needs, and incomplete knowledge of concepts and institutional arrangements, which resulted in a developmental process that has deviated significantly from the ideal. The developmental process can be separated into two stages. The original stage was dominated by an in-house development of an automated cartographic system designed to meet a specific objective, while the second stage involved the creation of a full-scale set of hardware and software capabilities in anticipation of demand. Both these stages necessitated a close partnership between the state and the university. The second stage drew upon the experience gained during the first. It is clearly recognized that several obstacles remain before the system can be declared a fully institutionalized success.

The First Stage: Coastal Mapping Program

The original cartographic system was basically created in a vacuum by programmers who were attempting to meet a loosely defined objective stated by the Coastal Council. The resulting digitizing and plotting system met the objective for a display and led to the production of a series of updated maps. Nevertheless, the first development faced a number of obstacles that limited its probability of success. While the obstacles listed below pertain to the South Carolina experience, they are probably symptomatic of any such undertaking:

1. Unclear specification of system needs by the user

2. Limited understanding of geographical data concepts on the part of users
3. Poor understanding of geographical data concepts on the part of designers
4. Overselling of system capabilities
5. Unclear demarcation between research and development and production
6. Physical distance (of 120 miles) between users and production staff
7. Unclear definition of responsibilities
8. Difficult verbal communications between users and production staff
9. Poor hardware performance
10. New hardware components
11. Evolution of geographical data-base concepts

Many of these obstacles were to be expected and could have been resolved only through what Dueker and Talcott (1977) consider to be an incremental approach. In fact, one theory in public administration suggests that this type of evolution is characteristic of any learning experience that necessarily involves a great deal of "muddling through" (Lindblom, 1959).

Second-Stage Development: Information System

In the summer of 1977 a serious research effort began to conceptualize and specify the requirements for a sophisticated multipurpose geographical information software system. Unlike the original design stage, this effort was more systematic. Of course, a number of changes had occurred since 1974 when the first system had been developed. From the viewpoint of the coastal mapping program the most significant changes were

1. The evolution of a serious body of literature regarding computer cartography and geographical information procedures
2. A significant improvement in polygon-based geographical data-handling procedures
3. Considerable experiences regarding the capabilities and limitations of automated methods by both users and designers
4. The involvement of geographers and cartographers in the conception and design of a new system.

Each of these factors greatly improved the chances for designing and constructing a successful system.

After a careful review of the relevant literature, considerable discussion with system users, administrators, and designers, and extensive interviews and consultations with other groups with similar needs, the basic system objectives were outlined. These goals suggested the need for a set of polygon-based procedures that would allow for

1. Flexible entry of point, line, and area data
2. Ability to handle various coordinate systems
3. Ability to analyze, manipulate, and display polygons
4. Ability to interrelate and model various data elements

Underlying the search process was the assumption that the state of the art had reached the point where a polygon-based system was feasible.

The development of specific components of the improved system was based on a positive assessment of the already existing system. These components included an excellent hardware configuration, an experienced programming staff, and an excellent data entry, editing, storage, and display system. The favorable appraisal mandated that any new software would be installed on the IBM mainframe and would have to be available in source code.

Pressures from various sources dictated that the step from the concept and design stages to the construction and operational stages would have to occur more rapidly than would have been desired. From the federal perspective South Carolina was in the final year of eligibility for 305 Coastal Zone Management funds. Future resources would be dependent upon the implementation and administration of the Section 306 Management Plan. On the state level there already existed a backlog of permit applications awaiting systematic evaluation. Therefore, the constricted timetable precluded in-house software development and forced us to search for a compatible system that could be installed at the University. Over a two-year period two major geographical information systems were acquired, installed, and put into production. A number of valuable interim products have been developed, and the staff has become well versed in the technical components of the systems.

In an effort to alleviate some of the organizational difficulties relating to the system a series of management changes have been implemented. Geographers and cartographers who are familiar with map design, spatial relationships, and applications have been installed in key positions to aid in supervision of map preparation, digitizing operations, and communications. Research and development staff have been separated from production operations. Responsibilities have been more clearly defined. For example, contractual arrangements, including specifications of inputs and outputs and scheduling, are being handled by the Office of Geographical Statistics of the Division of Research and Statistical Services. That office, which includes the state cartographer and state geographer, also provides the staff for the state's Mapping Advisory Committee. As such, it can provide an essential linkage between the university Computer Services Division and the various agencies. By serving as a liaison group, it can reduce ambiguities that often arise while also giving the staff of the Computer Center more specific guidelines and priorities.

User groups are now sheltered from direct communication with computer scientists. Promotion of the system is now being conducted in a more conservative fashion with considerable emphasis on demonstration projects that make use of existing capabilities. By having an operational system available, new users are able to clearly specify the products they desire without having to become involved in an expensive and time-consuming development process.

While this approach may sharply deviate from the ideal development models, it is essential to the future success of the system. By establishing the technical capability first, demand is now being created through the natural resource agencies. Fortunately the university and state have been able to cooperate in the production of the system.

The Role of Computer Graphics and Automated Geographical Data Handling

From its inception, the coastal mapping program has been premised on the assumption that automation would offer an efficient, rapid, and cost-effective approach to data collection and analysis. In fact, 24 percent of the 1974 Coastal Zone Management grant of $198,000 was devoted to a computer-oriented system in which "general inventory data were digitized, processed and stored" (South Carolina Coastal Zone Planning and Management Council, 1974). There was an underlying belief that the general concepts of computer mapping had advanced to a stage that could create a dynamic system that would enable the state to rapidly update various data items, as well as supply specific information for management decisions.

The evolution of the automated mapping system at the University of South Carolina was the result of a fortuitous series of circumstances rather than a well-designed plan. Late in 1974 it was decided that the original coastal mapping program operated by the Charleston County Planning Office had outgrown the county's computing resources. The digitizing and plotting equipment was then moved to the Computer Services Division of the University of South Carolina. The move permitted a greatly expanded computer capacity as well as an opportunity to develop on-line digitizing and editing capabilities. In addition to maintaining the excellent hardware facility, the university was committed to the further development of a graphics system that would serve both the public and academic communities. This continued commitment has been augmented and enhanced throughout the last six years.

The role of major state universities in the development of state-sponsored automated systems is a provocative one. It is difficult for a state-supported institution to ignore the needs of state agencies, especially when they are physically adjacent to each other in the same city. More important, public service activities have recently assumed an increasingly significant role in such universities. Consequently, the research and development activities of their faculty and staff reflect this growing interest. In fact, many significant developments in the field of automated cartography in particular and geographical data handling in general have emerged from just such institutional settings. Instead of viewing such public service activities as a necessary evil or a way to support themselves in the summer, an increasing number of researchers are finding that the state government represents an exciting real-world laboratory.

The development of the Coastal Mapping Program at the university was shaped by the constraints of already existing hardware and software systems. The university was basically a large IBM shop, oriented to batch processing. There was considerable disk storage, and IMS was available for data-base management. APL represented an interactive language that had graphics capabilities. Utilizing these resources, the graphics staff created a set of procedures for the input, graphical display, and editing of the data that included selective data retrieval and preparation for plotting. In fact, the on-line editing functions developed by the staff represent one of the only such APL-based systems in existence. Since many of the functions could be quickly displayed on a Tektronix storage tube, it was possible to demonstrate the system at remote locations via telephone lines. Subsequently the system has been enhanced through the addition of an IBM mass-storage device, an electrostatic plotter, backlighted digitizing tables, and, most recently, a Kongsberg 5000 Flatbed Plotter that has scribing capabilities. Software is now maintained through IBM's VSPC system.

Examples of Outputs from the Geographical Information System

During six years at the university the geographical information system has steadily improved its capabilities for the production of computer-generated outputs. The system presently can produce not only a variety of displays on different output devices but also a full range of sophisticated analytical tools. The overriding philosophy has been that automated cartography is but one component of the total geographical data handling picture. Accordingly, computer-produced graphics must be more than an art form generated on fancy equipment. The ultimate success of the system is a function of the ability of digital geographical data handling to be integrated into the planning and management process. The following examples illustrate the potential of these possibilities.

The original coastal mapping program was designed solely to revise outdated 7½-minute U.S. Geological Survey (U.S.G.S.) quadrangles. The digitizing and plotting system that was originally developed at the Charleston County Planning Council was based on the assumption that a map is a set of lines. Each line on the source materials was therefore designated by a certain line type. This scheme included linear features, such as roads and single-line creeks, as well as boundaries around natural and political areas. For example, the line surrounding a brackish marsh could be subdivided into a number of boundaries, such as lowmarsh/brackish marsh, brackish marsh/upland, and fresh marsh/brackish marsh. Each of these boundary types was given two numerical codes that identified the areas separated by the line. These codes were entered into the data base as the line was digitized. The display programs selected the specific line types from the data base and plotted them in a choice of four colors with a variety of line types (Figure 3-1).

With the passage of the South Carolina Coastal Zone Management Act it became obvious that planners and policymakers required more than visual display from the data base. For example, a specific requirement for the Coastal Zone Management Plan was an inventory of land use within the coastal zone. This necessitated the development of an information system that could treat geographical data as areas or polygons. Fortunately, in April 1978 the Geography Program of the USGS announced that the Land Use and Land Cover Maps for the coastal part of the state were available. The Geography Program also agreed to transfer and assist in the installation of their Geographical Information Retrieval and Analysis System (GIRAS), which was capable of inputting, analyzing, and displaying this information (Mitchell and others, 1977).

CHARLESTON QUADRANGLE

Coastal Zone Wetlands

Topographic

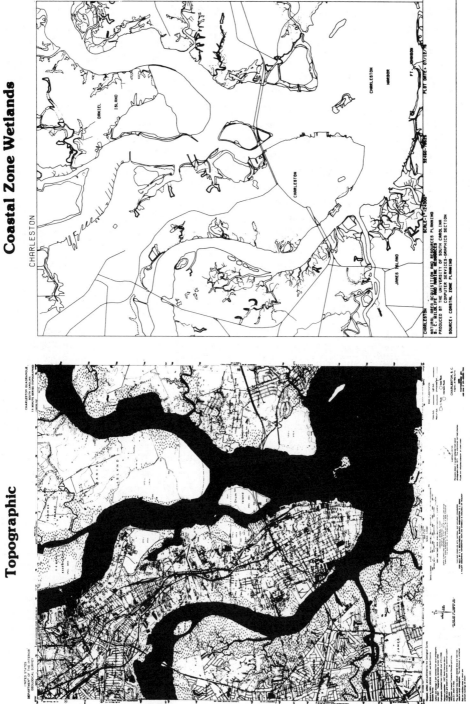

Figure 3-1 Comparison of the computer-generated Charleston, S.C. quadrangle with the original U.S.G.S. version.

When GIRAS arrived in June, it was evident that the installation, testing, and production efforts must overlap one another. Only a considerable effort by the personnel of the Geography Program and the university would make the transfer and installation of the software possible. The importance of the data to the management plan, coupled with the desire of the U.S.G.S. to have their data utilized in the project, motivated substantial efforts by both groups. Considering that some parts of the software were still being developed, and that the U.S.G.S. is not in the software transfer business, the transfer went quite smoothly, and the programs were operational within two months.

The GIRAS software was immediately utilized to create the maps and statistics required for the Coastal Zone Management Plan. Digital files, supplied by the U.S.G.S., combined with files digitized in South Carolina, formed the basis for a Level I (Anderson and others, 1976) land-use and land-cover map for an eight-county region along the state's coast (Figures 3-2 and 3-3). Scribes of the Level I land-use categories and a finer Level II wetlands map originally compiled by the Coastal Council were produced on a Kongsberg plotter. These two maps were combined to produce the final photographic product.

In addition its graphics capabilities, GIRAS was employed to overlay the land-use file with both political boundaries and the critical area boundaries of the coastal zone. These overlaid grid files were then used to generate a detailed inventory of land use and land cover both within and outside the critical zone for each county (Figure 3-4). Thus, after a period of only five and a half months, the GIRAS software had been successfully transferred, installed, tested, and put into production.

The acquisition of GIRAS represented a major step in meeting a number of software needs, as well as aiding in production of excellent interim products. The state is presently involved in a cooperative program with the Geography Program to digitize the remainder of the land-use/land-cover data for the state. These data, combined with the capabilities of GIRAS, will constitute an extremely fertile base for analysis of land use.

The acquisition of GIRAS and the subsequent development of the products for the Coastal Council were independent of a search for a commercially available software system. In fact, the installation of GIRAS occurred concurrently with the development of a detailed demonstration project for the evaluation of the PIOS and GRIDS systems of the Environmental Systems Research Institute (ESRI). After considerable research, it had been determined that the ESRI software systems most closely met the specified modeling and analytical capabilities within the hardware constraints of the university. The demonstration project was designed to evaluate the performance of these capabilities on a detailed set of tasks.

The demonstration project consisted of a simulation of a search for a potential site for a barge terminal in a coastal area. The inputs for the analysis required the digitizing of fourteen different variables for a four-guadrangle area in Georgetown County, S.C. These variables included land use/wetlands, soils, elevation, zoning, utilities, flood-prone areas, and water quality, in addition to selected point data, such as historical sites and rookeries. Thirteen additional variables, including slope and distance measures, were generated from the original variables through the various programs in the GRIDS system. The resultant 27-layer data file, consisting

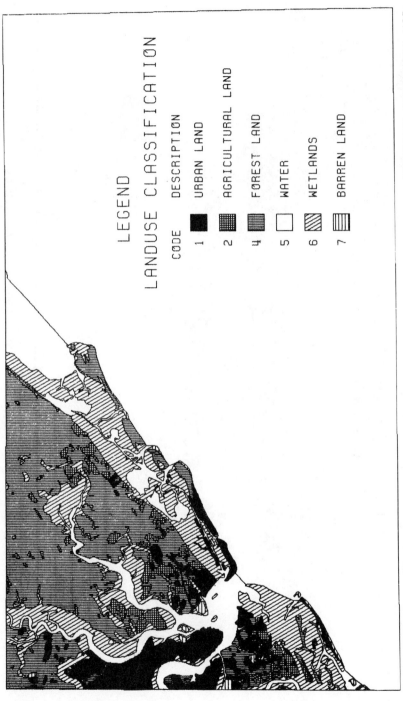

Figure 3-2 Level I landuse and land-cover map of the James Island, S.C. quadrangle generated by GIRAS on an electrostatic plotter.

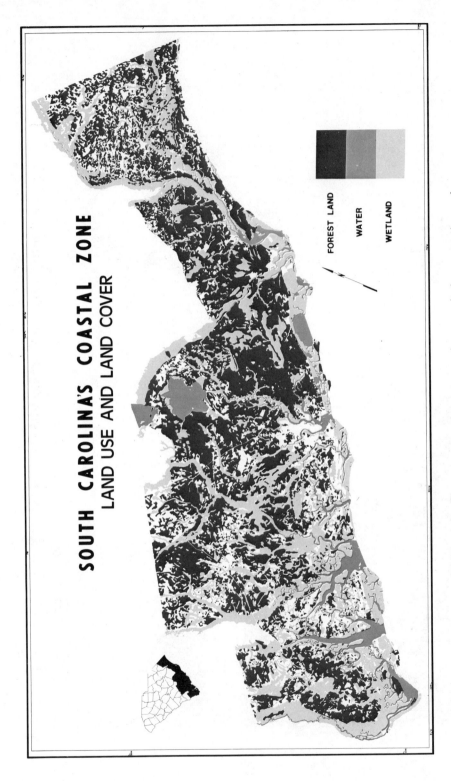

SOUTH CAROLINA'S COASTAL ZONE
LAND USE AND LAND COVER

FOREST LAND

WATER

WETLAND

Figure 3-3 Three composite screened open-window negatives of Level I landuse and land-cover produced from scribes plotted by GIRAS software.

42

LAND USE LAND COVER STATISTICS

		URBAN OR BUILT UP LAND	AGRICULTURAL LAND	IMPOUNDMENT	RANGELAND	FOREST LAND	FORESTED WETLAND	SALT MARSH	BRACKISH MARSH	FRESH MARSH	WATER	BARREN LAND	TOTAL BY COUNTY
JASPER	CRITICAL	168	15,340	2,724	0	28,081	4,170	33,606	2,301	2,508	5,347	415	94,660
	NON–CRITICAL	5,743	52,400	3,500	7,966	132,627	121,649	107	0	4,028	1,964	3,242	333,226
	COUNTY TOTAL	5,911	67,740	6,224	7,966	160,708	125,819	33,713	2,301	6,536	7,311	3,657	427,866
BEAUFORT	CRITICAL	24,928	64,137	2,212	455	69,081	59,692	128,635	1,357	621	47,492	4,528	403,138
	NON–CRITICAL	30	9,337	2,066	0	10,389	5,572	23	0	902	752	1,137	30,208
	COUNTY TOTAL	24,958	73,474	4,278	455	79,470	65,264	128,658	1,357	1,523	48,244	5,665	433,346
COLLETON	CRITICAL	49	9,297	10,834	119	24,267	12,670	19,956	10,170	1,059	7,822	89	96,332
	NON–CRITICAL	8,066	143,014	9,212	603	264,295	148,976	0	0	7,125	1,533	2,215	585,039
	COUNTY TOTAL	8,115	152,311	20,046	722	288,562	161,646	19,956	10,170	8,184	9,355	2,304	681,371
DORCHESTER	CRITICAL	405	899	45	0	18,336	12,117	0	439	862	49	148	33,300
	NON–CRITICAL	9,282	75,249	0	158	155,341	89,749	0	0	0	1,167	4,201	335,147
	COUNTY TOTAL	9,687	76,148	45	158	173,677	101,866	0	439	862	1,216	4,349	368,447
CHARLESTON	CRITICAL	38,499	86,515	11,941	326	120,132	16,091	131,311	10,523	4,178	52,171	6,387	478,074
	NON–CRITICAL	13,528	8,018	0	0	87,366	44,032	272	320	822	919	910	156,187
	COUNTY TOTAL	52,027	94,533	11,941	326	207,498	60,123	131,583	10,843	5,000	53,090	7,297	634,261
BERKELEY	CRITICAL	40	2,827	21	0	7,710	6,217	0	814	243	3,568	0	21,440
	NON–CRITICAL	24,856	79,464	4,273	1,631	345,673	117,359	0	464	7,681	70,802	2,379	654,582
	COUNTY TOTAL	24,896	82,291	4,294	1,631	353,383	123,576	0	1,278	7,924	74,370	2,379	676,022
GEORGETOWN	CRITICAL	4,787	7,159	7,741	100	24,325	13,940	10,227	8,262	3,798	21,667	830	102,836
	NON–CRITICAL	10,961	43,382	4,019	0	273,032	95,693	0	0	19,946	8,718	978	456,729
	COUNTY TOTAL	15,748	50,541	11,760	100	297,357	109,633	10,227	8,262	23,744	30,385	1,808	559,565
HORRY	CRITICAL	8,471	227	0	0	7,927	711	1,849	0	0	1,038	978	21,201
	NON–CRITICAL	21,665	199,502	0	0	297,130	187,251	0	0	727	2,085	2,718	711,078
	COUNTY TOTAL	30,136	199,729	0	0	305,057	187,962	1,849	0	727	3,123	3,696	732,279
TOTAL BY LAND USE	IN ACRES	171,478	796,767	58,588	11,358	1,865,712	935,889	325,986	34,650	54,500	227,094	31,155	4,513,177
	SQ. MILES	268	1,245	92	18	2,915	1,462	509	54	85	355	48	7,051

Figure 3-4 Area statistics for coastal countries generated by GIRAS AREASUM program.

43

of one-acre cells, was the basis of subsequent analytical operations. The graphical capabilities of ESRI software were tested through the digitizing, editing, and mapping of each of the variables (Figure 3-5).

The major objective of the test was to evaluate the analytical or modeling capabilities of the software through an analysis of the "suitability" of various parts of the four-quadrangle area for a barge site. Suitability was defined by the planning staffs of the Coastal Council and the Division of Research and Statistical Services. One aspect of this test was to determine whether the planning professionals could actually relate to the type of input necessary to model the complex interrelationships among the variables. This involved the generation of a number of different suitability maps from simple forms completed by the planners (Figure 3-6).

An additional part of the demonstration involved the evaluation of the potential impacts of the expansion of an existing highway and railway network. Once again, the planning staffs determined the criteria for "conflicts" with proposed routeways. The route evaluation procedure determined which categories of each variable the route traversed and then calculated the associated level of "conflict." Finally, resultant measures of conflict were displayed on a linear graph, which visually highlighted the nature and location of areas of "conflict" along a given route (Figure 3-7).

A positive assessment of the ESRI software led to its installation and to subsequent on-site training of personnel during January and February of 1979. A software linkage between PIOS and GIRAS facilitates the use of the capabilities of both of these systems. Eventually, the system will combine the GIRAS digitizing and polygon-creation programs as the basic input system, while the PIOS interface will enable the creation of multivariable files for use by the versatile ESRI modeling routines. Graphical display can include both the electrostatic grid mapping of ESRI and the GIRAS plotting routines for the creation of high-quality graphics on the Kongsberg plotter. The exact configuration will continue to evolve over time, however, as both systems are written in FORTRAN, and a great number of possibilities for combination and modification exist. These software additions have provided great opportunity for integration by the graphics staff of the university's Computer Services Division. In a research setting, which the university must always remain, a turnkey system or one that is not available in source code would have been unacceptable. The successful culmination of this search process clearly demonstrated that transferable systems exist outside the purely research and development environment.

STATE-LEVEL APPROACHES TO GEOGRAPHICAL INFORMATION SYSTEMS

As the 1980s get under way, it is useful to reflect on the status of geographical information systems at the state government level. While there is considerable optimism in the field of automated cartography, the successful implementation of integrated information systems as actual working tools still remains somewhat in doubt. During the 1970s significant progress had been made in terms of hardware capabili-

LAND USE/WETLANDS GEORGETOWN SOUTH

Electrostatic Plot

Flatbed Plot

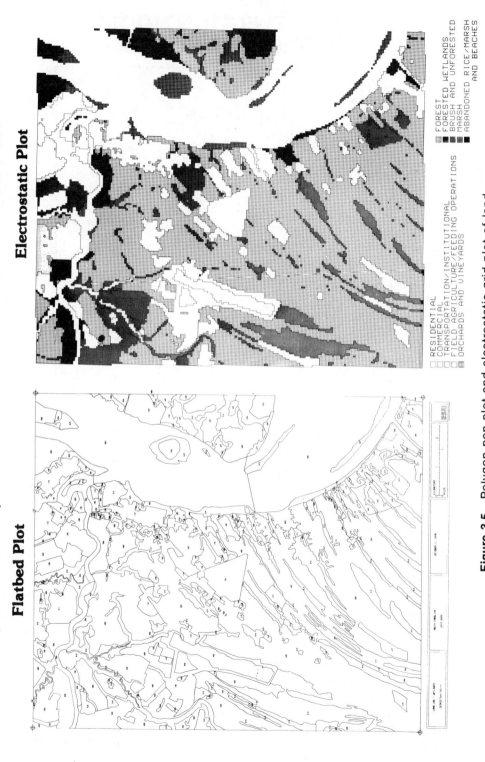

Figure 3-5 Polygon pen plot and electrostatic grid plot of land-use/wetlands generated by ESRI software.

45

SITE SELECTION MODEL
GEORGETOWN SOUTH

☐ VERY LOW SUITABILITY
▦ LOW SUITABILITY
■ MODERATE SUITABILITY
■ HIGH SUITABILITY
■ VERY HIGH SUITABILITY

Figure 3-6 Barge site suitability model generated from 27-variable file with ESRI software.

ties for the display of geographical data. Electrostatic and colored ink jet plotters, color film records, color video terminals, and high-precision plotters with photoheads have eliminated the criticism of the aesthetic quality of early computer mapping products. Recent experiences clearly demonstrate that, even outside the realm of federal mapping agencies, fully automated procedures can generate products equal in quality to those produced by conventional manual methods. Ray Boyle (1979) may well have been correct when he stated at AUTO CARTO III, "Over the next five years your tools will have become all that you need as we presently see automated cartography." Nevertheless, the history of the implementation of geographical systems has not been a good one. In fact, Guinn and Kennedy (1975)

ROUTE EVALUATION GEORGETOWN SOUTH

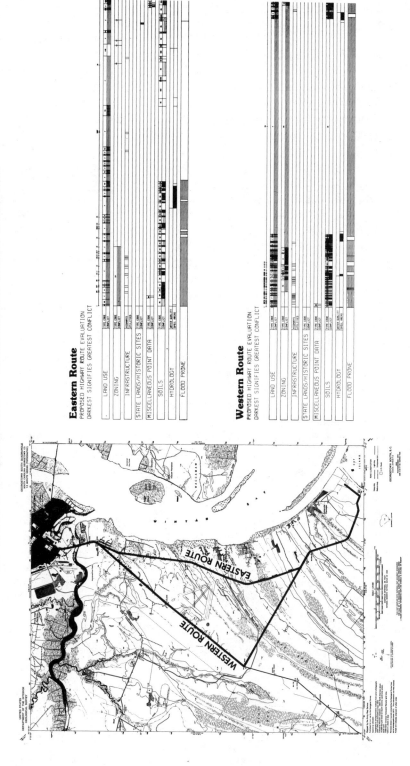

Figure 3-7 Route evaluation model generated from 11-variable file with ESRI software.

suggest that "failures of automated systems don't just dot the thirty-year history of the application of computing equipment to human endeavors, they all but blanket it!" They suggest that early land-information systems failed for the following reasons: lack of established user community; less-than-comprehensive technical understanding by system developers; limited understanding by users of such things as time schedules and output formats; difficult institutional settings; and unrealistic aspirations. In general, little has been altered in these conditions.

Prospects for the successful integration of geographical information systems at the state level are dependent on demand, appropriate justification, and a realistic definition of what is involved. The development of any new system must be justified on the basis of whether it is faster, cheaper, or better than an existing approach. Statewide geographical information systems should never be sold on the premise that they are quicker than conventional methods. The compilation, digitizing, and editing of large regions with complex polygonal coverages are enormously time-consuming processes whose benefits will become apparent only over time. It is also difficult to legitimately calculate a favorable benefit/cost ratio for such a technological alternative without including long-term reductions in personnel, which is not always a desirable policy. Therefore, the future success of statewide geographical information systems depends on their ability to improve upon the quality and type of analysis presently being practiced. For example, the Minnesota Land Management Information System is based on the philosophy that "Success should only be measured in terms of information delivery" (Robinette and Nordstrand, 1978). Only when imaginative new approaches to site-selection and/or impact analysis, feasible only with digital processing, become accepted norms will the widespread adoption of the technology be witnessed. The site-suitability and corridor analyses included in the ESRI demonstration (Figures 3-6 and 3-7) indicate the value of the investment of time and money. It would be inconceivable to manually generate those products from the available 27 layers of data at a one-acre resolution, and then to further rapidly generate a new set based on a different set of criteria.

A recent survey by the National Conference of State Legislatures (1979) indicates that state government continues to be an active arena for geographical information systems development (Table 3-1). The approaches chosen by each of the eighteen states vary enormously, as do the organizational entities in which the systems are housed. For example, the table reveals that such systems may be found in a state planning office, department of commerce, department of natural resources, or even part of the legislative branch of state government. Technical capabilities are presently available to meet the tremendous needs for such systems. The ultimate success of these systems, however, depends on their ability to handle the problems that lie beyond the hardware and software.

While it is easy to accept the fact that a successful system is more than hardware and software, rarely is it fully comprehended that a system must include the four major subsystems outlined by the IGU Commission on Geographical Data Sensing and Processing in its classic 1972 discussion (Tomlinson, 1972). Of those four subsystems–management, data processing, data analyses, and information system use–only one deals specifically with automated data processing. A more recent report by the same commission defines a geographical information system in

Table 3-1 EXISTING STATE-LEVEL NATURAL RESOURCE INFORMATION SYSTEMS

System Name	Acronym	Organizational Structure
Alabama Resource Information System	ARIS	Alabama Development Office
Arizona Resources Information System	ARIS	Arizona State Department of Land
Georgia Resource Assessment Program		Department of Natural Resources
Iowa Water Resources Data System	IWARDS	Iowa Geological Survey
Louisiana Areal Resource Information System	LARIS	Office of State Planning
Maryland Automated Geographic Information System	MAGI	Department of State Planning
Minnesota Land Management Information System	MLMIS	State Planning Agency
Mississippi Data Management System		Research and Development Center
Montana Geo-Data System		Department of Community Affairs
New Jersey Geographic Base File		Division of State and Regional Planning
New York Land Use and Natural Resources Inventory	LUNR	Department of Commerce
North Carolina Land Resource Information System	LRIS	Department of Natural Resources and Community Development
North Dakota Regional Environmental Assessment Program	REAP	Legislative Council
Ohio Capability Analysis Project	OCAP	Department of Natural Resources
South Carolina		Division of Research and Statistical Services
South Dakota Land Resource Information System	LRIS	State Planning Bureau
Texas Natural Resources Information System	TNRIS	Department of Water Resources
Virginia Resource Information System	VARIS	Office of Commerce and Resources

Source: National Conference of State Legislatures, *Remote Sensing: A Review of State Landsat Applications,* Vol. 2, No. 9 (February 1979).

a functional context as "a chain of steps that leads from observation and collection of data through analysis to use in some decision-making process" (Calkins and Tomlinson, 1977). Failure to recognize this holistic definition remains a persistent problem for sucessful implementation.

The Next Step

Presently a sense of cautious optimism prevails in South Carolina. The state's needs are great, and efforts must be made both to eliminate duplication and to utilize modern technology to fullest advantage. Within the last year legislation has been passed that mandates the establishment of common base maps and geodetic controls. These are essential first steps in the data-acquisition stage. In addition, the governor has established a State Mapping Advisory Committee. This committee, consisting of more than twenty representatives from public and private organizations throughout the state, provides a forum for the exchange of information about map products and information needs of the state. While its primary purpose is to advise the governor and the USGS, it is also to promote a common approach to the general geographical data needs of the state. There remains an established commitment within the state's Division of Research and Statistical Services, Office of Geographical Statistics, for the further development of the system. The involvement has received endorsement in the budgetary considerations of the University Computer Services Division and through major sponsors within the legislature. Strong linkages to the academic departments of the university continue. The Geography Department provides advice and consultations on matters of cartography, system design, and remote sensing. The acquisition of software capabilities has provided an excellent basis for research projects within the university, as well as pilot projects and demonstrations for various agencies. The production of the Coastal Zone Land Use and Land Cover map, and the demonstration projects with ESRI, represent meaningful by-products of the developmental process.

The data input, analysis, and display systems are now well established. Further, there is a realization that many obstacles remain before the system will deserve a service bureau status. In the fall of 1979 the governor requested that the Mapping Advisory Committee undertake a detailed study of need for such a system and make recommendations regarding future developments. We are optimistic about the future role of the system and the benefits that will accrue to the state.

REFERENCES

AMERICAN SOCIETY OF PLANNING OFFICIALS, *Information/Data Handling Requirements for Selected State Resource Management Programs.* Washington, D.C.: U.S. Department of the Interior, 1975

ANDERSON, J. R., E. E. HARDY, J. T. ROACH, and R. E. WITMER, *A Land Use and Land Cover Classification System for Use with Remote Sensor Data,* U.S. Geological Survey Professional paper 964. Washington, D.C.: Government Printing Office, 1976.

BOYLE, RAY, "Digital hardware: mass digitization," *Proceedings of the International Conference on Computer-Assisted Cartography: AUTO CARTO III.* Falls Church, Va.: American Congress on Surveying and Mapping, 1979.

CALKINS, H., and R. F. TOMLINSON, *Geographic Information Systems, Methods, and Equipment for Land Use Planning, 1977.* Ottawa: IGU Commission on Geographical Data Sensing and Processing, 1977.

DUEKER, KENNETH, *Geographic Data Encoding Issues.* Iowa City: University of Iowa Institute of Urban and Regional Research, 1975.

_____ and R. TALCOTT, *State Land Use Planning Process Issues: Geographic Information System Implications,* Technical report 64. Iowa City, Iowa: University of Iowa Institute of Urban and Regional Research, 1975.

GUINN, C., and M. KENNEDY, *Avoiding System Failure: Approaches to Integrity and Utility.* Louisville: Urban Studies Center, 1975.

KENNEDY, M., and C. MEYERS, *Spatial Information Systems: An Introduction.* Louisville: Urban Studies Center, 1977.

LINDBLOM, Charles E., "The Science of Muddling Through," *The Public Administration* **19,** 79–88 (1959).

MITCHELL, W. B., and others, *GIRAS: A Geographic Information Retrieval and Analysis System for Handling Land Use and Land Cover Data.* U.S. Geological Survey Professional paper 1059. Washington, D.C.: Government Printing Office, 1977.

NATIONAL CONFERENCE OF STATE LEGISLATURES, *Remote Sensing: A Review of State Landsat Applications,* **2:**9 (1979).

ROBINETTE, A., and E. NORDSTRAND, "A Resource Information System Developed by User Applications," *1978 URISA Proceedings,* **1,** 255–267 (1978).

SOUTH CAROLINA COASTAL ZONE PLANNING AND MANAGEMENT COUNCIL, "An Application for a Program Development Grant to the Office of Coastal Environment," 1974.

TOMLINSON, R. F., ed., *Geographical Data Handling* (Symposium ed.). Ottawa: IGU Commission on Geographical Data Sensing and Processing, 1972.

Chapter 4

Program Evaluation and Policy Analysis with Computer Mapping*

Robert R. Bell

Gary C. Pickett

Joseph T. Scardina

Policymakers, like most decision makers, face the difficult task of evaluating needs and examining the impact of various resource allocations. Policymaking bodies must also implement decisions and communicate them to concerned groups and to other cooperating or affected agencies. The quality of the final result is to a large degree a function of the quality of analysis of the problem. Well-done analysis, however, may lose impact if improperly communicated. This chapter will examine the role computer mapping may play in policy analysis and will describe the advantages policymakers may gain from computer mapping systems.

*Portions of this chapter were presented at the Second International Conference on Computer Mapping Hardware, Software, and Data Bases, Harvard University, July 1979.

Representative "pictures" of geographic data (such as depths of river channels, sizes of mountain ranges, and economic profiles of regions) have been produced for many centuries. For centuries, too, administrators have used maps for decision making. While the computer "caused" rapid development in agencies' ability to generate data, management's ability to utilize computer-produced information has evolved more slowly. Computer mapping in many cases presents the opportunity for "quantum jumps" in the use and understanding of demographic information. In this sense, mapping is a communications process, whereby an agency can present a series of relevant maps depicting data requested by interested decision makers. The "pictures" created by the computer may be effective adjuncts to the support data and may present the data in a more readily understandable form.

Understandably, computer mapping is not normally a stand-alone process. Mapping systems are typically more effective when used with other analytic tools and procedures, with maps providing the vehicle for communicating the results of the analysis. Maps may be used to show relationships between geographic areas and to pinpoint high and low incidences of a variable. To higher-level administrators who are not familiar with the analytic techniques used or the geographic location under consideration, the maps (or "pictures") may be worth a thousand words, or a thousand pieces of statistical information. Mapping may therefore command more attention and encourage greater utilization of the data supplied by the agency.

Many mapping applications relevant to policy analysis have been described in the literature. Predicted population changes for the State of New York have been mapped for the 1980s and 1990s using Harvard University's SYMAP packages (Peucker, 1972). New York City's Geographic Information System has been designed to create maps of information on property worth, ownership, taxes, and value of property improvement (Savas, 1971). Las Vegas, Sacramento, and San Diego have used computer maps in subdivision planning (Bell and Wallace, 1973 and 1974). Researchers at the University of Waterloo have developed computer maps describing soil values and land development and have used such maps in legislative hearings on future land development (Peucker, 1972; Peucker and Chrisman, 1975). Planners in Cleveland used two- and three-dimensional color-coded mapping and plotting techniques to present information relating to the distribution of health-care facilities in the Cleveland area (Shannon, Bashshur, and Metzner, 1971). Other useful readings and applications may be found in Bell (1977), Dutton (1978), Kennedy and Myers (1977), Shostack and Eddy (1971), Smith (1971), and Tomlinson, Calkins, and Marble (1976).

REQUIREMENTS FOR MAPPING*

To be able to map with the computer, we must successfully complete four sequential tasks: (1) select and specify the data to be mapped; (2) link the data files to a geo-

*Much of the information in the next few sections was taken from Robert R. Bell and John B. Wallace, "Computer Mapping with Census Products," *Business and Economic Dimensions,* **8:2** (March–April 1972), 9–23.

graphic base file; (3) manipulate and organize the data to fit available programs and equipment; (4) decide on the cartographic features of the map to emphasize significant areas of interest. These steps are detailed in Figure 4-1.

Data Files

In order to select and specify the data, the user needs to decide which data best meet his or her needs. Because a large portion of the costs involved in the data handling and mapping process come from the development of programs, large-volume users may find it less expensive or less time-consuming to contract the problem out to private sources that specialize in data handling.

Users should consider all the data sources at their disposal, because useful maps often combine census and non-census data. Non-census data are generally massaged into a machine-readable form called a geophysical or geographic information system or data base. These data may be found at the local, state, or national level.

Many students of government have long held that public information systems must be improved if public agencies are to function effectively. Hearle and Mason (1963) summarized the problems of data coordination among state and local public agencies:

1. There is extensive duplicate collection and storage of the same information items.
2. Information collected by one function is often unknown to other agencies which could use it if they were aware of its availability and if it were in a form usable to them.
3. Because of jurisdiction or procedural problems, information items are not efficiently shared among functions and agencies.
4. Often data that would be useful to a department are not collected at all, even though another department could easily gather these data in the course of its regular operations.

The need for compatible, coordinated data bases and procedures has become more critical with the prospect of federal revenue-sharing programs, which will be successful only if urban planning is coordinated and based upon information derived across traditional bureaucratic boundaries.

To meet this need, federal funds have been made available to develop coordinated information systems and have produced geophysical data bases of varying designs. These systems, developed and operated in such urban areas as New York City, Tampa, and Los Angeles, enable each agency to obtain the geographically oriented data that are routinely gathered and maintained by all agencies in the city organization.

The design philosophy generally employs a centralized, user-oriented method of data interchange together with centralized tools for data analysis and display. In some cities decentralized satellite files are maintained by the respective agencies, while in other cities the systems are designed on the basis of a massive central reposi-

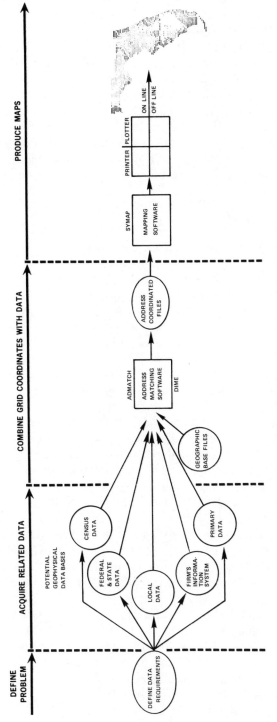

Figure 4-1 Decision steps in computer mapping.

tory of data. New York City's Geographic Information System (GIST) was designed to permit autonomous agencies such as Welfare, the Board of Education, and the Department of Health to maintain control of their own files.

The technology of geophysical information systems being developed by local public agencies also has important implications for private organizations. Society will benefit if private and public groups cooperate in the development and use of this information. Private organizations such as insurance companies, real estate agencies, and mortgage firms can contribute large amounts of data gleaned mostly from public sources. If private firms use the publicly developed systems, then development costs can be shared by many users, and duplication between private and public organizations will be avoided. But if cooperation among public agencies has been difficult to achieve, how much more difficult is private—public cooperation going to be?

Address-Matching Software

A basic requirement of automated mapping is that each point of interest be linked to its geographic location by means of grid coordinates—a uniform network of horizontal and vertical lines. Typical systems of grid coordinates are latitude and longitude, state coordinate systems, and the Coast and Geodetic Survey metric coordinate system. In each coordinate system every location has a unique numerical code. Selection of the proper coordinate system to use depends upon the scale of the map, the size of the area it represents, and the amount of detail to be represented. It is rarely practical to associate these coordinates with the data at the time the data are collected. Consequently, an ordinary geographic code such as street address or health area is associated with the data as they are collected, and an address-matching system is subsequently used to associate the coordinates with the data.

Address-matching systems generally consist of a geographic base file and address-matching software. The geographic base file consists of records that relate geographic codes such as street addresses, census tracts, and block numbers to various systems of grid coordinates. The address-matching software reads the geographic data-base files such as census tapes and local geophysical records, matches geographic codes with grid coordinates, and produces files that can be processed by mapping programs to produce maps.

The Census Bureau, in cooperation with the Harvard Laboratory for Computer Graphics and Spatial Analysis, has developed a series of manual and computer-oriented address coding systems to match data with their geographic locations. The Bureau's software can, with some modification, also be used to match the census data and non-census data.

One system, called Dual-Independent-Map-Encoding (DIME), uses a coding scheme that approximates all streets in an area as straight lines. Each line contains information about census tract or block number, a name (such as a street or railroad), and, if applicable, address ranges for each side of the line. Intersections or nodes are identified with map coordinates.

Another software package, ADMATCH (or Address Matching System), was developed by the Census Bureau to assist in assigning geographic codes to computerized files containing street addresses and is very useful in matching non-census with census data.

Computer Mapping Tools

After the agency has acquired a base file that has map coordinates attached, users must consider the type of maps they wish to make. Two mapping techniques are widely available: character-printed maps and line-drawn maps. Character-printed maps require character-printing software; line-drawn maps need plotting equipment. Since advanced techniques are available that perform both character-printing and line-drawing operations, users probably should acquaint themselves with the advantages of each.

Character-printed maps use a standard computer printer. The resulting map is basically a set of typewritten characters in one of two forms. The mapping variables may be printed at the center of the relevant area—often referred to as a spatial-order statistics map. The second form uses printed characters to shade the relevant areas to show relative concentrations of variables. In the gray-shaded map the computer depicts various characteristics of the map by using different symbols (such as X's for high occurrence and O's for low) or by shading through overprinting of characters. Where the area to be mapped is too large for the printer, the map can be produced in sections and brought together later.

The other general mapping technique uses plotting devices to make two- or three-dimensional line-drawn maps. The most commonly available line-drawn mapping equipment is the pen plotter. Maps produced by plotters range from simple diagrams to three-dimensional drawings. The type of plotter available limits the type of map that can be made. Plotters typically are relatively time-consuming in their work, in many cases requiring several hours to draw maps. Since the central processing unit may be tied up in directing the plotter, machine-time costs can be high.

An option now widely available is microcomputer mapping using cathode ray tube (CRT) technology. The CRT displays the map very quickly, much as a television picture tube does. The map can then be transferred to paper or microfilm for presentation, or it can be plotted.

Combining Features and Data

To be recognizable, a map must combine familiar boundaries and geographic features with the data being mapped. Two methods of defining boundaries and geographic features are available on computer-generated maps. The first method, which consumes much computer time, is to have the computer "digitize" the features and local boundaries and print them at the same time it prints the data.

The second and probably more feasible alternative is to provide the computer with the geographic features already defined on the map paper. This paper can be set up to correspond with the geographic grid coordinates in the base file, and the computer's job is to project the two- or three-dimensional data profile onto the maps. Printed outline maps of this type can be obtained from commercial sources such as the Rand-McNally Company. Their maps identify geographic features such as county and city boundaries, railroads, and streams with their names. The Census Bureau provides enumeration maps for the areas surveyed by the census. These maps define census boundaries such as county lines, minor civil divisions, county civil divisions, places, tracts, wards, blocks, congressional districts, and enumeration districts for the area requested. Copies are available at the cost of reproduction.

The coordinates in computer memory can be processed by a projection routine to make them compatible with the size of map chosen. The computer-generated map is used as an overlay on the geographic outline map, and together the two present a recognizable and informative picture of the characteristics of the area.

Selecting and Specifying the Data

An important and difficult task in the computer mapping process is selecting the subject of the maps and the source of the data. The effective administrator will attempt to minimize wasted efforts of both programmers and machines by spending sufficient time and thought in specifying the validity and level of accuracy of the data to be mapped. The quality of the final maps is, at best, no better than the accuracy of the data used to produce them.

Two rules should be followed to assure valid, accurate data mapping. First, when possible, obtain data from professional sources. Consider the process of attaching necessary coordinates for any proposed map. These coordinates can be obtained manually from a commercial map or from a statistical reference, but the task is both boring and slow, with mistakes certain to occur. A better way is to use the Census Bureau data. The cost may be higher, but the Bureau is meticulous, and that is often worth the extra price. For more sophisticated data reductions and compilations, many firms around the country are in the data-bureau business. They use census and other basic data as input to create special tabulations for their customers. Although not always as careful as the Census Bureau, the better of these firms can be more responsive to the user's particular needs.

The second rule of data collection is never to overstate the quality of the data. For example, many maps use data on federal spending obtained from the federal agencies. But when an agency reports how much it spent in a county, that figure may not include the money that went directly to the state and was reallocated to the county. The map that uses such data will show significantly more money going into the state capital than is actually spent there, and less in the county.

Whenever a map is made, the possible deficiencies in the data should be specified. Often the person for whom the map is being made is interested in using it, at least partially, as a persuasive tool to support an idea or substantiate a situation to other people. If he or she is blocked, not by a weakness in the idea, but by a deficiency in the data, the user will lose confidence in the maps.

DESCRIPTION OF THE TENNESSEE TECH MAPPING SYSTEM

The purpose of our mapping system is to enable our organization to generate graphic output, specifically maps, containing information relative to program and policy decisions. The mapping system uses the Tektronix Industries 4051 Graphics

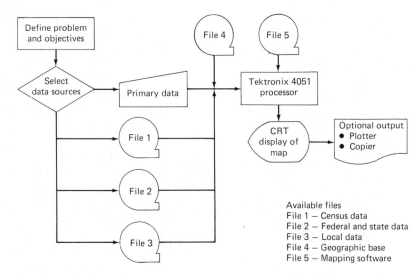

Figure 4-2 Elements of the graphics system.

System, combined with a digitizing unit, digital plotter, and copying unit. This system creates plotted maps, together with hard-copy maps reproduced from the CRT image. The entire hardware package cost is approximately $20,000. Data files have been compiled from the State Department of Economic Development, the state *Statistical Abstract,* the Upper Cumberland Development Commission, and other county and city agencies in the region.

Data manipulation prior to entry to the mapping system is done on a Burroughs 6700 computer system. Appropriate data (typically in rank-order or density form) are then placed on magnetic tape and are entered into the mapping system. The user then selects an appropriate mapping base (state, region, county, city), manipulates the data into appropriate mapping form, and creates the desired map on the CRT. If modifications are deemed necessary, appropriate reprogramming and/or data manipulation is performed. After the CRT map is judged acceptable, the system produces a copy of the map on the plotter or through the copying unit (see Figure 4-2). In its current state, the mapping system can create a hierarchy of maps for various stages in the decision process. In stage 1, the system can develop an atlas of the state, showing the relative distribution of a variable across all 95 counties. It can also isolate the state's economic development regions and create comparative maps between or within them. After regional areas have been evaluated, the mapping system will produce maps for selected counties in the fourteen-county Upper Cumberland Development Region. Finally, with the direct digitizing unit, the system can create a map showing any particular area of interest.

METHOD DESCRIPTION

The initial design objective was to develop a reasonably fast mapping technique that could be run on a stand-alone basis using a microcomputer graphics system. The method developed is capable of producing five different shading densities in predefined areas of a particular state, county, or regional map. The overall approach is to generate the coordinates for a series of horizontal shading lines for each area to be shaded. Once these coordinates are stored, the desired shading density can be achieved by drawing all or alternate numbers of the shading lines. This particular approach was selected in order to minimize the memory and time requirements for drawing and shading a map, which could include as many as 100 different areas. It is also necessary to generate the coordinates for drawing the boundaries of the various regions of the map.

The software consists of three separate routines. The first routine is used to input and store the coordinates of the various area boundaries. This requires a digitizing device, such as a digitizing plotter or a graphic tablet. The latter was used in this work. As many as 100 separate boundaries with as many as 29 points per boundary can be input using this routine. This number is more than ample to represent the state map of Tennessee and the boundaries of all 95 counties. All of these data can be contained in approximately 26K bytes of random-access memory of the graphics microcomputer. In order to minimize drawing time, boundaries are not associated with individual areas, thus eliminating the need for duplicate drawing of boundaries common to adjacent area. The map showing all the boundaries could be drawn in approximately 40 seconds on the CRT display of the graphics system.

The second routine is used to generate the endpoint coordinates of the shading lines for each area of the map. It is highly desirable to store these coordinates rather than computing them each time shading is required. There are two methods for generating these shading coordinates. One involves digitizing the total boundary for each area and then computing the coordinates for shading lines of a given spacing. The other simply requires direct digitizing of the endpoint coordinates from a grid of closely spaced horizontal lines superimposed on the map. The digitizing time for both methods is approximately the same; however, the first method is more flexible, since it allows sets of shading lines of different orientations to be generated with a resulting increase in possible shading densities. The second method is more straightforward and easier to implement. The second method was used in the applications described in this paper. As many as 30 horizontal shading lines per area for 100 different areas can be generated using this routine. The digitizing time for the 95 Tennessee counties was approximately one hour. The shading lines require approximately 26K bytes of random-access memory. The data for these first two routines is stored on magnetic tape for use in the actual mapping routine.

The third routine is used to perform the actual mapping graphics. Integer shading densities between 0 and 4 are used to specify the shading for each area. Nonzero shading densities are input for the appropriate regions. The boundary coordinates are read from the magnetic tape and the area boundaries are drawn. Next the shading coordinates are read from magnetic tape, and the areas with nonzero density values are shaded. The total drawing and shading time for typical maps such as those shown in the following section is approximately 120 seconds on the CRT display. Although it was not incorporated into the present routine, composite shading is also possible using sets of shading lines of different orientation.

RESOURCES REQUIRED

The computer hardware consisted of a Tektronix 4051 Graphic System microcomputer with the maximum 32K bytes of random-access memory and a built-in 300K byte magnetic tape unit. The peripherals consisted of a Tektronix 4662 digitizing plotter, a Tektronix 4956 Graphic Tablet, and a Tektronix 4631 Hard Copy Unit. The system was interfaced to a Burroughs 6700 host computer but did not require this interface for any of the mapping routines. All the mapping software was developed by the authors.

AVAILABLE MAPPING OPTIONS

The present mapping system presents users with a number of options. Although the system is not interactive, the user selects from an initial "cafeteria" list of options. Selection often is a "staged" decision process, with secondary decisions dependent upon outcomes of initial selections.

Choice of Mapping Reference Areas

Users also have several mapping options available. Statewide maps can be created, outlining selected data on a county-by-county conformant map. Users may also select a "regional highlight" option, which shows reference boundaries for all counties but maps data into only a selected number of counties (usually a specific region). Examples of this type of map are shown in Figures 4-3, 4-4, and 4-5.

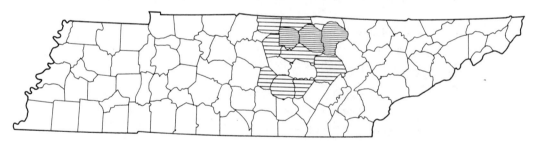

Figure 4-3 Relative tax ratios, upper Cumberland region.

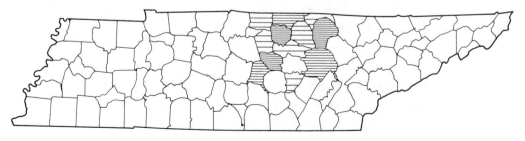

Figure 4-4 Available shading densities.

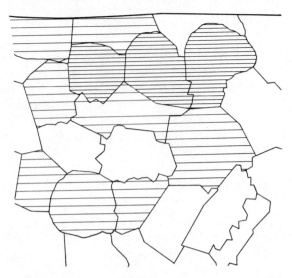

Figure 4-5   Fourteen county relative tax ratios.

Maps can also be made of "average" characteristics for each of the economic development regions in the state, and users may select maps that "depict" averages across the development regions. Users may also request that any combination of counties be mapped, with other counties drawn with no shading. Maps showing intracounty variations of data can be created for certain counties. Finally, the digitizing option allows the creation of certain other special maps upon user requests.

- Choice of geographic area:
    - state
    - regional highlite with state references
    - region
    - intraregion highlite with region or state references
    - intracounty highlite
- Selection of data items:
    - existing data base
    - primary data
- "Overlay" mapping to combine (integrate) data items:
    - "location potential" surfaces
- "Zoom" (or window) mapping
- Plotter or CRT copy maps
- Multicolor mapping
- Modification of density functions
- Histogram support charts

Figure 4-6 Selectable functions for economic development mapping system.

Data Selection

As Figure 4-6 indicates, users can select data from several available sources or can request primary data collection. The existing data base includes statistical information from federal and state abstracts, together with local data gathered by city and county governments and development commissions.

Overlay Mapping

Several persons have suggested that "overlay" maps showing combinations of data may be more useful for some decisions. Consequently, maps can be produced showing data that have been statistically combined using rank-order and other techniques.

Window (or "Zoom") Mapping

The 4051 terminal offers users the ability to zoom in on a specific region, producing maps that focus only upon a specific portion of an initial map. The use of the "window" command creates a new enlarged map of the area of interest. Because of low usage of this option, several problems still exist; these are discussed later in this chapter.

Plotter or CRT Copy Maps

After maps have been created on the CRT, two copy options are available to the user. The map may be reproduced using the digital plotter, which allows an initial map size of 11 by 17 inches. Since maps may be produced section by section, this option does not set an upper limit on the final size of maps. A second option uses the copying unit, which produces 8½-by-11-inch reproductions of the CRT image.

Multicolor Mapping

The availability of the digital plotter gives the option of creating maps of several colors. This involves manual changes of plotter pens of various colors and consequently is very time-consuming. Even with the time sacrifice, color offers an attractive alternative to black-and-white maps.

Modification of Density Functions

Exisiting software uses a class-interval function that automatically divides the data range into five equal steps. Obviously, in some situations the data can be portrayed more effectively with varying interval sizes. The system can easily be modified to create density functions from any five specified intervals. When density is combined with the color option and with various cross-shading techniques, the number of potential map variations is tremendous.

Histogram Support Charts

Statistical data summaries are normally provided to support the maps. Users may also request histogram (frequency) charts if they wish.

PROBLEMS ENCOUNTERED

A major, although not uncommon, problem involves the combination of many data bases into one coordinate system. In a given region, population demographics are reported by census tracts; shopping centers and transportation nets are reported by zoning areas of corridors; private sources may report by mailing address or zip code; banks may code data by service area. In many cases these various levels of reporting cannot be broken down into more specific criteria.

Many decisions hinge upon subjective inferences regarding interactions among data at various levels. This suggests that the resulting information system may be "layered," having data sources at several different reporting levels. The research or decision objective must then specify the level at which the data may be obtained. Our long-term objective is to provide an interactive mapping system that interfaces the present system with a data hierarchy in the Burroughs B-6700 system. Analytic techniques and mapping technology will then be part of the same general system, and many mapping alternatives not presently available will be used.

IMPLICATIONS OF THE MAPPING PROJECT

Obviously, the development of a small-scale mapping project such as this one does not entail the degree of sophistication present in many mapping systems. In many ways the project is still in its infancy with differentiated data analysis and mapping hardware and with two-dimensional black-and-white mapping techniques. The system does demonstrate, however, the feasibility of low-cost mapping projects. The field is not entirely in the domain of well-funded development groups.

Further Applications

It is obvious to the authors that computer mapping has applications in many areas where the need is just becoming apparent. Agency managers are slowly becoming aware of the tremendous potential for communication this technique offers. It is also apparent that mapping continues to move out of the laboratory into more and more real-world, day-to-day operations. The characteristics of relatively low-cost hardware and the availability of software such as that described in this chapter make this type of analysis attractive to even small organizations with little computing expertise. Computer mapping capability is within the grasp of agencies that traditionally utilize the computing resource only for clerical processing. The output, moreover, because it is graphical in nature tends to overcome the "implementation shock" that accompanies quantitative output generated by sophisticated management science models. In effect, managers can conceptually grasp what has been accomplished—and so the "black-box phenomenon" describing the user-machine relationships of earlier computing generations is virtually nonexistent.

Another factor of particular interest is that similar applications can be accomplished by simple interfacing of plotters or appropriate visual display devices with existing minicomputers or small processors. Managers of smaller agencies with limited resources will likely find this alternative attractive, since the incremental cost for the upgrade can be minimized, perhaps shifting the cost/benefit ratio dramatically. When compared to the purchase of a total stand-alone graphics system, this option becomes especially attractive.

A Final Note on System Effectiveness

This mapping project was designed to produce simple, straightforward, relatively inexpensive maps on an existing computer system. Having accomplished that purpose, it can now be used to produce economic and demographic maps for the region. The authors are convinced that local development administrators view computer mapping as a communications breakthrough, and that this mapping system will play a role in the continued economic development of our region.

REFERENCES

BELL, R. R., "Marketing Information Systems—Design Requirements Associated with the Application of Computer Graphics to Bank Site Location," *Proceedings,* American Institute for Decision Sciences, National Meetings, Chicago, October 1977.

————and J. B. WALLACE, "Decision-Oriented Computer Mapping Systems," *Business and Economic Dimensions,* November–December 1973 and January–February 1974, pp. 22–30.

DUTTON, G., ed., *Harvard Papers on Geographic Information Systems,* 8 vols. Reading, Mass.: Addison-Wesley, 1978.

HEARLE, E., and R. MASON, *A Data Processing System for State and Local Governments.* Englewood Cliffs, N.J.: Prentice-Hall, 1963.

KENNEDY, M., and C. R. MEYERS, *Spatial Information Systems: An Introduction.* Louisville: University of Louisville, Urban Studies Center, 1977.

PEUCKER, T. K., *Computer Cartography,* Resource Paper 17. Washington, D.C.: Commission on College Geography, 1972.

————and N. R. CHRISMAN, "Cartographic Data Structures," *The American Cartographer,* **2:**1 (1975), pp. 55–69.

SAVAS, E. S., "GIST—New York City's Geographic Information System," *Government Data Systems,* September–October 1971.

SHOSTACK, K., and E. EDDY, "Management by Computer Graphics," *Harvard Business Review,* November–December 1971, pp. 52–58.

SHANNON, G., R. BASHSHUR, and C. METZNER, "The Spatial Diffusion of an Innovative Health Care Plan," *Journal of Health and Social Behavior,* September 1971, pp. 216–226.

SMITH, D., *Industrial Location: An Economic Geographical Analysis.* New York: John Wiley, 1971.

TOMLINSON, R. F., H. W. CALKINS, and D. F. MARBLE, *Computer Handling of Geographical Data.* Paris: The Unesco Press, 1976.

Chapter 5

A Graphics-Oriented Computer System To Support Environmental Decision Making

H.V. Giddings

ABSTRACT

In 1974 the energy shortage resulting from the Arab oil embargo created a new dimension for states in the Upper Midwest—large-scale energy development. While these states historically have been involved with managing major environmental impacts, their efforts in the past centered primarily on water and land use (because, for example, the primary air pollutants are soil particles).

North Dakota, like many western states, tends to be schizophrenic in its approach to energy development. The continued mechanization of farming operations combined with lack of industrial activity has caused a long-term decline in the state's population. North Dakotans have become accustomed to watching their sons and daughters move out of state to seek employment; hence, jobs resulting from energy development are extremely important. North Dakotans also tend to have a strong conservation ethic and are inclined to reject the ideas of large strip mines, loss of animal habitat, degradation of air quality, and the like. Further, increased energy development means competition for one of the state's most important resources—water. Small municipalities want rural water systems developed, while dryland farmers look to irrigation as a way to end their dependence on rainfall, which is all too often insufficient. The energy industries need water for plant cooling, slurry pipelines, and other industrial uses. In the end, the water-use issue likely will create more public concern than other environmental issues.

Most people realize North Dakota has substantial coal reserves; however, the state's mineral resources go far beyond that. In 1978 North Dakota had one of the most actively explored oil fields in the United States. The state also faces pressure to develop potash, uranium, and gravel deposits. Considering North Dakota's rural lifestyle and sparse population (most counties have less than 12,000 inhabitants), it is not surprising that the effects of large-scale development, both good and bad, are substantial.

For some years a small group of legislative leaders recognized the need for a "scientific and technological" capability to assist the decision-making process in general and the state legislature in particular. Given the conservative nature of the state, that concept did not have sufficient legislative support) be implemented. In 1975, however, impending large-scale coal development provided the necessary impetus. The North Dakota Regional Environmental Assessment Program (REAP) was created

> . . . for the purpose of establishing and carrying on research in regard to North Dakota's resources and areas of governmental activity or responsibility for the purpose of assisting in the development of new laws, policies, and governmental actions and providing facts and information to the citizens of the state.

When the Forty-fourth Legislative Assembly created REAP, it took a novel and radical step. At that time, REAP was unique among state efforts to bring science and technology into the decision-making process. It was made part of the legislative branch of government and was to be responsible to a committee, the Resources Research Committee, comprised of legislators, state agency personnel, university faculty, an industry representative, and a citizen at large. The effort was radical when one considers that the initial funding of $2 million was part of a total state government budget of only $442 million—a significant portion of the state's budget devoted to a vaguely defined program with an estimated six-year development cycle.

If, in 1975, one had conducted a poll of people knowledgeable about REAP, the consensus would have been that "REAP will collect all data about North Dakota, feed the data into a huge computer, and answer any question dealing with the quality of life in North Dakota." While that statement itself is naive, it is consistent with the unbelievably unrealistic expectations many politicians hold for science and technology with respect to aiding decision making.

Given the common perception of REAP as a huge computer and data base capable of answering essentially any question, it should be clear that REAP's first hurdle would be to properly define its role and activities. That process commenced on June 1, 1975, when Dr. A. W. Johnson began his duties as REAP's first director. He identified four major tasks to be undertaken:

1. To develop an adequate data base on the environmental, economic, and sociologic characteristics of North Dakota

2. To design and implement a computer-based information system capable of meeting the needs of, and being used by, decision makers

3. To design and implement assessment/modeling systems capable of forecasting the implications of alternative development activities on the environmental and social characteristics of North Dakota

4. To design and implement a mechanism for monitoring changes in the characteristics of North Dakota

While those four goals were more specific than the legislation, they also represented a task that could never be fully accomplished. In order to further limit REAP's scope of activities, three parallel studies were initiated. Teams of experts organized into Technical Task Forces (TTFs) were used to define limits of what could be accomplished, given the state of the art with respect to environmental research and the existence of necessary data. A total of 92 technical experts from both state universities (49), state agencies (22), federal agencies (18), local government (1), and industry (3) worked for slightly more than three months, producing a set of eleven reports that contained recommendations for priority baseline data-collection studies and modeling projects, as well as the cataloging of current applicable research efforts. The second design activity consisted of teams of users called REAP User Specifications Teams (RUSTEAMS). Fifty-three potential users (31 from state agencies, 6 from federal agencies, 12 from the universities, 1 from industry, and 3 from local government) were organized by discipline and asked to specify the "outputs" required from the system, the input data requirements, processing and analysis requirements, frequency of use, and response-time requirements. Their effort yielded a 2750-page report. Finally, an in-house study was conducted to determine the state of the art with respect to natural resource systems, composite mapping, and graphics as used in environmental analysis.

To this point, system design activity followed a traditional course. Experts defined the universe of possible activity, while users indicated priority needs. From this effort grew the concept of the "REAP system," which, in reality, was a methodology for meeting the information needs of decision makers. One portion of that "system" is a computer capability. Other portions include links with the state universities for research, cooperative data-collection efforts among state agencies, and numerous coordination efforts.

Like the legislative concept of REAP as a huge computer system containing all the data about North Dakota and able to answer any scientific or technical question, the vision of a computer system comprised of all data and programs identified by the TTFs and RUSTEAMS would be a naive one. A glance at just a few of the 92 "top-priority outputs" (Table 5-1) will illustrate the major analysis and programming effort required to produce those outputs. Further, the data needed to support those outputs are measured in hundreds of billions of characters and in the years of effort required to collect and keep current. Further, consider the reliability of TTF and RUSTEAM efforts. Members of either group were rarely familiar with any but the

Table 5-1   SELECTED TOP-PRIORITY OUTPUT REPORTS

Air Quality/Meteorology

Ambient Air Quality Data on North Dakota
Emission Inventory Data on North Dakota
The Meteorology and Climatology of North Dakota: Climatology
    Water Balance
The Meteorology and Climatology of North Dakota: Atmospheric
    Stability—Wind Information
Climatic Extremes and Other Weather Hazards in North Dakota
Trends of Air Quality in North Dakota
Emergency Measurement of Air Quality in North Dakota
Effects on North Dakota's Air Quality by Proposed Development
Expected Air Pollutant Emissions from Proposed Development in
    North Dakota
Maximum Allowable Pollutant Emission Densities in North Dakota
Prevention of Significant Deterioration (PSD) Air Quality Increment
    Accounting System for North Dakota

Animals

Animals of North Dakota
Unique/Rare or Endangered Species of North Dakota
Biotic Communities of North Dakota
Population Trends of Animals in North Dakota
Strip Mined Area Potential for Wildlife Habitat in North Dakota
Engineering Development Impact on Wildlife in North Dakota

Geology

Disturbed Land of North Dakota
Topography of North Dakota
Economic Mineral Deposits in North Dakota
Drill Hole Data of North Dakota
Oil and Gas Statistics for North Dakota
Surface Geology of North Dakota
Geological Aspects of Mined Lands in North Dakota
Trends in Mineral Economics in North Dakota
Geological Constraints on Development in North Dakota

most primitive data processing applications (such as payroll and personnel). They simply did not have a conceptual framework that would allow them to provide detailed assistance in the design of an automated system. The most frequent request, for example, was to simply "see" raw data printed in a report.

One of the first design concepts was a perception of REAP as a *focal point* for information. This subtle change in orientation had wide-ranging practical ramifications. For example, water data are retrieved upon demand from the United States Geological Survey's system in Reston, Virginia; commercial time-sharing services and networks are considered an integral part of the "REAP" computer system. Literature searches are performed using a combination of in-house automated capabilities, the state library, the university libraries, federal reference systems, and commercial bibliographic reference systems. The goal was to create a computer system that, to a user, appeared to "have all the data about North Dakota and be able to perform any needed analysis," while the in-house portion consisted only of those capabilities that cost and response considerations justified.

While the in-house computer system represents only a portion of the total REAP system, it was a major developmental effort. The remainder of this report will discuss the development of that system, its functional capabilities, and its uses. It is important to note that the in-house computer system is simply one of a number of tools that REAP makes use of to meet its mandate—the provision of timely information to decision makers.

FUNCTIONAL DEFINITION

In theory, the intersection of (1) the needs assessment provided by the RUSTEAM effort, (2) the state of the art with respect to environmental research and existence of necessary data, and (3) the state of the art with respect to automated systems define the automated outputs REAP should attempt to produce. However, even if the lack of precision in the various definitional efforts were ignored—which would be disastrous—the cost of the analysis and programming effort required to directly implement the desired capabilities would be far beyond the level of funding REAP could expect or—more to the point—would have the nerve to request.

At this stage of the design effort, REAP made the first of many iterations between "top-down" and "bottom-up" design.* Activities to this point had proceeded in a top-down fashion (i.e., the initial goal of "automate everything" was subdivided into outputs. . .which were subdivided into programs. . .which were subdivided into algorithms, and so on). The bottom-up step involved abstracting the algorithms required to produce the various outputs, grouping similar algorithms, and finally producing a generalized functional description of a set of capabilities that provides the necessary processing. The difference in approaches is more than semantic. In the case of the top-down effort, the primary focus was on specific

*While the various software components were designed separately in a traditional top-down manner, software was implemented in a bottom-up fashion that transcended component boundaries. This approach, which substantially reduces the number of lines of code written, and as a result, the time to implement the system, and improves the reliability of the resulting software products, is the subject of an unpublished paper by the author: Giddings, R.V., "Design of Automatic Systems: A Case Study."

inputs and outputs. In the case of the bottom-up effort, the emphasis was on synthesizing generalized algorithms that operate on classes of data to produce classes of outputs.

The functional capabilities defined by this bottom-up design effort can be divided into two classes—those that resulted from user specification efforts (either directly or by logical extension) and those imposed by REAP. Seven general capabilities evolved from user requests: queries (reports containing "raw" data), maps (in various scales, projections, and so on), statistics (identified most often by a request to determine a trend), charts and graphs (primary end users are not technicians; rather, they are legislators, mayors, state agency officials, and the like, who desire readily understandable outputs), calculator capabilities (for simple engineering problems that exceed the capability of a small calculator but are within the programming capabilities of the technician needing the results), composite mapping (although other than visual overlaying was not requested), basic geographical capabilities (area computations, windowing, and so on), and models (a wide variety of requests to answer "What if. . . ?" types of questions). REAP imposed three capabilities: a large data base (capable of handling spatial data and large amounts of alphanumeric data), communications (networking and remote job entry), and in-house digitization. Finally, the various capabilities had to be tied together in a straightforward, user-oriented manner.

Before discussing systems capabilities in detail, it is worth noting one of two design objectives that were not met. Originally, it was thought that decision makers (legislators, mayors, state agency officials, and so on) would have direct terminal access to the REAP system for the analyses they needed. Conceptually, that would have been possible. Had the REAP design proceeded in a top-down manner, decision-makers could have been provided with a detailed description of the various system outputs and with instructions for using a terminal to request a particular output. However, the system consists of a number of generalized capabilities that must be tailored to a given application (e.g., a generalized statistical capability requires the user to specify the statistical test to be used, input data, and so forth). While most of the generalized capabilities are simple to use, understanding the implications of their use requires sophistication (consider, for example, the difference between performing a linear regression and knowing what the result means!). It is unlikely average legislators would have the required skills—or would desire to have them.

THE DATA BASE

The most important aspect of the REAP system is the data base. Consider for a moment the requirements that had to be met: it must be capable of handling polygon, grid, or cellular data, as well as large volumes of alphanumeric data; it must support on-line data, off-line data, and archiving; data retrieved from other sites must be easily loaded and purged; it must be "self-documenting" (because many users have terminals located hundreds of miles away); it must meet rigorous security requirements; it must take into account that there are no universally accepted "best data"; and it must take into account that most of the data loaded will be in "error." (While one should require data about an employee's payroll history to be precise, what is the probability that one will know absolutely the location of all coal beds in North Dakota?)

The concept of "best data" brings into focus the second design criterion that REAP failed to meet. Legislators thought that the REAP effort would result in a standardization of data collection and, more importantly, the standardization of data used in environmental analysis. The concept was that, if everyone used the same data, verification of results would be greatly simplified—which is obviously true and would greatly assist regulatory agencies. As should be readily apparent, the insurmountable difficulty is in determining what data should be used (i.e., what are the "best" data?).

Being "best" is not an intrinsic property of data; rather, it is a judgment we apply to data with respect to a specific use. Rather than asking that all data collection conform to the most stringent requirements that could be envisioned, REAP chose to assign the user the responsibility for determining whether data obtained from REAP were the "best data" for any specific use. This approach required that REAP develop a mechanism for describing data in sufficient detail to allow such judgments to be made. It also required that the user be capable of making such judgments.

REAP has developed a data-base management system (DBMS) that meets all the criteria described earlier. It is a modern DBMS in every sense (i.e., it has a complete set of utilities including table-driven routines that load, verify, and update the data base; has its own access methods; performs accounting; performs data compression; converts to standard units; produces performance statistics; provides extensive security features; supports on-line, off-line, and archived data; and has a dictionary and directory to allow program physical independence as well as device independence).

While the internal structure and functioning of the REAP DBMS should be of interest to computer scientists studying data-base management techniques, our description here will be limited to the structure of the data base as seen by the user. To a user, the data base consists of data (maps, alphanumeric data, and so on) *and* detailed descriptions of data, all of which are organized into "titles." The construct of a title, defined to be a theme of data from a single source, is basic to understanding or using the data base. All data-base operations refer to titles or elements of titles.

Part of every title is a detailed description, intended to be sufficiently precise to allow a user to decide whether the data are suitable for a given use. Because all data-base operations require the use of a title, a user is forced to explicitly decide on suitability or to avoid the decision (i.e., not read the descriptions of the data when they are written to the terminal).

While every title contains a detailed description of data, the data may not reside in the data base. Many titles describe archived data, data residing at other computer sites, or even data that are not in machine-readable form. While this may sound strange, it provides a convenient method for a machine-readable inventory of data sources (see "BROWSE").

The system recognizes two classes of titles: p-titles for spatial data and d-titles for alphanumeric data. Functionally, every d-title is associated with a unique p-title. For example, "1970 Census Data" could be a d-title associated with a p-title called "1970 Civil Census Divisions," while livestock production data may be associated with a p-title called "Townships." Any given p-title may have more than one d-title associated with it. For example, the p-title "Townships" may have d-titles "Livestock Production," "Land Cover," and "Crop Production" associated with it.

The use of "titles" solves a number of data management problems. For example, if a map of coal beds is found to be in error, a new map is entered as a new title. The descriptive text in the title that is in error is changed to indicate that a better map exists. Since we create new titles rather than change existing data, we can continually update the data base while preserving an orderly and stable user environment.

One final note: repetitions of data do not necessarily imply a proliferation of titles. For example, a water quality monitoring station that is collecting repeated measurements will not require a new title for each set of measurements; rather, as long as the instrumentation for that site remains the same, the resulting sets of data are stored in the same title and identified with a unique date and time. (If the instrumentation were changed, a new title would be created, because there would be a new theme of data.)

BROWSE

BROWSE provides access to the descriptive information stored as part of each title. Conceptually, BROWSE can perform two functions: list the descriptive information for a title and perform keyword searches. As with most high-level keyword search capabilities, boolean selections are allowed (e.g., "Economics and Mercer" will produce a list of titles keyworded as "economics" and as relating to Mercer County). The appendix to this chapter gives a complete description of the BROWSE language. Like all REAP-developed software, it is designed to be run interactively, prompts the user, and provides extensive "help" in its use.

Three types of keywords are stored in the data base: standard keywords for title subject-matter areas; names of counties and planning regions (a speed-up for the very common request, "What data do you have about my county?"); and title-specific keywords (any additional keywords that seem to be appropriate). The standard keyword scheme is available upon request.

Information about titles produced by BROWSE is intended to be sufficiently detailed to allow determinations about suitability for any given use (see Figures 5-1 and 5-2). Information presented about p-titles includes descriptions of the information, source, and limitations on use (e.g., known errors, titles containing "better" data); an indication of whether the data reside on-line, off-line, or have been archived, are available for remote job access at another site, or are not in machine-readable format (in which case a contact person's name and address are provided); scale; resolution; keywords; date digitized (if appropriate); date loaded into the data base; and finally, if the user is at a graphics terminal, a map showing the State of North Dakota and the borders of the 53 counties with the area covered by the p-title shaded in.

SOURCE:

PROCESSED DIGITIZED DATA ORIGINALLY OBTAINED FROM
COMPUTER RESEARCH CORPORATION, ARVADA, COLORADO. THE ORIGINAL
DIGITIZATION WAS BASED ON A VARIETY OF SURVEYS, THE PRINCIPAL ONE
BEING THE U.S. ARMY MAP DEFENSE SURVEY.

DESCRIPTION:

A MAP OF ALL THE QUARTER-QUARTER SECTIONS OF NORTH DAKOTA.

USE AND ACCURACY:

BECAUSE OF UNCERTAINTIES IN THE ORIGINAL LAND SURVEYS, ONE
SHOULD BE CAREFUL WHEN USING THIS MAP FOR DETAILED
LOCATIONAL NEEDS IN THE SISSETON INDIAN RESERVATION AREA
(LAKE TRAVERSE LAND) IN SARGENT AND RICHLAND COUNTIES IN THE
SOUTHEASTERN CORNER OF THE STATE. QUARTER-QUARTER SECTIONS
ARE GENERATED BASED ON THE METHOD THE SURVEYORS WERE
SUPPOSED TO FOLLOW, BUT IN SEVERELY DISTORTED SECTIONS, THE
COMPUTER-GENERATED MAP WILL NOT COINCIDE WITH THE ACTUAL
QUARTER-QUARTER SECTIONS AS SURVEYED.

KEYWORDS:

*ALL P-TITLES	*,*GEOGRAPHICAL BOUNDS	*,*LAND SURVEY	*
*POLITICAL BOUNDARIES	*,*POLITICAL ENTITIES	*,*QUARTER-QUARTERS	*
*RECTANGULAR SURVEY	*,*SECTION	*,*SOCIAL	*
*SOCIOECONOMIC DATA	*,*STATE	*,*STATE GRID	*

TYPE	P-TITLE.
DATE DIGITIZED	YEAR 1979 DAY 170 AD
DATE UPDATED	YEAR 0 DAY 0 AD
SCALE	1 : 126720
STATUS	DATA STORED ONLINE
CLASS	POLYGON.

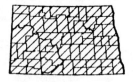

BOUNDARY

QTR-QTRS

Figure 5-1 P-title descriptive information.

Information presented about d-titles includes descriptions of the information, source, and limitations on use; location (e.g., on-line, off-line); keywords; whether the data are homogeneous over the area described; and the name of the associated p-title. For each data element in a d-title the following can be displayed: element name, description, original units, transformed units, whether there are "missing

TITLE: LCA-DATA

SOURCE:

ORIGINATED FROM TWO SATELLITES LAUNCHED BY THE NATIONAL AERONAUTICS
AND SPACE ADMINISTRATION (NASA): LANDSAT-1 AND LANDSAT-2. NINETEEN
INDIVIDUAL SCENES COVERING NORTH DAKOTA WERE SELECTED FROM THE EROS
DATA CENTER IN SIOUX FALLS, SOUTH DAKOTA. THESE LANDSAT SCENES WERE
THEN PROCESSED AND CATEGORIZED BY BENDIX AEROSPACE SYSTEMS DIVISIONS
IN ANN ARBOR, MICHIGAN, UTILIZING THEIR MULTISPECTRAL DATA ANALYSIS
SYSTEM (MDAS).

DESCRIPTION:

ACREAGES OF EACH TYPE OF LAND COVER FOR
EVERY QUARTER-QUARTER SECTION IN NORTH DAKOTA. TEN LAND COVER TYPES
ARE REPRESENTED: BUILT UP LAND, CROPLAND, MIXED PASTURE, FALLOW
LAND, EXPOSED SUBSOIL, RANGELAND, FOREST, WATER, WETLAND, AND BARREN
LAND. AN ADDITIONAL CATEGORY SUMMARIZES LAND THAT COULD NOT BE
CLASSIFIED (UNCATEGORIZED).

USE AND ACCURACY:

DATA ARE SUITABLE FOR BROAD REGIONAL ANALYSIS ONLY. IT SHOULD NOT BE
USED FOR SITE-SPECIFIC ANALYSIS DUE TO THE POOR RESOLUTION OF THE
LANDSAT SYSTEM (1.12-ACRE MAXIMUM RESOLUTION)AND SUBSEQUENT LIMITA-
TIONS IN PROCESSING THE DATA. FOR MORE INFORMATION, A BROCHURE EN-
TITLED "LAND COVER MAPS OF NORTH DAKOTA" AND REAP PUBLICATION NO.
77-5 "LAND COVER ANALYSIS OF NORTH DAKOTA" ARE AVAILABLE THROUGH THE
REAP OFFICE AT 316 NORTH 5TH STREET, BISMARCK, ND 58505 (TELEPHONE
701-224-3700). LAND COVER ANALYSIS MAPS FOR THE STATE AND FOR EACH
COUNTY ARE ALSO AVAILABLE THROUGH THIS OFFICE.

TITLE: LCA-DATA

ELEMENT NAME: BARREN

DESCRIPTION:

ACRES OF BARREN LAND FOR EVERY QUARTER-QUARTER SECTION IN
NORTH DAKOTA. THIS CATEGORY INCLUDES SAND AND GRAVEL PITS,
BEDROCK QUARRIES, AND STRIPMINED AREAS.

USE AND ACCURACY:

DATA ARE BEST USED FOR BROAD REGIONAL PLANNING ONLY. BECAUSE
THE DATA ORIGINATED FROM 19 LANDSAT SCENES HAVING A SEASONAL
RANGE OF 45 DAYS AND A YEARLY RANGE OF FOUR YEARS, GROUND
CONDITIONS OFTEN CHANGED SIGNIFICANTLY. THEREFORE, IN SOME CASES
DRIED UP LAKE AND SLOUGH AREAS MAY BE CLASSIFIED AS BARREN LAND.
ALSO, IN SOME AREAS WHERE NEW GROWTH IS OCCURRING, THE AREA
UNDER DEVELOPMENT MAY APPEAR TO BE BARREN LAND WHERE THE
TOPSOIL HAS BEEN REMOVED.

UNITS:

THE RESOLUTION OF THE LANDSAT SYSTEMS IS 1.12 ACRES (I.E. THE
SIZE OF THE PICTURE ELEMENT, OR "PIXEL").

Figure 5-2   Sample D-title descriptive information.

values'' (and, if so, an indication of the value that represents a missing value), heading for use in reports, accuracy, scale factor, and others. (Much more information about elements is contained in the dictionary but is not needed by the user. For example, a user need not know whether an element is a real number, integer, character string, or a vector of numbers, integers, or character strings.)

BROWSE's operation can be mastered in a matter of minutes, and, since all other data-base capabilities use title names and the symbolic name for elements of titles, it is necessary as well as informative. Of course, a user cannot ''browse'' data restricted from that user because of security requirements.

QUERY

While the data-base management system and BROWSE were logical consequences of the user needs assessment, QUERY was a direct response to the need most often expressed—a report containing ''raw'' data. QUERY is a high-level, interactive, prompting, general-purpose, query language. It is unique in its ease of use and its language constructs for expressing relationships between spatial data (p-titles) and alphanumeric data (d-titles).

When performing a query (which, of course, results in a report) a user specifies a report title; the p-titles and d-titles of interest; the universe to be searched; selection criteria; a range of collection dates and times for data that are collected repetitively (e.g., data from an automatic air quality monitoring station); and the symbolic names of elements to be reported. While this sounds confusing, less than a half hour of instruction is required to master QUERY's use (see the Appendix).

Figure 5-3 illustrates a simply query that will produce the name of the permit holder, legal description of the permit area, and amount of water authorized for all irrigation water permits that authorize use of more than 20 acre-feet of water.

One of the more powerful features of the query language is its capability to process varying length vectors of numbers or characters. For example, the symbolic name SPECIES may represent a list of all the raptors found in a given study area. The statement ''PRINT SPECIES'' produces a report in which the entire list is printed for each selected study area (polygon). Further, the statement SPECIES = ''SWAINSON'S HAWK'' is well defined. Specifically, the entire vector for each study area is searched for an element ''SWAINSON'S HAWK.'' If any such element is found, that study area is selected.

```
REPORT TITLE
IRRIGATED LANDS
$$$
USING P-TITLE = WPERMITS, D-TITLE = PERMITD
CONSIDER ALL POLYGONS
SELECT ("TYPE" = "IRRIGATION" and "AMOUNT" > 20)
PRINT POLYGON-NAME, "NAME", "LEGAL DES"
STOP
```

Figure 5-3   Sample query.

Reports are automatically formatted with headings—even when the amount of data to be printed exceeds the width of the output device. Summary data or summary counts can also be obtained.

MAP

MAP draws maps on either graphics displays or plotters. In its most basic mode, a user simply indicates the name of a p-title and a fully annotated map is produced. If desired, however, a user can specify the coordinate system to be used, scale, map dimensions, shading, multiple grid systems, character fonts, shading, windowing, and so on (see Figure 5-4). Maps are stored in the data base with plotting codes for each polygon, line, or point. Standard U.S. Geological Survey map symbols (for roads, railroad tracks, and so on) are used when appropriate.

Since MAP has been interfaced to the output of QUERY, its capabilities are greater than is readily apparent. For example, a query resulting in a list of polygon

```
PLEASE INPUT COMMAND ... ?
USING P–TITLE 'COUNTIES'
PLEASE INPUT COMMAND ... ?
TURN ON ANNOTATION
PLEASE INPUT COMMAND ... ?
DRAW
PLEASE INPUT COMMAND ... ?
```

Figure 5-4 A simple map.

names for water permits that have been issued for irrigation purposes could be used as input to MAP. The result would be a map of irrigated lands.

Maps can be produced on mylar to allow visual overlaying. While this manual overlaying of maps is not elegant, it is useful to a great number of state agencies that will never receive the funding for a graphics display. For agencies that can afford it, MAP can provide visual overlaying at a graphics display.

GAP

While discussions about geo-based computer systems tend to focus on how intersections, unions, and related computations are performed, no one involved in the user design effort could visualize that such computations were feasible or how they could provide useful analysis. This lack of understanding, and concomitant lack of interest, resulted in a low priority for "packaging" these algorithms. Specifically, the various algorithms have been developed and tested (owing to the bottom-up implementation process) and the data base has been designed to assist these computations (i.e., minimum containing rectangles are stored for p-titles, polygons, and chains; areas and length are stored for polygons and lines, respectively; and statistics are produced to allow a determination of when the results of intersections and unions should be stored as new p-titles in order to avoid redundant computations). At the time this chapter was written, however, a high-level command language, GAP, to tie the various algorithms together had not been finalized.

A lack of experience with respect to user needs has made it difficult to structure such a language. As users become familiar with the various system capabilities and can begin to articulate their needs with respect to this type of analysis, the command language will be implemented. Owing to the bottom-up software development process, this is not a difficult or time-consuming process.

INTEGRATED SOFTWARE

While the REAP system implementation resulted in a major software development effort, an attempt was made to avoid "re-inventing the wheel." The major trade-off involved is software development time and cost versus a loss of consistency among the various capabilities (i.e., purchased software does not interfere to the data base and would not use language constructs similar to those developed by REAP). Part of the consistency problem is solved by the monitor (discussed below). The database interface problem is solved with a query-language option that produces reports without headings that can be easily processed by purchased software (i.e., data are extracted from the data base and formatted for use by purchased software, rather than purchased software being interfaced to the data base).

Purchased software includes the Statistical Package for Social Scientists— SPSS (a widely used, generalized, statistical program); HARRIS Computer System's APL, BASIC, and FORTRAN (HARRIS provides excellent versions of all three); PASTA from the Harvard Lab for Computer Graphics and Spatial Analysis (digitization software); Integrated Software Systems Corporation's DISSPLA (for

REAP's device-independent graphics), and TELL-A-GRAF (a high-level, user-oriented language to produce charts and graphs that must be seen to be appreciated).

While the list of purchased software, combined with BROWSE, QUERY, and MAP, sounds like a confusing conglomeration, in practice it is not. Each package has a distinct function and a distinct command language designed to facilitate that function. Because there is little overlap in either function or language, there is little chance for confusion among capabilities.

THE MASTER MONITOR

With any interactive computer system, a user must learn a basic command language (job control or operating system command language). Typically, this is the most difficult task for a novice, because the functions that must be performed bear little direct relationship to the problem being solved (e.g., to a novice, allocating files and invoking programs is not directly related to a least-squares analysis). The REAP Master Monitor, an extension of the HARRIS operating system, handles tasks such as terminal identification, file assignment, batch job submission, program invocation, and security. However, a user with absolutely no previous computer experience can perform all monitor functions, once given a password and told that "Return" must be pressed at the end of each line. To date, no one has required instruction in the use of the monitor!

A SET OF TOOLS

Whenever a tour of the REAP in-hour computer system is given, someone asks, "What does the computer do?" The difficulty associated with answering this question has always been embarrassing. Had REAP elected to write a number of programs that took specific inputs and produced specific outputs, the answer would have been simple. The individual who asked the question would have been provided a list of outputs. Unfortunately, the answer is not that simple.

In reality, REAP has developed a large data base and a set of powerful user-oriented tools that can perform a variety of analyses. What the system "does" is really a function of two variables: the data available for analysis, and the creativity and analytic capability of the user.

A TYPICAL EXAMPLE

Rising population and a perceived increase in crime rates in the coal-impact counties led the North Dakota Supreme Court to consider restructuring and expanding North Dakota's court system. REAP was asked both to provide the analysis necessary to determine the extent of any such impacts and to prepare a synopsis of that analysis suitable for use during legislative committee hearings.

The charts shown as Figures 5-5 through 5-10 are some of those used to illustrate potential impacts under high (BLM Level II), medium (BLM Level I), and low (BLM baseline) scenarios of development. They were useful in reducing economic

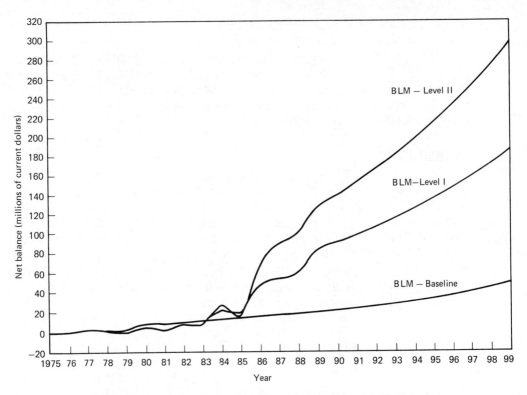

Figure 5-5 Projected state net fiscal balance for North Dakota by year for three development scenarios.

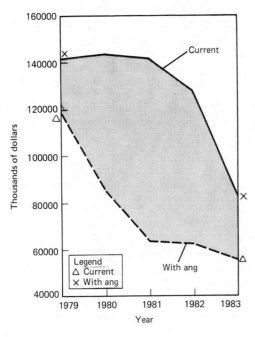

Figure 5-6 REAP economic demographic model RED 1.4 regional economic activity— project-related business activity.

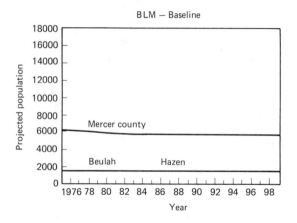

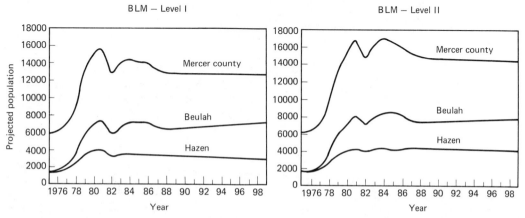

Figure 5-7 Population projections by year for three development scenarios.

and demographic information from REAP's models, research conducted at North Dakota State University, and several other sources to a readily understandable level.

CONCLUSION

REAP has found that graphics can be effective aids to the decision-making process and that they are highly desired by users. REAP has also found that the whole area of psychological effects of graphics must be explored. Specifically, what impact does the type of graphic, layout, and choice of color have on the message conveyed to the decision maker? Understanding such psychological effects is vital when one is trying to reduce a great amount of detail to a few graphics in order to illustrate a point to a decision maker who has little time for detailed analysis.

To date, there has been insufficient user experience to determine the adequacy of the descriptive material stored in the data base, the completeness of the set of analytic tools being provided, and the eventual completeness of the data base. This latter area is of special concern in light of REAP's loss of funding. While agency

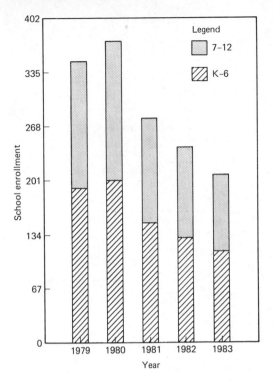

Figure 5-8 REAP economic demographic model RED 1.4 Beulah population projections—school enrollment—current level of development.

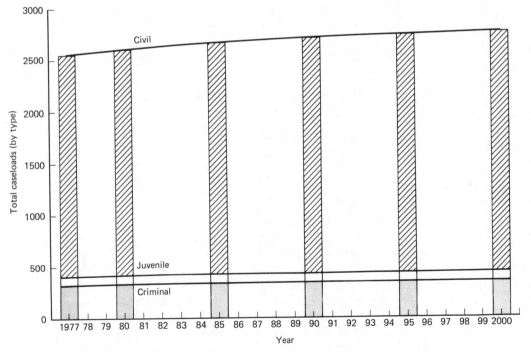

Figure 5-9 First judicial district projected total court caseloads.

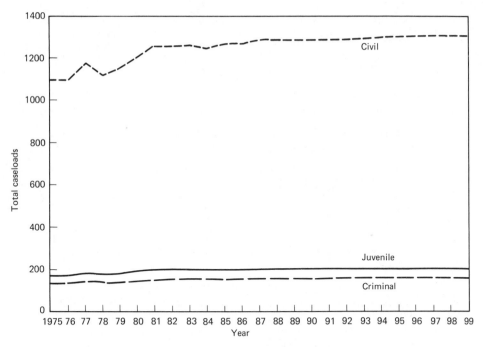

Figure 5-10 Sixth judicial district projected total court caseloads.

funding has assured the continued operation and use of the computer system, no single agency has REAP's mandate to oversee the development of a comprehensive environmental data base. Presumably, the data base will grow in various directions as needed data are added by state agencies. A fortunate, but unintended, consequence of the data-base structure (i.e., the use of titles and provision of detailed descriptions of the data) is that a stable environment can be maintained under such circumstances.

REFERENCES

BATTELLE, *North Dakota Regional Environmental Assessment Program.* Battelle, Columbus Laboratories, 1975. 113 pp.

GIDDINGS, R. V., *An Evaluation of Natural Resource Systems, Composite Mapping Systems, Graphics Packages, and Other Related Animals.* Bismarck: North Dakota Regional Environmental Assessment Program, 1976. 7 pp.

_____, *Alternative System Architecture.* Bismarck: North Dakota Regional Environmental Assessment Program, 1976. 20 pp.

_____, 1979. *REAP System Design Specifications—Draft.* Bismarck: North Dakota Regional Environmental Assessment Program, 1979. 150 pp.

_____, J. R. REID, and F. L. LEISTRITZ, *System Analysis Details Report,* Vol. 1. Bismarck: North Dakota Regional Environmental Assessment Program, 1976. 97 pp.

IBM. *N.D. REAP System Requirements and Conceptual Design.* Gaithersburg, Md.: International Business Machines, Federal Systems Division, 1975. 175 pp.

———, *N.D. REAP System Analysis and Plan Report.* Gaithersburg, Md.: International Business Machines, Federal Systems Division, 1976. 164 pp.

JOHNSON, A. W., J. R. REID, and F. L. LEISTRITZ, *Technical Task Force Reports.* Bismarck: North Dakota Regional Environmental Assessment Program, 1975. 196 pp.

REAP. *REAP User Handbook.* Bismarck: North Dakota Regional Environmental Assessment Program, 1978. 200 pp.

REID, J. R., and R. V. GIDDINGS, U.S. Geological Survey: "Water Data and the North Dakota Regional Environmental Assessment Program," *Proceedings of the First Membership Conference of the National Water Data Exchange (NAWDEX),* 1978. 11 pp.

———, F. L. LEISTRITZ, and R. V. GIDDINGS, *System Analysis Details Report,* Vol. 2. Bismarck: North Dakota Regional Environmental Assessment Program, 1976. 2750 pp.

———, ———, and ———, "ND-REAP, An Information and Analysis System for an Energy Exporting State," *Proceedings of the International Congress of Energy and the Ecosystem,* July 1978. Elmsford, N.Y.: Pergamon Press, 1978. 10 pp.

Part II

COMPUTER GRAPHICS
FOR REGIONAL
POLICY ANALYSIS

Chapter 6

Use of Computer Graphics In Policymaking

Alan Paller

ABSTRACT

Explosive growth in the use of computer graphics has spilled over into the policy-making process. Today, federal policy analysts and corporate executives are finding computer graphics to be valuable, reliable aids to the policymaking process. This chapter looks at computer graphics in the policymaking process from five vantage points. First, it looks at the reasons for the growth of the computer graphics field that makes this tool available for policymakers. Second, it provides two examples of successful use of computer graphics in policymaking. Third, it shows where graphics fit in the policymaking process. Fourth, it provides some criteria for choosing the right chart. Finally, it presents an action plan for implementing computer graphics in a policymaking environment.

Despite many promises from suppliers of computer graphics hardware and services, the growth of computer graphics during the sixties and early seventies was disappointing. Only after 1976, and especially after 1978, did the field begin to assume major significance. In reviewing the history of computer graphics, four features stand out as the principal barriers to its growth. It is because each of these four barriers has been broken that data representation through computer graphics has begun to show explosive growth.

Barrier I: The High Cost of Equipment

During the middle sixties and even into the seventies, the price of entry into the computer graphics field was, at a minimum, tens of thousands of dollars. Many researcher organizations spent hundreds of thousands on equipment in order to explore the world of computer graphics. Today, in contrast, digital plotters cost as little as $2500, can be linked between standard terminals and telephone lines, and can transform a standard terminal into a graphics work station. Similarly, IBM's making available a color computer graphics terminal for less than $200 per month radically altered the economics of the color computer graphics field, cutting by a factor of almost five the cost of interactive color computer graphics hardware. Hardware costs have dropped both for black-and-white and for color; even instant 8-by-10-inch color prints and 35mm slides are now available on equipment that costs as little as $12,000.

Barrier 2: Low-Quality Output

The charts produced by early computer graphics products were of such low quality (e.g., jagged lines and poor lettering) that most of them had to be sent to a graphic artist for tracing before they could be used in a publication or presentation. Because of this expensive additional step, the expected cost savings of using computer graphics for publication or presentation were not realized. During recent years, however, the quality of graphics produced by the reasonably priced computer equipment has improved markedly. The new equipment, even at low cost, can make smoother lines at higher speeds and can generate black-and-white printed output that rivals the products of graphic designers. Color film recorders can now make color slides that are as good as the very best produced by graphic artists. Similarly, the software used to produce computer graphics, especially the DISSPLA and TELL-A-GRAF software packages (available from Integrated Software Systems Corporation in San Diego, California), offer more than 50 graphic arts lettering styles as well as a variety of line widths, textures, shadings, and bar chart organizations that were unavailable even a few years ago. Together, the advances in hardware and software eliminate the need to have computer graphics redrawn by graphic artists.

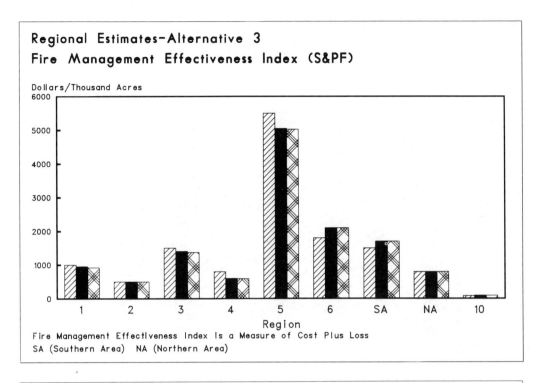

Regional Estimates–Alternative 3
Fire Management Effectiveness Index (S&PF)

Dollars/Thousand Acres

Fire Management Effectiveness Index is a Measure of Cost Plus Loss
SA (Southern Area)   NA (Northern Area)

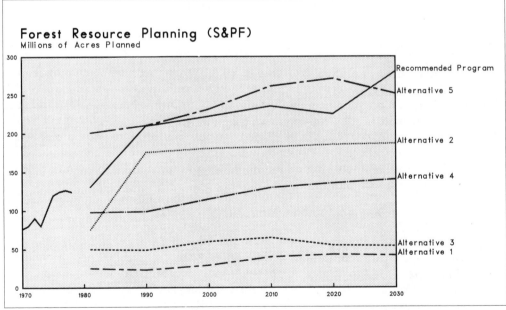

Forest Resource Planning (S&PF)
Millions of Acres Planned

Figure 6-1 An example of higher quality charts available from DISSPLA using $6,000 plotter.

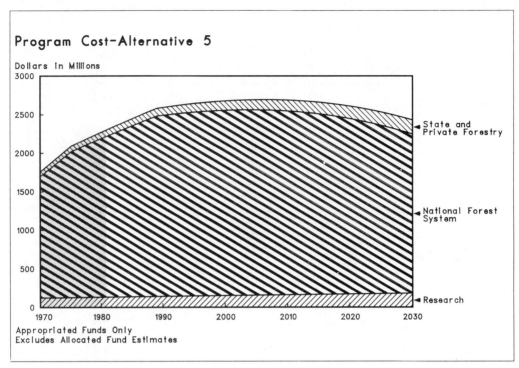

Figure 6-1 (Continued)

Barrier 3: Dependence on Programmers

In the early days of computer graphics, highly qualified computer programmers were needed to make even the simplest chart with a computer. The amount of time necessary for programming and debugging was exorbitant, and the extra time involved in implementing changes made computer graphics an inflexible tool. Today, languages such as TELL-A-GRAF make it possible for secretaries, analysts, and management staff to make their own charts, using English-like commands. These packages have allowed the graphics programmer to specialize in integrating graphics into other information systems.

Barrier 4: Lack of Demand from Management

Although computer graphics were widely available in the sixties and seventies, only a small number of organizations decided to use them. A principal reason given was that there was "no demand" for such tools from management. Today, most analysts realize that the demand *was* there but had not been expressed, because the people who could have used graphics did not know that computers could produce them. These potential users did not read the computer magazines and were not aware computer graphics existed. After computer graphics equipment manufacturers, and especially the color graphics terminals manufacturers, began to advertise in such magazines as *Business Week, Fortune,* and *Forbes,* there was a massive in-

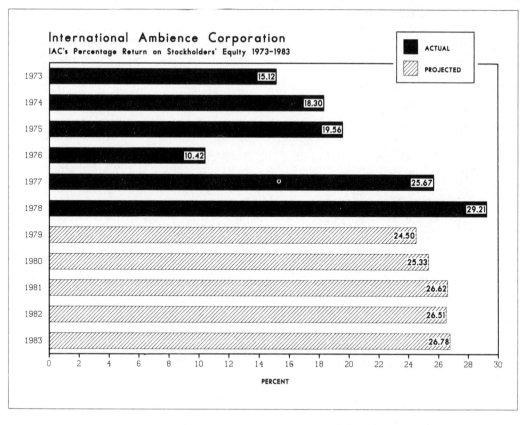

Figure 6-2 An example of boardroom graphics.

crease in demand for computer graphics. A good description of management's interest came from George Blake, Vice President of Finance for Anderson Clayton, who said in *Harvard Business Review,* "Of all the frustration of business life, the most aggravating and persistent is the flood of paper. I used to wade through a 100-page monthly budget report. Now I get a better picture from just one set of graphs."

EXAMPLES OF COMPUTER USE BY POLICYMAKERS

Policymakers are found in both government and commerce. Although stereotyped as solitary thinkers, most policymakers spend the majority of their time listening to presentations by others and developing policy from information thus gained. Therefore, the quality of presentation affects the impact of data on the decision-making process.

Three examples will illustrate the value graphics can add to the presentation of raw statistics. One example comes from the congressional review process, one from the management of a Fortune 100 corporation, and the third from the judicial review process.

The Special Action Office for Drug Abuse Prevention

In the early seventies a new federal initiative was launched to combat drug abuse in the United States. Congress had previously authorized large amounts of money, which were distributed among dozens of programs in eight federal agencies. The Special Action Office for Drug Abuse Prevention was established by the White House to attempt to coordinate the hundreds of millions of dollars being spent by those agencies each year. But coordination, which included authority to veto grants made by the individual programs, required congressional approval. The Special Action Office was successful in obtaining coordination authority from the House of Representatives but was stymied by Senator Hughes and his Subcommittee on Alcoholism and Drug Abuse in the Senate. Senator Hughes apparently felt that the individual program managers were doing a fine job of planning new programs, and that the Special Action Office would simply constitute another layer of bureaucracy.

The director of the Special Action Office had tens of thousands of pieces of data about the activities of each of the federal agencies, but he knew that a book of raw data given to Senator Hughes would be unlikely to change the Senator's mind.

Some of the members of the Special Action Office had seen computer-generated maps and decided to attempt to use large computer-generated graphics in hearings before Senator Hughes' subcommittee. A charting and mapping project was designed to make use of the vast amount of detailed data that had been collected to present in a comprehensive portrait of Drug Abuse Prevention expenditures; the portrait would demonstrate (1) that the Special Action Office thoroughly understood the dimensions of all the existing grant programs, and (2) that there was indeed a need for coordination. Seven different types of maps were produced, some showing data for metropolitan areas, others data for states. The maps showed total expenditures per capita or total expenditures per estimated number of addicts and also showed which agencies were spending the money, how much, and for what. Most of the maps used simple pie charts positioned on the city or state where the money was being spent. The size of each pie was proportional to either the total number of dollars or dollars per capita spent, and the pie was color segmented to show the percent of the expenditure being made by each federal agency.

The maps prepared were very large, measuring approximately 3½ by 6 feet, so that when shown during the hearings, they could be seen from a distance and would receive the full attention of the members.

The maps did their job! When Senator Hughes saw them, he said, "That's the first time a federal agency has done its homework before it's come up before my subcommittee." Shortly thereafter, Senator Hughes' subcommittee approved the Special Action Office's charter.

There are two reasons why the maps worked. First, they showed the proper data in a nontechnical format that could be easily understood by the audience: most people are familiar with maps. Computer printouts can rarely accomplish the same goal, because printouts appear overwhelming to people unfamiliar with their format. Second, the maps were carefully designed to illustrate the points that needed to be made. *Too often graphics are made to illustrate data without the essential prior decision of what purpose the graphics should serve.*

The Equal Employment Opportunity Commission Action Against AT&T

Before the Equal Employment Opportunity Commission (EEOC) had the power to sue employers in Federal District Court, it was authorized to intervene before regulatory agencies in an effort to bring about more equal employment opportunity. Under this authority, in 1970 the EEOC intervened before the Federal Communications Commission (FCC) to attempt to force the American Telephone & Telegraph Company (AT&T) and its operating companies to make available more employment and advancement opportunities for women and minority groups. In particular, EEOC claimed that there was a nationwide pattern of discrimination against women; that women were channeled into a particular set of jobs; and that those jobs had no room for substantial upward mobility. Men, on the other hand, were allegedly channeled into jobs that had opportunities for major management responsibility.

EEOC asked the Federal Communications Commission to delay AT&T's request for a rate increase. The FCC responded by saying that it would not delay the request but would set up a bifurcated hearing process in which it would, in two separate hearings, hear the EEOC charges of discrimination and the AT&T request for rate increase. FCC would judge each independently. If a finding of discrimination was reached and was not appropriately addressed, future rate increase hearings would be affected.

The attorneys directing the AT&T Task Force at the Equal Employment Opportunity Commission realized that the case would turn, in part, on how the statistical analyses of employment practices were perceived by the Federal Communications commissioners. EEOC retained several of the nation's most prominent labor economists and statisticians; AT&T retained others of equal competence. The EEOC attorneys realized early that, by means of esoteric changes in the analyses and models being used, one expert economist could make another's look suspect; and, if the economists and statisticians began arguing in technical terms, the FCC commissioners who had to decide the case might not be able to determine what patterns existed.

To avoid this problem, the leader of the EEOC Task Force requested a series of cross-tabulations that would show the pattern of concentration of women and minorities in limited job groups to be a nationwide phenomenon. However, even these cross-tabulations could be very difficult for nontechnical audiences to fully understand, so a second set of computer printouts, this time generated by digital graphics plotters, was requested to present the cross-tabulations so that nontechnical audiences could see the patterns. A series of bar charts were used to show the concentration of men and women in large job categories. Pie charts were used to show (1) the share of total wages each affected group might have received, and (2) the share actually received by the affected group. Other charts were selected for other analyses.

The most fruitful presentation technique used in this case was the conversion of some of the computer-generated charts into computer-generated maps. Each map took one of the chart types and showed, for each of 25 operating companies around the country, the summary graphic located at the operating company's headquarters. The maps were too large to be reproduced effectively here, but their results can be

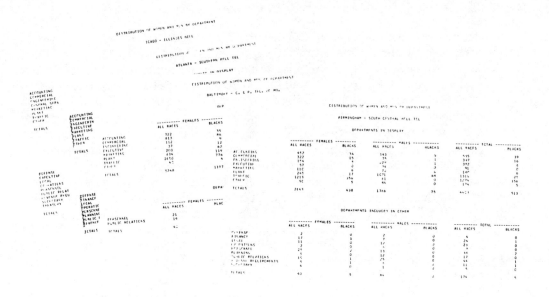

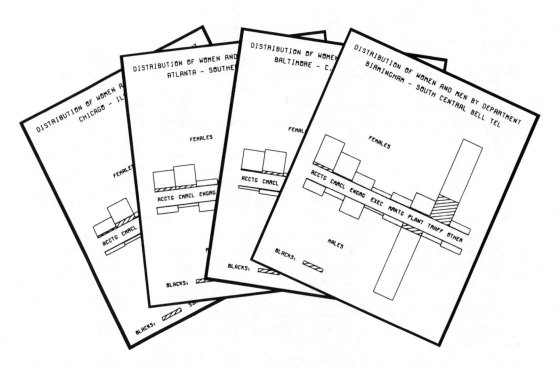

Figure 6-3 Example reprinted from the FCC record showing difference in legibility of tables and charts for showing patterns. (The poor print quality was in the record.)

described. EEOC took each of the maps and placed them on the wall of the Federal Communications Commission hearing room before an important meeting. Each map was covered with brown paper before the hearing began. The EEOC attorney took the lead attorney for AT&T around the room, lifted the brown paper on each map, and showed how it would be quite easy for a nontechnical audience to see the nationwide pattern in the statistics. After seeing the third such map, the AT&T attorney is said to have responded with a four-letter expletive. The case was settled a few weeks later.

In public presentations the lead attorney for the EEOC has noted the power of these graphics to prevent the attorneys from hiding behind confusing testimony of statisticians and economists.

THE PRINCIPAL ROLE OF GRAPHIC DISPLAY IN POLICYMAKING

Each of us who has participated in federal policymaking exercises has developed his or her own model of the process. To understand the role of graphics in the process, one needs to know the policymaking model used by the writer. Here is mine.

The policymaking process—at least the final phase that actually leads to a new policy—has four major phases:

1. *Performing the staff work,* in which the federal analysts and their supporting organizations prepare assessments of existing programs and alternative changes, so that new policy may be grounded on a thorough understanding of the past.

2. *Drafting the new policy paper,* in which leaders among the analysts, with some participation from the ultimate decision maker, prepare a description and justification for the new policy.

3. *Selling the policy,* in which the decision maker and staff present the new policy initiative to other federal agencies, to Congress, and to the Office of Management and Budget or the White House to obtain backing for the new program they have outlined.

4. *Implementation,* during which new regulations are written and the new policy is put into effect.

Graphics are most widely used in phases 1 and 3. That is, they are used when old programs are being analyzed and when the new program is being sold. This is because *their primary value is in transmitting understanding of a trend, pattern, or relationship.* Stated differently, graphics allow a person who understands the pattern shown in the data to communicate that pattern to another person who might not have had the benefit of months to thoroughly analyze the data. *The difference between good graphics and bad graphics is the difference between a graphic that communicates a pattern and one that the reader finds hard to understand, or finds easy to understand but in terms of the wrong pattern.*

In general, graphics are prepared in three modes:

1. As charts or maps contained in written reports, to highlight trends
2. As larger charts used in small-group presentations or in congressional testimony.
3. As overhead projections or 35mm slides

With today's technology, all three modes may be quickly and effectively prepared by computers.

Chart Books for Program Managers

Although new programs and new regulations receive the most attention, a large portion of an organization's policy is made by managers in everyday decision making. Many policymakers have used graphics in the "chart book" format for day-to-day decision making. A "chart book" is a collection of charts that represents an up-to-date picture of the operations of an organization. The chart book is used in several ways.

First, it is a quick reference book for managers to use in identifying problems that need immediate attention (this assumes that its production is extremely timely).

Second, once the user decides that a certain pattern needs to be addressed, the chart book becomes a means of informing subordinates and peers of the nature of the pattern. For example, a chart book developed by one of the nation's largest food cooperatives included a map showing the productivity of marketing staff in various counties. The map showed that sales in a particular region of the country were lagging. Senior management decided to terminate operations in that region and enclosed a copy of that page of the chart book in the memorandum closing the operation.

The third use for the chart book is one of image and trust building. In this role it is carried by the executive or left in a prominent place in the office. When meeting with outside analysts, clients, stockholders, financial analysts, and journalists, the executive uses the chart book as a tool for focusing the discussion. It contributes to the executive's image as a person who is totally familiar with the organization's workings, aware of relevant trends, and in a position to solve problems before they become crises.

Executives in both corporate and government organizations enjoy the benefits of chart books. At Bank of America, for example, chart books are widely used in management. A recent article points out their importance: "We use graphics extensively for internal reports. . . . They help make a point quickly. . . . A monthly report for the board of directors was at least fifty percent charts and graphs."

Choosing the Right Chart

Perhaps the most frequent error in using graphics is choosing the wrong chart. An example: The Legal Services Corporation (LSC) was interested in demonstrating to Congress the extent of coverage of their program. LSC had commissioned the preparation of a computer-generated map to show, county by county, the spread of the Legal Services program. The person who designed the initial map decided to use a dense black shading to show presence. Since a high priority for several years had been to obtain nationwide coverage, LSC found that, except for a couple of counties, the entire nation was covered and, therefore, the entire map was solidly black. What the designer failed to realize was that the director of LSC wanted Congress to understand that LSC had made progress but still had a long way to go. The map implied that the entire country was adequately covered and no further effort, or money, was needed—a conclusion the director did not want.

Another example of mistaken choice is the graph in Figure 6-4 showing the federal budget deficit. In the first chart the deficit line declines; but a closer look shows that the zero line is at the top of the chart, so that the declining deficit line actually reflects a larger deficit each year. The information would be better illustrated by the second chart, showing the depth of the deficit with bars.

The addition of graphics to a presentation, then, does not guarantee that the data will be effectively presented. Good presentations require graphics that are well selected and well designed.

ACTION PLAN FOR THE FIRST COMPUTER GRAPHICS PROJECT

Learning to use graphics in policymaking is not always easy. Requests for charts can be late, and data can be changed so often at the last minute that the systems people and graphics producers have difficulty coordinating their efforts. If you have the opportunity to inject graphics into the policymaking and program management processes of an organization, the following action plan is recommended.

Step 1: *Choose a situation that involves an important memorandum or briefing and that gives you at least four weeks to prepare the charts.* The forum should be an important one because staff otherwise will not give the project enough priority to make it work. Four weeks should be allowed because, the first time, it will take that long.

Step 2: *Find a helper.* The helper should be a person who has used graphics in a similar arena before and can help you select the most effective chart and the most effective method of producing it. Try to find someone inside your organization to act as your helper. If you try to use graphics the first time without such a person, you'll find that the hurdles are too large to overcome. You may end up dropping back to manual methods or using no graphics at all.

Step 3: *Collect and organize your data.* This may seem obvious, but we are often asked to generate charts for a briefing before the data are ready. If the situation is such that the data will be changing up until the last minute, you can still accomplish this step by obtaining a set of estimates of what the data will say. You can use the set of estimates for your sketches and planning and put in the final data at the last minute.

Step 4: *Decide on the key points to be made from the data.* To do this,

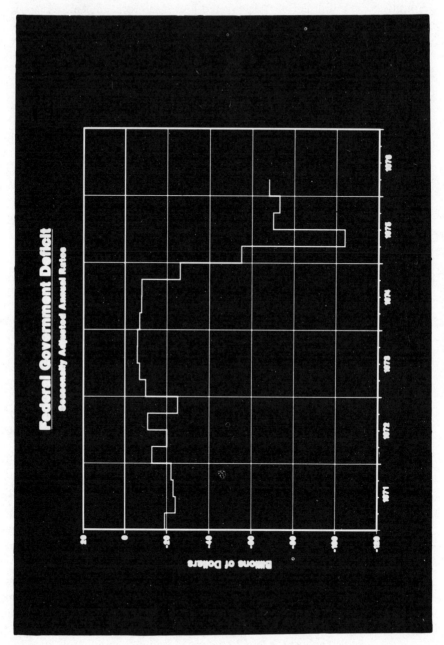

Figure 6-4(a)   Line chart.

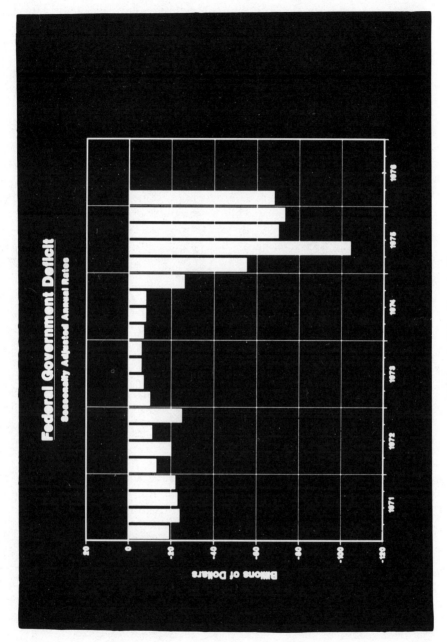

Figure 6-4(b) Bar chart.

consider the presentation you are trying to make, decide on its objectives, and then analyze the data to find the information that supports those objectives. Then write a one-sentence summary of the information you think the data in a particular table convey. If you cannot summarize the information in one sentence, you will not be able to make an effective chart. Once you have your key summary sentences and your back-up data organized, you are ready to move to step 5. (*Caution:* Limit the number of charts. Usually if you include more than ten kinds of charts, you will so weaken the emphasis given to each one that the audience will not have a chance to focus on the main points.)

Step 5:   *Prepare sketches.* Sketch the graphic that you think most effectively presents the data and makes the point.

Step 6:   *Take the sketches to a graphic artist.* Ask a graphic artist to look at your sketches and suggest improvements. It will help if the graphic artist is familiar with the computer graphics techniques that will be used; that way, the artist will not choose a design that requires unusual altering of the computer program. At least a few graphic artists are available who know what computers can and cannot do, and more are learning each day.

Step 7:   *Take the improved sketches to a representative of the ultimate audience.* (This is a very important feedback step.) Take the charts, after improvement by a graphic artist, to someone who understands the views of the people who will be receiving the presentation or the memo. Ask that person to look at the sketches and tell you where you may be incorrect or may be raising an issue that will undermine the presentation. Listen very carefully, because this is the one chance you may have to test the charts before they are finally presented.

Step 8:   *Program the computers to prepare the final graphs.* You may have noticed that we have not involved the computer until this final step. Most computer people turn these projects around and start by programming the computer. Such activity can lead to too much wheel-spinning and to the preparation of charts that are not needed, either because (1) the graphic artists find that the charts were poorly designed, (2) the audience thinks the charts are poorly developed, or (3) the charts did not illustrate the important points to be presented. If, on the other hand, you go through the first seven steps, this computer step will be cost effective.

The computer graphics field is growing at a great rate. IBM, Digital Equipment Corporation, Hewlett-Packard, and other large computer firms have entered the field. Top-level managers and policy analysts have begun to demand charts in lieu of, or in addition to, tables. Systems developers and management information systems staff should view this new development as a major opportunity to increase their visibility in their organization and to help make the computer more valuable to the policymakers. The real value of graphics is that they amplify the worth of data. Considering the amount of money spent today on gathering and tabulating data in information systems, amplification through the use of graphics can be worth a great deal of money to the people financing the data collection.

Chapter **7**

Regional Environmental Analysis and Assessment Utilizing the Geoecology Data Base* †

R. J. Olson

J.M. Klopatek

C.J. Emerson

ABSTRACT

Regional analysis and assessment studies examine the spatial, temporal, and functional characteristics of geographic areas whose size and boundary configurations often depend on the definition of a particular problem. Thus, reference may be made to ecological, urban, economic, political, or abstract regions. The fundamental steps in regional environmental assessment include characterizing the regional environment, determining potential stress areas in the region, and evaluating possible impacts from the perturbation being assessed. Computer car-

*Research sponsored by the Office of Technology Impacts, U. S. Department of Energy, under contract W-7405-eng-26 with Union Carbide Corporation.

†Publication No. 1389, Environmental Sciences Division, Oak Ridge National Laboratory.

102

tography is a valuable tool within each step to provide displays, for visual interpretation, of resource data or analysis results. Evaluation techniques may include statistical procedures, simulation models, or systems analysis. However, having data available at uniform resolution and proper scale is a key factor in regional studies. Three examples are presented, each using different analysis methods and computer graphics, that utilized the Geoecology Data Base as the key data source.

To address environmental problems at the regional scale, the county-level Geoecology Data Base was developed at Oak Ridge National Laboratory (ORNL). The data base provides information on many aspects of the environment for common spatial cells, thus accommodating a variety of analysis needs and methodologies. Using selected variables from existing data sources, a standardized digital data base was created for the conterminous United States. Over 1000 variables on file for county-subcounty units provide data on terrain, water resources, forestry, vegetation, wildlife, agriculture, land use, climate, air quality, population, and energy. This paper describes the data base and illustrates the utility of the county-level data base with three examples.

The Geoecology Data Base is utilized in conjunction with statistical analysis (SAS) and computer cartographic display (SYMAP, EZMAP, etc.) programs both to characterize regional environmental systems and to delineate possible environmental impacts. Much of the effort involved in creation and expansion of the Geoecology Data Base consists of obtaining and editing diverse inventory and monitoring files. An integral aspect of this activity is the promotion of data exchange through increased awareness of available data and development of more efficient exchange methods. Data base inventories and exchange standards are described as a joint product of the eight Department of Energy (DOE) laboratories.

The three examples involve regional environmental assessment and planning studies conducted by the Environmental Sciences Division (ESD) at ORNL. First, future patterns of projected levels of SO_2 are overlaid on SO_2-sensitive agricultural crops and forest resources. Second, those areas of potential natural vegetation of the United States as modified or replaced by current land use are depicted. Finally, an ecological evaluation of potential wilderness areas using a number of county-subcounty ecological parameters is discussed. These applications demonstrate the versatility of county-level digital files, such as the Geoecology Data Base, coupled with computer cartography in conducting regional environmental studies.

GEOECOLOGY DATA BASE

The Geoecology Data Base was created by selecting variables from extant sources and storing them in a standardized, county-level (Olson and Goff, 1976; Olson et al., 1980). The County-Level Integrated Data Base (CLIDE) used within the CEQ UPGRADE system also uses this approach (CEQ, 1979). The emphasis has been to apply the data base to ongoing research needs through collaboration with specific projects. However, the data base can be assessed directly by investigators. Expanding and updating of the data base is also done according to project needs and funding with the Environmental Sciences Division.

The Geoecology Data Base was designed to meet the needs of regional environmental studies while accommodating the format of the majority of available environmental data. The data base concept of being able to easily overlay thematic data stored at a common spatial unit (counties) for use in regional models was established during the NSF-funded International Biological Program (Figure 7-1) (Burgess and Kern, 1973). A prime consideration was to have a flexible, user-oriented system which could be developed, utilized, and upgraded with minimal costs.

Regional studies require data at various spatial scales (cell sizes) and for different geographic regions. Counties were selected as the primary geographic cell. They represent well-defined spatial units that can be selected or aggregated, based on various regional definition. Crop-reporting districts, state climatic divisions, land resource regions, air quality control regions (AQCRs), water subareas, standard metropolitan statistical areas (SMSAs), Bureau of Economic Analysis areas (BEAs), and states all represent areas defined in terms of aggregates of county units. Furthermore, counties or regional aggregates of them are often the political

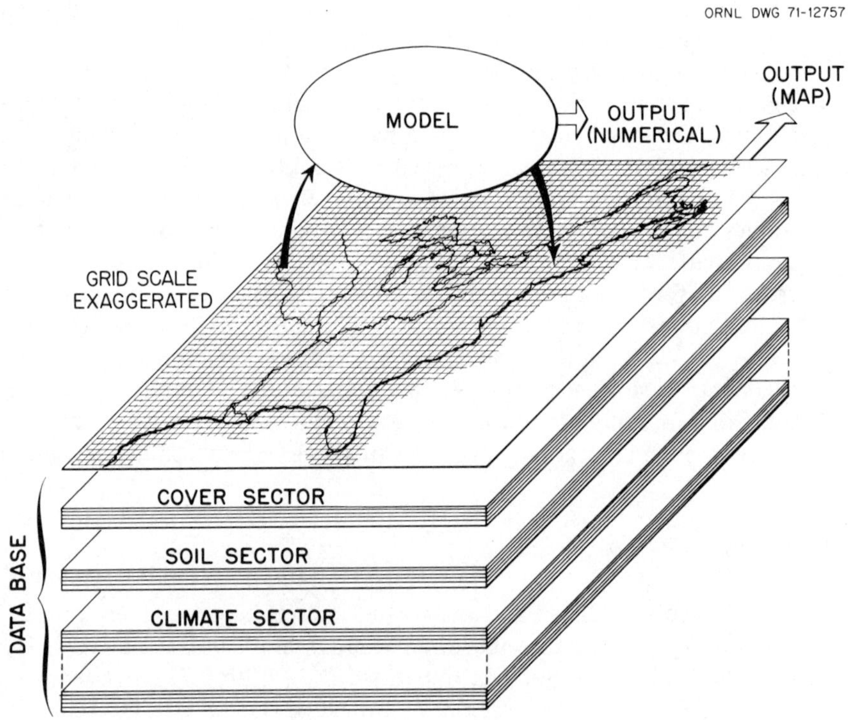

ORNL DWG 71-12757

BIOME RESOURCES MODEL

Figure 7-1

units for implementing policy. In addition, a large amount of environmental data is available as county statistics. Large (and often ecologically more heterogeneous) counties are less desirable as spatial cells for regional analysis. Subcounty units, based on physiographic considerations, have been designated for the larger counties in the eastern states (e.g., Florida, Maine, Minnesota) in order to store data in more environmentally homogeneous cells. Remaining to be done is subdivision of the large western counties. Independent cities, such as those found in Virginia, have been combined with appropriate county units, as environmental data are normally not available for these smaller urban areas.

Most data sets within the data base provide geographic coverage, or are being expanded to such coverage, to include the conterminous United States (3071 county units). More comprehensive coverage exists for the sixteen southern states (1388 county units). The Federal Information Processing Standards (FIPs) state and county codes are used exclusively for county geocodes.

The temporal aspect of each data set was selected to reflect the most current conditions. In the case of rapidly changing sources, data sets contain observations from a series of years. The reference year for most files lies between 1965 and 1978. Agricultural productivity, bird populations, air quality, and population are examples of files with several years of data. Land-use changes occur very rapidly for certain areas, but current data are not available at the county level to define these changes. Climatic data sets include monthly, 30-year norms to allow definition of the annual climatic cycle.

The data base is organized into thematic sectors that contain data sets. For example, the agriculture sector has a data set for crop statistics and another for livestock statistics. Each data set contains a set of variables such as state and county identifiers, reference year, and data items. Data sets are usually created by selecting variables from a single data source. Within the Geoecology Data Base, data sets consist of either one or multiple observations per county unit to minimize storage requirements. With single observations per spatial unit, each computer record contains all the variables for a county. As an example, within the forest resource data set, each county has an observation containing acreage estimates for each of the twelve major forest types in the East, even though not all forest types occur in each county. Data sets with multiple observations per spatial unit include mammal, bird, tree, and vegetation lists. In these cases there is an observation per county unit for each species or type that occurs within the county rather than a single observation containing a variable-length species list. Data sets with multiple observations are often very large and are stored on magnetic tapes rather than online disk units.

The current status of the Geoecology Data Base is summarized in Tables 7-1 and 7-2, which indicate types of files, number of variables, and geographic coverage. Table 7-1 lists files with one observation per county, while Table 7-2 includes files with multiple observations per county. Using the average number of observations per county for data sets with multiple observations, there are currently over 1000 variables stored per county unit. For the South there are an additional 500 variables per county. The Geoecology Data Base also includes dictionaries to provide English translations of the codes used in the system and index files to define regions in which individual county units are located. Indices exist for climatic

Table 7-1

Table 7-1 NUMBERS OF VARIABLES BY GEOGRAPHIC COVERAGE FOR THOSE DATA SETS IN THE GEOECOLOGY DATA BASE ARRANGED WITH ONE OBSERVATION PER COUNTY UNIT

| Thematic Sector | Geographic Coverage* | | | Total Variables |
	South	East	U. S.	
Agriculture	24	73		97
Air Quality	15			15
Base data and indices	6		42	48
Climate		72	90	162
Energy	55		155	210
Forestry	49			49
Land	21		64	85
Population	25		44	69
Terrain		46		46
Total variables for data sets with one observation per county unit	195	191	395	781

*South—16 southeastern states; East—37 eastern states; U. S.—48 conterminous states.

Table 7-2 AVERAGE NUMBER OF VARIABLES FOR DATA SETS WITHIN THE GEOECOLOGY DATA BASE ARRANGED WITH MULTIPLE OBSERVATIONS PER COUNTY UNIT AND COVERING THE CONTERMINOUS UNITED STATES

Data Set	Number of Variables per Observation	Average Observations per County Unit	Average Variables per County Unit
Breeding bird surveys*	8	100.0	305
Ecoregions	6	2.4	8
Endangered Species	6	2.2	8
Land capability by land use	28	12.3	281
Mammal species ranges	6	8.2	4
Soil†	8	2.0	11
Tree species ranges	6	32.5	38
Vegetation, potential	8	2.5	13
Vegetation, adjusted	8	2.5	13
			681

*Breeding bird surveys are based on 1825 routes within the United States.
†Soils data cover only the eastern states.

divisions, crop-reporting districts, land resource areas, forest inventory units, air quality control regions, water subareas, and others.

Computer System

The Statistical Analysis System (SAS) (Barr and others, 1976) provides a user-oriented file management system with extensive statistical capabilities (Olson and Strand, 1978). Interactive editing and retrieval are available in SAS. SAS also has the flexibility to interface user-written programs to the system for direct access by an SAS program. Each file in the data base is stored as an SAS data set with the directory that contains descriptive information for each variable. The 55 online data sets occupy over 10 million bytes of storage.

SYMAP is used to produce contour maps utilizing county centroids as data points and county statistics for data values. Conformant maps consisting of shaded county polygons are produced with the EZMAP program developed by the Geographic Systems Group at ORNL. All storage and processing are accomplished on an IBM 360/91 computer at ORNL.

Data Resources

An extensive effort is required to find appropriate data sources and to reformat them to create a data base such as the Geoecology Data Base. This experience has also been shared by other agencies requiring county-level thematic data to conduct regional studies (Morris and Novak, 1979). The Interlaboratory Working Group for Data Exchange (IWGDE) was established in 1976 to increase the sharing of data resources among the eight DOE-funded laboratories (Benkovitz, 1978). Based on the Geoecology Data Base experience and IWGDE participation, inventories of available thematic data, problems encountered in large thematic files, and data exchange standards being developed by IWGDE are discussed by Benkovitz.

Information centers are available to automatically search keywords and abstracts for books and literature on a variety of topics. However, they do not usually contain descriptions of thematic digital files. Such files are usually created, maintained, and not widely documented by mission-oriented agencies to fulfill their specific needs. Diligent searching and personal contacts are required to find these unique and very useful data sets.

Inventories of spatial data at ORNL have been published periodically since 1975 (Shriner and others, 1978), and a combined inventory of 820 data bases, graphics packages, and models from the eight national laboratories has been published (Shriner and Peck, 1978). These and similar inventories provide a means to locate potential sources of thematic data files. However, it must be appreciated that the custodians for most of these files are actively involved in research and development programs and are not oriented to fulfilling requests on data files.

Our experience with extant data has emphasized the need for extensive data checking. Data problems encountered include erroneous data, missing data, wrong county identifiers, and inconsistent county identifiers such as geocodes for independent cities or other areas (e.g., Yellowstone National Park). The most fruitful ways to determine errors are:

1. Using the data
2. Generating thematic maps
3. Searching sorted lists
4. Calculating univariate statistics
5. Associating two or more independent files.

Although users of a data set may eventually find errors, we have found that a preliminary thematic map of a variable will quickly display possible inconsistencies through irregularities in the spatial pattern. In addition, SAS is used to generate ordered listings and simple statistics that often indicate questionable values.

One of the most thorough methods to discover errors is to combine two independent files by county and check for inconsistencies. Based on ecological relationships, tree species occurrence can be checked against potential vegetation types with a county; for example, many tree species do not grow in areas classified as prairie. Another example of cross-file checking would be comparing county acreages as given in most files. Most files that contain an estimate of total county area do not agree with the 1970 census values used as our base county acreage. Some of these differences stem from the classification of small and large water bodies within an inventory or from real changes in county boundaries. However, in other cases it has been exceedingly difficult to resolve differences in the elementary statistics of county size.

The experiences described above have led to the development of data exchange guidelines by IWGDE. Members of IWGDE have published data exchange standards (Benkovitz and Wiley, 1977; Brooks and others, 1978) and are extending these conventions to accommodate various geographic-based files. These guidelines specify the format for a data definition file that describes the contents of the associated data file. The software to write and read the exchange files has been implemented for IBM, CDC, PDP, and NOVA computers as a prerequisite for efficient data exchange. The current standard is under consideration by the American National Standards Committee, X3L5 (Information Interchange Data Descriptive File ANSI X3L5/78-62), to be adopted as a formal ANSI standard.

To minimize editing and reformatting efforts, the IWGDE has drafted a set of conventions for the content of thematic files. Conventions include exchange standard format, five-digit FIPS geocodes for county units, definition of independent city/county aggregations, metric units of measure, missing value codes, and documentation standards (Benkovitz, 1979). As files become converted to conform to these conventions, they would be designated as reference data bases. Reference data bases would be created by persons familiar with the subject content and actively using the file, so that errors and inconsistencies would be minimized. Table 7-3 lists currently available data bases that IWGDE considered essential to regional studies. IWGDE is not creating this set of reference data bases but has proposed the conventions that would yield a set of compatible, useful, thematic data bases for the nation.

APPLICATIONS OF THE GEOEOCOLOGY DATA BASE

Air Pollution Impacts

One of the activities of the Environmental Sciences Division (ESD) is to predict and evaluate environmental impacts from energy technologies. As part of this role, ESD studies possible future environmental impacts in the South from the expanded use of coal. One of the primary impacts from burning more coal appears to be the in-

Table 7-3 EXTANT SPATIAL DATA BASES PROPOSED BY THE DOE INTERLABORATORY WORKING GROUP FOR DATA EXCHANGE AS CANDIDATE REFERENCE DATA BASES*

	Data Base	Year	Geographic Unit	Original Source
1.	Population (by age, sex, race)	1950	Counties	Census
		1960	Counties	Census
		1970	Counties	Census
		1975	Counties	Census
		1980	Counties	Census
2.	County and city data book	1972	Counties, cities	Census
		1977	Counties, cities	Census
3.	MED–X	1970	Counties, cities	Census
4.	Mortality rates (53 causes)	1968–1972	Counties	NCHS
		1973–1976	Counties	NCHS
5.	Air quality control regions	1975	Counties	EPA
6.	Point source emissions	1974–1978	Aggr., points	EPA
7.	Ambient air quality	1974–1978	Points, AQCR's	EPA
8.	PARAP (population at risk to air pollution)	1974–1976	Counties	LBL
9.	Weather station locations	—	Points	NOAA
10.	Weather surface observations	1800s–1980	Points	NOAA
11.	Monthly temperature and precipitation for state climatic divisions	1931–1980	County Aggregates	NOAA
12.	Wind roses	—	Points	
13.	Watershed boundaries	—	Polygons	USGS
14.	Water quality (STORET, WATSTORE)	—	Points	USGS, EPA
15.	Water quality (NASQAN)	1974–1980	Basins	USGS
16.	Land use from conservation needs inventory	1976, 1977	Counties	USDA
17.	Agriculture production	1979	Counties	USDA
18.	Endangered species	1981	Counites	USF&WS, BNL
19.	BNL energetics atlas	1972–1974	Counties	BNL
20.	Generating utility reference file	1981	Points	DOE
21	Coal reserves	1977	Counties	DOI
22.	County outlines	1980	Counties	Census
23.	Census tract boundaries	1970	Tracts	Census
24.	World data bank II	1977	Polygons	

*Updated 1982

creased levels of sulfur dioxide (SO_2), which causes injury to certain agricultural crops and forest (timber) resources.

To estimate the potential impacts of increased levels of SO_2 on vegetation, we used maps generated from long-range trajectory models based on coal-use scenarios for 1985 (Davis, 1978). Estimates of SO_2 levels were transcribed from a rectangular grid to county centroid coordinates and mapped with SYMAP (Fig. 7-2a). Since it was almost impossible to ascertain what effect ambient SO_2 levels would have on macroscale systems, the map of predicted 1985 levels was overlaid with maps of the vegetation most likely to be impacted. This was done for soybean cropland (Fig.

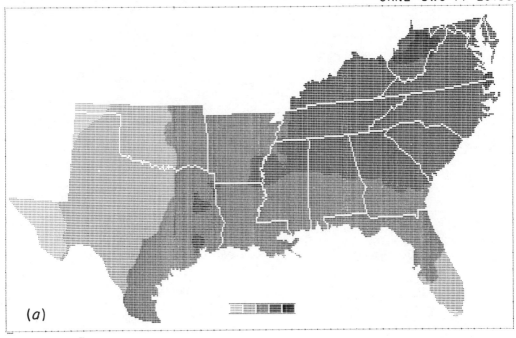

(a)

Figure 7-2(a)

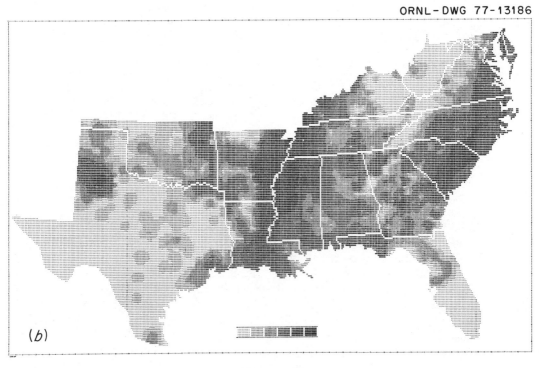

(b)

Figure 7-2(b)

ORNL-DWG 77-20842

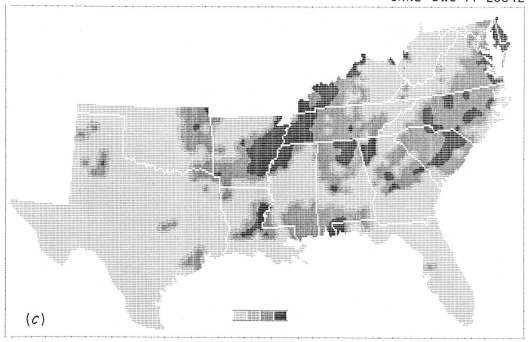

(c)

Figure 7-2(c)

ORNL-DWG 77-13189

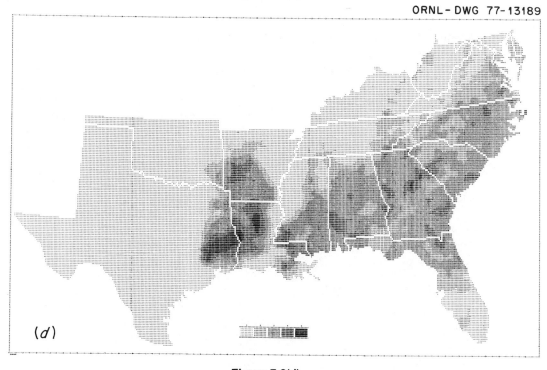

(d)

Figure 7-2(d)

7-2b) and softwood forests (predominantly pine species), because they are known to be sensitive to SO_2 pollution. The darkest regions on the resulting maps indicate the coincident areas with the highest crop productivity (Fig. 7-2c) or highest softwood productivity (Fig. 7-2d) and the highest levels of atmospheric SO_2.

While the role of emissions from coal-fired electric plants in the magnitude and occurrence of these SO_2 levels may be debated, it is likely that the effluents from steam electric plants will interact with those from other industrial and urban sources. Thus, while the SO_2 levels depicted here may not cause acute vegetational injury, they may, when combined with ambient SO_2 levels, cause severe chronic injury. Furthermore, levels represent annual averages for county cells, so that there still may be periodic episodes that result in acute injuries to the vegetation. The darkest areas on the computer-generated maps indicate areas of justifiable concern. For example, if just those counties that are darkest on the SO_2-soybean map (Fig. 7-2c) were to suffer a 10 percent drop in yield, the result would be a loss $0.6 \times 10^6 \text{ m}^3$ (17 million bushels), or over \$100 million per year. Although the results are very general at this point, they indicate a substantial potential impact of SO_2 on pine forests and soybean yields. This coupling of the Geoecology Data Base to the synagraphic mapping systems demonstrates not only the applicability of the data base, but the versatility of the combined systems for regional analysis.

Natural Vegetation and Land Use

The need to incorporate information on land use and vegetation into regional studies prompted the use of extant data in order to determine the amounts and types of natural vegetation existing within the United States. The preservation of natural vegetation is an integral part of the U. S. Forest Service's Roadless Area Review and Evaluation program (RARE-II) (USFS, 1978). This program allocates roadless areas to wilderness as part of the National Wilderness Preservation System or to other land uses based on many criteria. In an ecological analysis of RARE-II tracts (Klopatek and others, 1980), we developed estimates of natural vegetation types adjusted for current land use. The amount of a particular vegetation type occurring on a RARE-II tract was compared to the adjusted estimate of the amount of that vegetation type occurring in the United States. This measure of vegetation uniqueness was one of several factors used to identify ecologically similar tracts that would be used to resolve land-use conflicts while preserving all natural vegetation types.

The determination of the loss of natural vegetation was accomplished in four steps. The first involved acquiring county information on the amount of potential area that could be occupied by each natural vegetation type. Vegetation data were digitized from Kuchler's (1964) map of Potential Natural Vegetation of the United States. The area of each vegetation type in each county in the United States was measured by using either planimeter or a dot grid method. These data were then stored in the Geoecology Data Base.

The second step was to obtain current estimates of land-use practices for county units. The 1967 Conservation Needs Inventory (CNI) (USDA, 1971) land-use data, stored in the data base, were aggregated to give land-use estimates for agriculture, pasture, range, forest, other nonfederal rural land (not classified as

LESS THAN 20   20 TO 40   40 TO 60   60 TO 80   MORE THAN 80

Figure 7-3

cropland, pastureland, rangeland, or forest), urban build-up, water, and federal land. Urban, water, and federal subdivisions of the noninventory acreage were obtained from Iowa State University Statistical Laboratory. The acreages were normalized to the 1970 census county acreage.

In the third step, probabilities were assigned to vegetation types that defined their probability of conversion to other land-use types. The probabilities of being converted to agricultural land, pasture land, or water areas (reservoirs) were assigned to the respective vegetation types based on a number of sources (Klopateck and others, 1979). For all large western urban areas (>10,000 ha) the county urban areas were keyed, through visual interpretation, to the potential vegetation that they replaced. For all counties containing urban areas in the vegetationally more homogeneous, smaller eastern counties, the total urban land was subtracted proportionally from the potential vegetation types occurring in the county. The same was done for the CNI "other nonfederal land" category.

Finally, a FORTRAN computer algorithm was developed to subtract the CNI county land-use data from the appropriate potential natural vegetation types occurring within the county. Figure 7-3 graphically depicts the percentage of potential natural vegetation still existing in the conterminous United States today. The results give a fairly accurate and indeed startling portrayal of the area occupied by natural vegetation. The spatial pattern of remaining natural vegetation areas reinforces the suggestion that preservation action is urgently required to protect many vegetation types. The entire results of this study are discussed in a paper by Klopatek and others (1979). From a pragmatic viewpoint this example represents a melding of extant and empirical data within the data base to produce results that can be used to analyze and assess regional environmental problems.

Wilderness Area Evaluation

As mentioned, ESD was involved in ecologically rating the U. S. Forest Service's 2686 roadless tracts, which totaled nearly 25 million ha (62 million acres) in the National Forests. The Department of Energy was concerned with both the energy-resource potential of the RARE-II sites and environmental values. The DOE funded this project to evaluate both the ecological and energy values of the tracts, which ranged in size from one to several hundred thousand hectares and occurred from Puerto Rico to Alaska. Evaluation of these tracts required the development of a sophisticated methodology as well as extensive data bases.

Expression of the ecological value of a wilderness area involved (1) identifying important natural resources located within the area, (2) determining the magnitude of those resources, and (3) computing the area quality value. The area quality value combines a particular resource's magnitude and importance. This procedure results in a value that can be compared to similarly derived values for other sites.

Based on a number of considerations, four major parameters were chosen to construct a quantitative ecological index of a tract of land located anywhere in the United States (Klopatek and others, 1980). These were

1. Vegetation: the vegetation communities according to Kuchler's (1964) system adjusted for current land uses as discussed in the previous section

2. Avian communities: the species and abundance of birds

3. Mammal communities: The species of mammals present

4. Endangered or threatened species: the occurrence of such species and whether or not the area provides critical habitat for the species

Each wilderness tract was evaluated within a hierarchical framework to provide the capacity to search for tracts of similar value when wilderness/development conflicts arose. All parameters were evaluated at national, regional, ecoregion, sectional, and individual tract levels. The 54 ecoregions of the United States (Bailey, 1976), representing broad areas considered to be ecologically homogeneous, were used to define ecological strata within which alternative tracts could be selected. The combining of values for various levels provides a measure of how a particular tract's resources relate to the whole country. Tracts containing a nationally or regionally rare resource would be given a high rank for the attribute. Mathematically, the ecological index reflects a filtering of information from one level to another. Thus, by combining values for all the parameters at all levels, we can calculate an overall ecological index for each roadless tract.

An application of the methodology is shown for ecoregion M3112, the Douglas fir region of the United States (Fig. 7-4). This figure displays the overall

OVERALL ECOLOGICAL INDICES
M3112

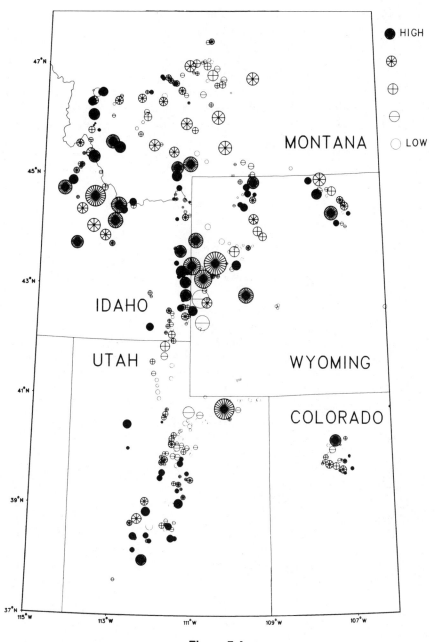

Figure 7-4

ecological indices, which are composites of the vegetation, mammal, avian, and endangered species rankings. The size of the circle is proportional to the size of the tracts. The most dense circles indicate that the tract ranked in the upper 20 percent of all tracts; the open circles indicate a ranking in the lower 20 percent. As can be seen, the upper level·ratings of the tracts are area- and state-independent. These ecological ratings were then compared with the energy rating of these tracts (this area contains the Rocky Mountain Overthrust Belt, a region claimed by industry to have the potential for greater oil and gas reserves than the Alaskan North Slope). Potential decision conflicts between tracts that received high energy and high ecological ratings were noted for alternative or mitigation strategies. The methodology developed for the ecological analysis and evaluation of the RARE-II tracts can thus be viewed as a trade-off analysis to help resolve environmental and energy resource conflicts. This application demonstrates the flexibility of the Geoecology Data Base in combining statistical analysis and computer mapping. It shows the relative comparison of tracts of land that are either subcounty in size or multicounty in area.

DISCUSSION

In October 1975 a week-long workshop on energy-related regional analysis was held in Oak Ridge, Tennessee, with participants from most of DOE-funded National Laboratories. Within the workshop, a task force on regional environmental data bases drafted a statement that stressed the need for interagency cooperation and coordination in developing a national environmental "data base." The goals were to minimize costly duplication of inventory and data management efforts, provide needed information for rational resource development, and promote optimal resource inventory design. The task force recommended a "distributed data base" concept, with the extensive data files continuing to reside in the responsible agencies. Creating a huge centralized data center was not considered feasible or desirable. Those agencies involved in environmental analysis and assessment, such as DOE, the Environmental Protection Agency, and the Council on Environmental Quality, could then assemble and synthesize a data base of selected variables from the distributed data files. The resulting data base would hopefully have quick response capability, spatial and temporal standardization, and high exportability.

The Geoecology Data Base represents a county-level file that has been created by selecting variables from distributed data bases and doing extensive editing to standardize the data base. We demonstrated, by example, that county-level data bases can be flexible enough to meet the needs of various regional studies. Furthermore, we described the conventions for data exchange and standardized reference data bases that are being implemented by the DOE Interlaboratory Working Group for Data Exchange. These guidelines are available for use by persons creating and willing to share thematic data files. With additional review, these standards can be adopted by the community of agencies involved in compiling and applying these data bases. With these standards, updating and expanding the Geoecology Data Base or similar data bases with new data will become a trivial task.

Computer cartographics is an integral part of the analysis and display of regional environmental assessment. Each of the examples utilized different display techniques according to the analysis needs. The artistic considerations of computer-generated maps will continue to improve with more sophisticated design and the addition of color. However, the need for appropriate data will continue to be a prime consideration for regional environmental assessments.

REFERENCES

BAILEY, R. G., *Ecoregions of the United States.* Ogden, Utah: U. S. Forest Service, 1976.

BARR, A. J., J. H. GOODNIGHT, J. P. SALL, and J. T. HELWIG, *A User's Guide to SAS 76.* Raleigh, N. C.: SAS Institute, Inc., Sparks Press, 1976. 329 pp.

BENKOVITZ, C. M., ed., *DOE Interlaboratory Working Group for Data Exchange Progress Report—October 1978.* BNL-51071. Upton, N. Y.: Brookhaven National Laboratory, 1979.

_____, and R. A. WILEY, *Using System 2000 with Proposed ANSI Standards for Data Exchange.* LA-UR-77-2739. Los Alamos, N. M.: Los Alamos Scientific Laboratory, 1977.

BROOKS, A. A., F. D. HAMMERLING, and B. N. McNEELEY. *User's Guide for an IBM PL/1 Implementation of Level 1 of the Proposed American National Standard Specifications for an Information Interchange Data Descriptive File.* ORNL/CSD/TM-74. Oak Ridge, Tenn.: Oak Ridge National Laboratory, 1978. 111 pp.

BURGESS, R. L., and L. H. KERN, eds., *Progress Report 1971–72, Eastern Deciduous Forest Biome, US-IBP.* EDFB/IBP-73/5. Oak Ridge, Tenn.: Oak Ridge National Laboratory, 1973. 326 pp.

COUNCIL ON ENVIRONMENTAL QUALITY (CEQ). *The County-Level, Integrated Data Extraction (CLIDE) Data Base Users Guide.* Washington, D. C.: President's Council on Environmental Quality, 1979. (Draft Report).

DAVIS, R. M. (project coordinator), *A Preliminary Regional Assessment of Coal Utilization in the South,* Vols. I and II. ORNL/TM-6122. Oak Ridge, Tenn.: Oak Ridge National Laboratory, 1978.

KLOPATEK, J. M., J. T. KITCHINGS, K. D. KUMAR, R. J. OLSON, *An Ecological Analysis of the U. S. Forest Service's RARE-II Sites.* ORNL/TM-6813. Oak Ridge, Tenn.: Oak Ridge National Laboratory, 1980.

_____, R. J. OLSON, C. J. EMERSON, and J. L. JONES, "Land Use Conflicts With Natural Vegetation in the United States," *Environ. Conserv.* **6,** 191–199 (1979).

KUCHLER, A. W., *Potential Natural Vegetation of the Conterminous United States.* Am. Geog. Soc. Spec. Publ. No. 36. New York, 1964.

MORRIS, S. C., and K. M. NOVAK, eds., *Use of County Level Data in Health, Energy, Demographic, Environmental and Economic Analysis: Proceedings of a Computer-Based Conference, March 1977.* BNL-51041. Upton, N. Y.: Brookhaven National Laboratory, 1979.

OLSON, R.J., C.J. EMERSON, and M.K., NUNGZSSER, *Geoecology: A County-level Environmental Data Base for the Conterminous United States.* ORNL/TM-7351. Oak Ridge, Tenn.: Oak Ridge National Laboratory, 1980.

_____, and F. G. GOFF, "Development and Applications of a Regional Environmental Data Base for Southeastern United States," in B. DREYFUS, ed., *Proceedings of the Fifth Biennial International CODATA Conference,* New York: Pergamon Press, 1976.

_____, and R. H. STRAND, "Management of Diverse Environmental Data with SAS," in *Proceedings of the Third Annual Conference, SAS Users Group, International,* pp. 200–206. Raleigh, N. C.: SAS Institute, Inc., 1978. 320 pp.

SHRINER, C. R., ed., A. A. BROOKS, R. M. DAVIS, F. A. HEDDLESON, P. E. JOHNSON, C. A. LITTLE, A. S. LOEBL, R. J. OLSON, L. J. PECK, B. C. TALMI, J. A. WATTS, and D. L. WILSON, *Spatial Data on Energy, Environmental, and Socioeconomic Themes at Oak Ridge National Laboratory: 1977 Inventory.* ORNL-5395. Oak Ridge, Tenn.: Oak Ridge National Laboratory, 1978. 69 pp.

_____, and L. J. PECK. *Inventory of Data Bases, Graphics, Packages, and Models in Department of Energy Laboratories.* ORNL/EIS-144. Oak Ridge, Tenn.: Oak Ridge National Laboratory, 1978. 281 pp.

U.S. Department of Agriculture (USDA). "National Inventory of Soil and Water Conservation Needs, 1967," Statistical Bulletin No. 461, 1971.

U.S. Forest Service (USFS), *RARE-II, Draft Environmental Statement: Roadless Area Review and Evaluation.* Washington, D. C.: USDA Forest Service, 1978. 112 pp.

Selecting New Town Sites in the United States Using Regional Data Bases

Jack Dangermond

THE PROBLEM

In the last nine years Environmental Systems Research Institute (ESRI) has had a series of clients ask for help in selecting appropriate sites for the development of new towns. While in some cases the possible site locations had been defined for us in advance, in some instances the question was completely open, and a national search was conducted.

This paper describes the process we used in helping one of our clients perform such an open search to locate new towns in the United States. In this client's view a good deal of housing development, including new towns, is considered within too small a planning frame. By making piecemeal decisions about development, the private as well as the public sectors risk mistakes because of a lack of proper perspective. Developers in the past could not afford—or believed they could not afford—to take this larger view; thus their projects often fell victim to local pressures, unforeseen regional forces, or unexpected changes in the pattern of overall regional growth.

In our view, planning within a larger national and regional frame of reference is now made possible by use of automated Geographically Based Information Systems (GBISs), which include both vertically and horizontally integrated data resources. To create a regional data base for southern California, for example, we used data from federal, state, and local government sources (vertical integration); we also used state-level data from several state agencies and county-level data from a number of different counties (horizontal integration).

The overall selection process we shall describe includes a national screening effort, a regional screening, a search for locales within a region, and finally an analysis of specific sites. Each level of the process has somewhat different features, which will be described here, but we will concentrate on a regional screening we performed for southern California.

THE METHODOLOGY

Figure 8-1 is an overall flow diagram of our methodology. It indicates four general phases in the work effort: national screening, regional screening, local assessment, and site analysis.

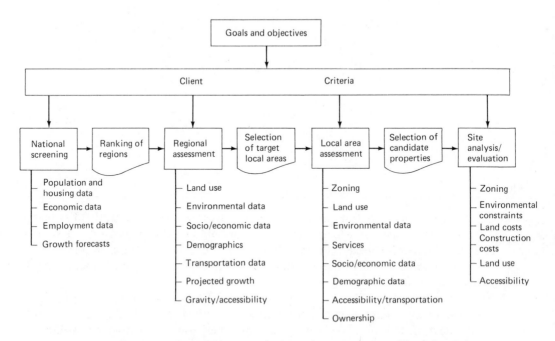

FIGURE 8-1 Flow diagram of screening process, with data examples.

The Process for Selecting the Region Studied

Figure 8-2 is an overall diagram of the data characteristics for each phase of the screening process. While the first phase—the national screening, using data for the various regions of the country—was not actually a part of the present project, we want to sketch the means by which southern California was selected as a region with high potential for locating new towns.

Over a period of eight years ESRI and our client on this project have developed means for using census and other data in order to screen the United States for potential new town sites. The process began with the decision that new towns would best be sited near existing metropolitan areas. In order to study these areas, especially from a socioeconomic point of view, we believed it desirable to have access to an existing automated data base. The U.S. Census provided a framework for this data base.

All Standard Metropolitan Statistical Area (SMSAs) with populations of more than 250,000 were selected for detailed study. From the census data a number

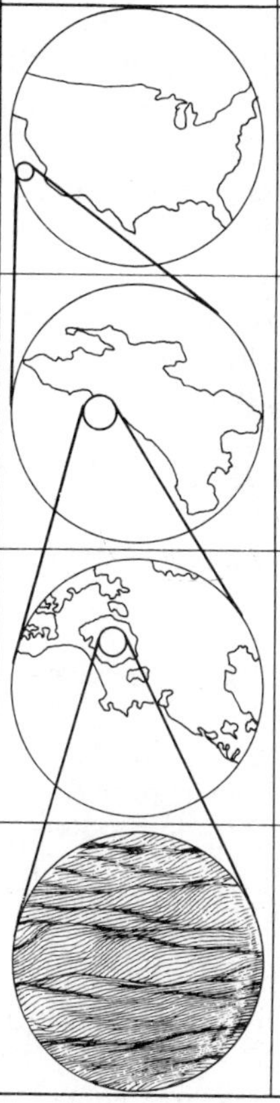

	Area	Size	Scale	Resolution
Countrywide assessment		Total country	1:10,000,000	Metropolitan area
Regional assessment		Thousands of square miles	1:250,000	100–200 acres
Local area assessment		Hundreds of square miles	1:24,000	5–10 acres
Site assessment		Square miles	1:2,000	1–2 acres

FIGURE 8-2   Data characteristics for screening.

of indicators were chosen that we believed were related to the potential success of new-town development. These related to the growth potential of the region, the age distribution of the population, familism, employment, existing housing stock, age of the housing stock, income, and so on. Using these indicators, we ranked each of the SMSAs according to its relative likelihood of supporting new town development. The results were displayed by means of statistical tabulations for each SMSA and for each variable. An overall ranking was also created, and from this southern California was selected as one of the top half-dozen metropolitan regions in terms of potential for needing and supporting this type of major new development.

General Outline of the Process of Regional Analysis for New Town Sites

First, it should be understood that the client's organization was carrying on investigations, especially of socioeconomic factors, that paralleled ESRI's work on locational factors of other kinds.

The general process involved, first of all, the selection of significant geographic indicators (such as land use, topography, and flood hazard areas) and their weightings, which would be used in making the locational decisions. The next step was the collection, reformatting, and interfacing of existing data and the creation of new data that described significant geographic variation according to these selective indicators. These mapped data were next automated and placed in computer files in the form of a GBIS for the southern California region. Finally, by means of automated overlay analysis, the products of the earlier tasks were used to rank all the areas within the region as to their appropriateness for the location of new urbanization. The results of this overlay analysis were then presented as computer-drawn color maps, statistical tabulations, and a report. A data bank containing the results and the raw data on which they were based was created, together with interfaces between it and various other sources of data.

The Study Area

The region examined in this project included about 12,000 square miles of southern California (see Figure 8-3).

Data Collection, Image Acquisition, and Base-Map Creation

To begin, ESRI acquired USGS topographic map sheets of the area at a scale of 1 : 250,000; these served as the planimetric base for the interpretation of the satellite imagery, for mapping, and for automation of the data.

Because of the regional scale of the project it was feasible to use satellite imagery—together with collateral data—as the basic source from which recent data on land use and land cover would be gathered. Landsat imagery provided both color infrared and black-and-white scenes of the region at a scale of 1 : 250,000 with nominal resolutions of 70 m and 30 m, respectively.

Collateral data relating to land use and environmental conditions were acquired from a wide variety of sources. It was necessary that the data be current,

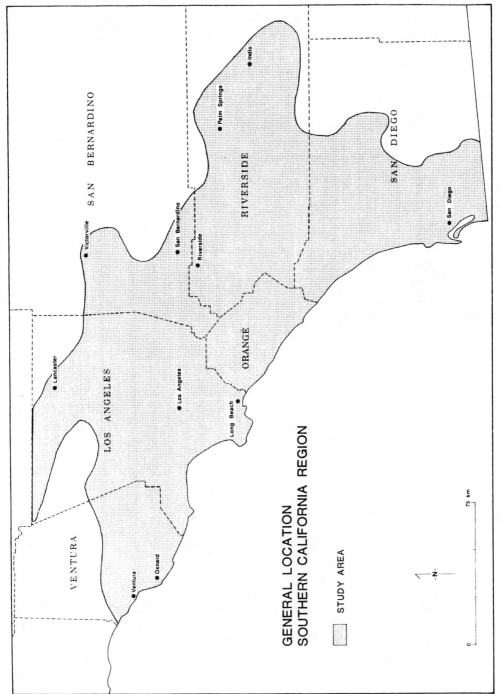

GENERAL LOCATION
SOUTHERN CALIFORNIA REGION

STUDY AREA

FIGURE 8-3   General location southern California region.

consistent, and reliable and that they provide full coverage for the region. Among the kinds of data gathered were USGS Land Use (LUDA) maps, California Department of Fish and Game maps of areas of special biological importance, Federal Aviation Administration Noise Contour Maps for airports, Southern California Association of Governments (SCAG) and Comprehensive Planning Organization (CPO) maps, and a wide range of other data from equally reliable sources.

Image Interpretation

The satellite imagery was used to manually (visually) interpret and map eight classes of land use (including residential, commercial, industrial, general urban, agriculture, natural, water, and public land) and to delineate a variety of environmental phenomena.

Data Integration and Mapping

The data derived from satellite imagery as well as those derived directly and indirectly from collateral sources were integrated and mapped using a modification of the Integrated Terrain Unit Mapping (ITUM) approach (see Hydrologic Engineering Center, 1978) that ESRI has developed, in conjunction with a comprehensive software system (see below) for manipulation and interpretation of terrain variation.

Manual mapping was done at a scale of 1 : 250,000, with the data resolved to the imagery and rectified to the topographic base maps.

Map and Data Automation

The data on the manuscript maps were automated by a process of X,Y-coordinate digitizing. Points, lines, and polygons were recorded using ESRI's Polygon-Intersection-Chain (PIC) system (see Appendices in Dangermond, 1978a). Edit plots of all the automated data were checked against manuscript maps and collateral data to insure accuracy.

Data Conversion to Grid-Cell Format

The locational analyses used in this project required automated grid-cell overlay approaches. Thus it was necessary to convert the polygon, line, and point data to grid-cell data. To accomplish this we used ESRI's GRIPS (Grid Information from Polygon System) software. This converts from X,Y-coordinate data to grid format automatically, using any appropriate cell size (see Figure 8-4).

The polygon data were first converted into grid-cell data using a uniform 155-acre grid-cell network (approximately 48,000 cells for the study region). This 155-acre grid was used chiefly for making test maps during the overlay analysis process. For final graphics a grid-cell size of 7 acres was employed. To create the 7-acre grid-cell files we reprocessed the original polygon, line, and points files using GRIPS; a grid file of approximately *one million* 7-acre cells resulted for the regional study area.

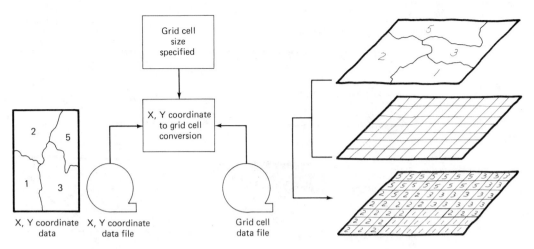

FIGURE 8-4 Converting X, Y coordinate data to a grid cell data file.

Computer Modeling

ESRI, working with the client, developed a series of computer models in order to analyze the data and derive from them information as to which locations were most suitable for urbanization of the kind a new town represents.

Some of the models were of the capability/suitability type; in such analyses the computer was directed to overlay a series of data variables and consider them simultaneously as they pertained to individual grid cells within the region. (The individual variables were selected because of their importance in indicating the capability or suitability of a location to support new towns.) Figure 8-5 illustrates the principle of overlay analysis. The computer can also weight the relative importance of each variable according to decision rules; these rules were supplied by client and ESRI personnel.

Other kinds of models are possible using this software; it is not uncommon for regional-scale planning projects to require 25 to 30 separate models. The major elements considered in this project were access to major highways (a search); a gravity model in which accessibility to residential, commercial, and industrial land uses was examined; an environmental constraints and opportunities map; and a map showing those areas where growth is projected to occur and in which undeveloped land now exists. These various maps were then overlaid on one another to obtain a combined measure of accessibility, capability, and suitability.

Computer Mapping

The results of the various modeling efforts were displayed on a series of computer-directed color maps, created in grid-cell format with a cell size of 7 acres. A matrix of 4 million items was used to generate each map, since for these final maps a total of four different modeled variables was used.

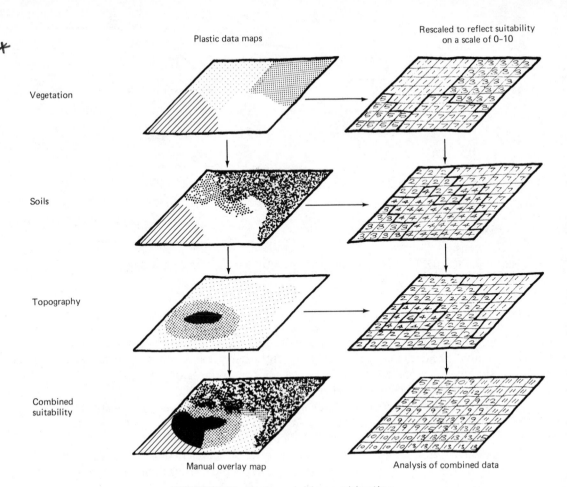

Plastic data maps

Rescaled to reflect suitability on a scale of 0-10

Vegetation

Soils

Topography

Combined suitability

Manual overlay map

Analysis of combined data

FIGURE 8-5 Data variable combination.

These color maps were used by the client to select areas within the region for further study as potential sites for new towns.

Further Analysis of Candidate Areas for New Towns

When the selection of tentative local areas (200 to 800 square miles) that seem suitable for new towns has been made, the next step involves repeating the regional process in a more refined manner. This process is outlined below.

With the candidate areas selected, a detailed data window is created at an enlarged scale (normally 1 : 24,000). To create such a focused data base we can either window the original data file with greater resolution, interface an existing data field, or create a new data bank at finer resolution. In the latter case we repeat steps similar to those performed at the regional level.

Instead of satellite imagery we use aerial photography to provide the additional detail required by the enlarged scale of mapping. New data, particularly socioeconomic data on the local area, are usually required at this scale of analysis.

These data are gathered from appropriate agencies and reformatted as needed for mapping and other kinds of automation. Real estate evaluations are usually done by the client's own professional staff. Where field work of other kinds is required, it may be done by the client, by ESRI, or by other consultant organizations.

Overlay analysis is again performed, using models, decision algorithms, and weightings of variables arrived at in meetings with our client. The results of these analyses are again mapped, at this larger scale, with display in the form of various colored maps of the types described earlier. Using these maps, candidate sites within the localized study areas are identified for detailed site investigation.

Detailed Site Analyses

This final geographic analysis parallels the previous two efforts in many regards; we shall describe only the differences.

Because this is a site-level assessment, the scale of mapping and analysis is generally about 1 : 1000 to 1 : 3000. Data are gathered with sufficient resolution to be useful for development of general land-use plans and to perform environmental assessment. Appropriate aerial photography is used to provide data on details of land use, vegetation cover, and other data that are visually interpretable. Collateral data on natural site features, such as soils data, topographic slope, engineering and basic geology, and hydrology, are gathered at an appropriate resolution and are incorporated into the data base. Automation of the data in X,Y coordinates or grid cells then follows.

The next step involves the computer mapping of these data. (Figure 8-6A and maps 1–7 of Figures 8-6B and 8-6C present typical computer maps resulting from a detailed site investigation.) Preliminary models that identify areas of natural hazard (flooding, mass movement, and so on), ecologically sensitive areas, areas with high erosion potential, and the like are combined to create the final suitability models. Then weighted interpretive models are created to identify the capability and suitability of the site to support housing, roads, recreation areas and facilities, conservation areas, open space, and so forth. The results of these analyses are also displayed as a series of computer maps in various forms to assist planners in the actual layout of the potential new town on the candidate site. (Maps 8, 9, and 10 of Figures 8-6C and 8-6D illustrate interpretive mapping using the data base shown elsewhere in Figure 8-6.)

When these analyses are complete, the client's planners can be fairly confident that a new town can actually be built on the site, that the environmental and engineering problems have been taken into account, and that they might proceed to actual land acquisition with considerable confidence.

Resources Required

Hardware. ESRI used a PRIME 400 system with four digitizing stations for this project (shown in the Appendix).

Software. For this project we used our own ESRI software system (shown in the Appendix). Color maps for final graphics were produced using ESRI's COLOR-

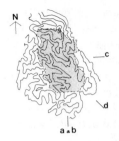

The illustrations presented on this page and the following pages are 3-dimensional drawings of the topographic surface of the site. The drawings are produced using the computer and pen plotter: they display the general topographic relief of the property. The first drawing (a) depicts the view directly north across Goshoke Lake and up the main valley of the site. The second drawing (b) depicts the same north view orientation but from a lower view altitude.

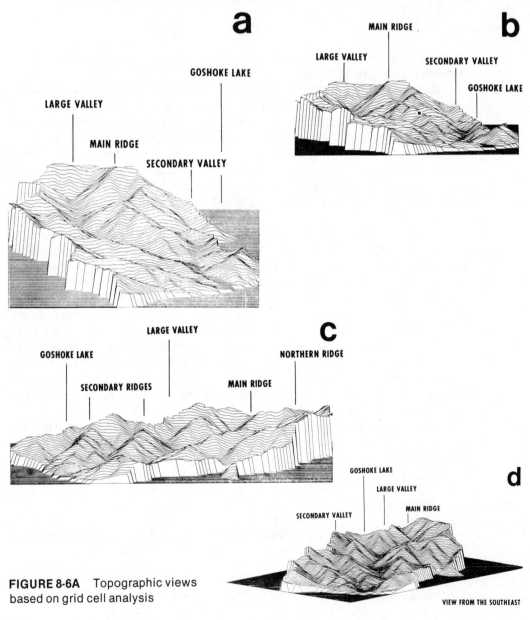

FIGURE 8-6A Topographic views based on grid cell analysis

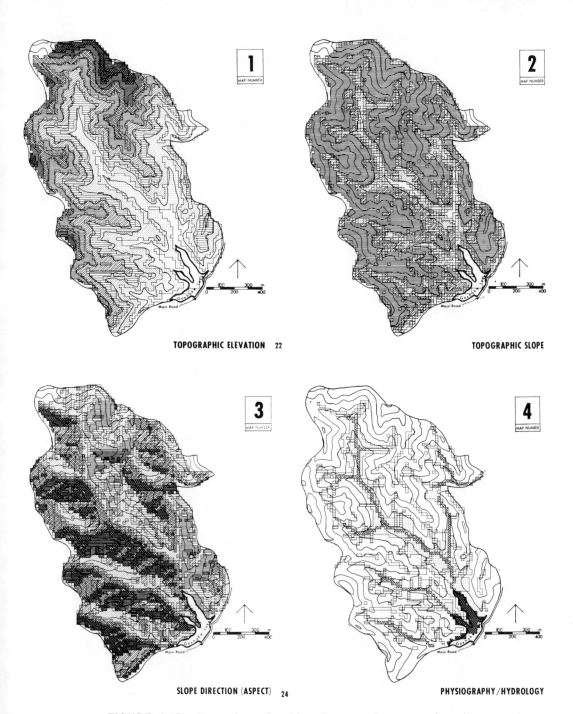

FIGURE 8-6B Examples of grid cell computer maps for site analysis.

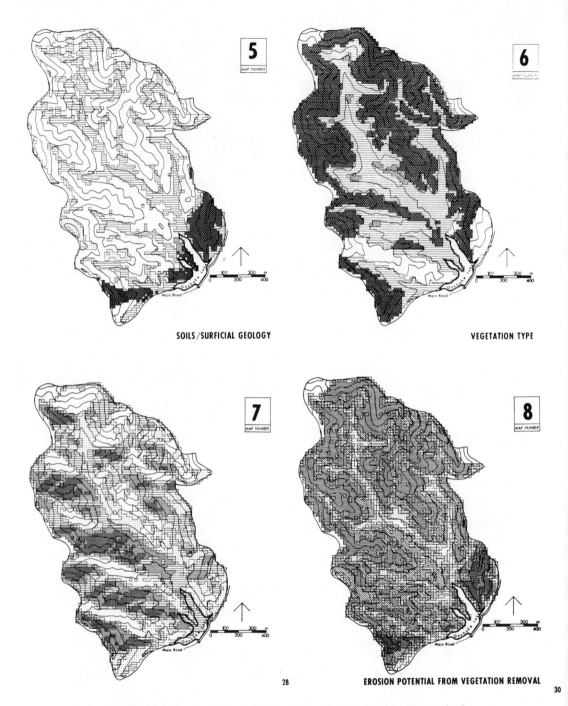

SOILS/SURFICIAL GEOLOGY

VEGETATION TYPE

EROSION POTENTIAL FROM VEGETATION REMOVAL

FIGURE 8-6C Additional grid cell map examples for site analysis.

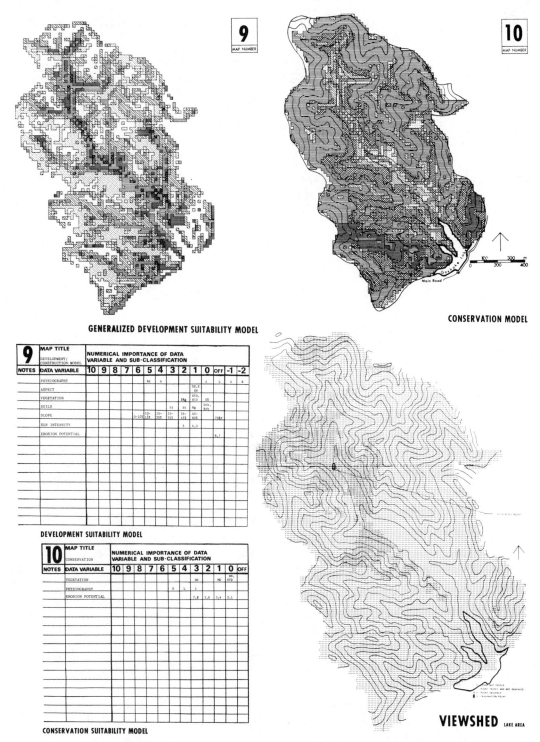

FIGURE 8-6D Examples of a grid cell modeling in site analysis.

MAP software and a DICOMED(R) color film recorder. (Source code for all ESRI software is available for purchase.)

Other. This entire project was completed in about twelve weeks—four of them taken up in waiting for satellite imagery to be delivered. Nine persons worked on the project at ESRI, including professional staff, photointerpreters, digitizer operators, and data processing staff. Total cost to the client for the project was under $40,000. Obviously such a tight schedule and low cost would not have been possible if many of the basic data required had not already existed.

THE ROLE OF COMPUTER GRAPHICS IN SOLVING THE PROBLEM

Some Special Characteristics of the Methodology

To be responsive to the needs of our client we used a methodology based on an automated GBIS (Geographically Based Information System), automated overlay methods to analyze the GBIS, and computer graphics to display the results.

This methodology was characterized by a number of important features, listed below.

1. *All* locations within the study region were considered, since all were stored in the data base. Moreover, the decision made about *each* location was documented by means of the computer maps created.

2. Most of the important factors known or believed to influence the success of the new town siting decision (land use, land development patterns, projected growth patterns, environmental constraints, demographic characteristics of the region, and so on) were considered by the process. (Socioeconomic factors were chiefly considered in more localized analyses performed in a computer mapping process complementary to the present project but not discussed in this paper.)

3. The process used was a flexible one. It took into account both subjective decision factors and objective criteria (such as those based on engineering features of the sites).

4. The concerns of various governmental agencies at several levels of government were taken into account in the process. This was done by obtaining from the various planning and administrative agencies their maps showing where they believed development should and should not be permitted to take place; these maps were then integrated into the GBIS created for this project.

5. The process permitted both major and minor changes to take place in the decision criteria used *without* redevelopment of the basic data in the data base.

6. The system incorporated *automated* interfaces to various kinds of federal government information resources, including U.S. Census data, Depart-

ment of Commerce data of various other kinds, Landsat imagery, and so on.

7. An automated data bank of geographic information was created that can be reused, updated, and reinterpreted as needed.

8. The format of the data bank allows for future vertical integration of information with local, regional, and state government information.

9. The products of the system were color graphic displays, created by the computer, which made the basic information about the region and the results of the decision making understandable both to the planning professionals involved and to the client's decision makers.

Special Benefits of the Methodology

First, we doubt that this project could have been accomplished within this time frame except by computer processing of the data and computer mapping of the results.

Second, we believe that this approach brought increased rationality to the decision-making process. Because we could store and process the geographic information in its primary form, we could be considerably more quantitative and rational. Modeling, for example, required planners to make explicit their criteria for site selection. This encouraged the selection of objective criteria, based on real data about the area under study. Where subjective criteria were used in modeling, they also had to be made explicit. The ability to weight decision factors, which is part of the capability of the GRID modeling software, is also important in this context.

Third, automation made it possible for our client's professional staff to avoid the drudgery and minutiae characteristic of many manual approaches to regional planning, allowing them instead to concentrate on performing as professionals: creating ideas, making judgments, pursuing possibilities, proposing alternatives for decision makers. We believe that they found this methodology liberating and that they are enjoying the freedom it gave them.

Fourth, we believe that computer graphics allowed decision makers to place increased confidence in the reports presented to them. A decision maker often has to trust that such reports are reliable, or at most briefly probe into them in a few places. Computer graphics allowed the display of most of the raw data that were used in coming to the reported conclusions and also allowed the decision process and its results to be more fully revealed through graphic displays of intermediate and final results.

Fifth, computer graphics seems to us to be one way of "humanizing" the results of computer analyses. By avoiding the use of large reports filled with columns of computer-generated statistics and other data, computer graphics allowed decision makers to avoid becoming bogged down in mental ciphering. Instead they could use the remarkable ability of the human eye to recognize patterns in graphic displays: they could rapidly grasp the significance of even large and complicated displays. We believe this is an enormous advantage of map graphics over other forms of display.

The actual computer graphics produced for the client in this project are proprietary and cannot be published here; however, since they are similar in format to those we have produced for several other regional studies, we can include a few examples from those projects to suggest what the project's graphics were like.

Project Example

Figure 8-6 shows several kinds of maps that were produced in connection with a single project; they are representative of the kinds of computer graphics that might have been used in the regional study for our client.

Color Graphics

A series of color maps were produced in connection with the display of the suitability of various locales within the region to support new town development. These color maps were produced by the use of ESRI's COLORMAP computer software. This software provides for the output of data (stored in a grid cell or polygon format) on color film with the use of a DICOMED(R) image recorder. The image recorder generates color graphic representations in which color hues and tones represent areas of homogeneous data. The output of the image recorder is a film that can be used to produce slides, color photographic prints, and print plates for offset printing or the like. While 512 different colors can be displayed, we have found that simultaneous use of more than ten or fifteen is confusing. The software also permits the outlining of each homogeneous color by means of a black line; this makes the color map easier to interpret. It is our experience that many planners like the COLORMAP products because they are effective in presenting findings to decision makers or to the public.

Plotter Maps

Plotter maps, as shown in Figure 8-7, were used in this project mainly for editing polygon files.

Electrostatic Plotter Maps

To a considerable degree the characteristics of plotter maps are also associated with maps produced from grid-cell data by ESRI's ELECTROSTATIC GRIDPLOT and AUTOPLOT software. This software produces plotter-type maps (grid and polygon respectively) but does so by means of an electrostatic plotter, which is faster and cheaper than a pen plotter.

In the present project, however, electrostatic plots were largely replaced by color graphics because of the need for the highest quality obtainable, almost regardless of cost. Figure 8-8 is an example of electrostatic output for suitability/capability done for Los Angeles County.

FIGURE 8-7   Example of plotter map of land use.

Printer Maps

The least expensive means of producing computer maps of grid-cell data is to use the line printer under the control of various GRID system software. We used these maps for preliminary testing of models and examination of the effects of various modeling weights and variations. Printer maps were used because they can be produced within minutes at a cost of only a few dollars.

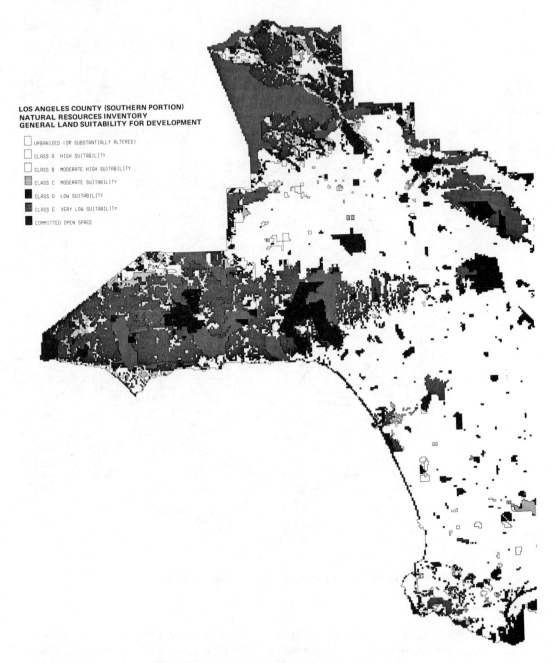

LOS ANGELES COUNTY (SOUTHERN PORTION)
NATURAL RESOURCES INVENTORY
GENERAL LAND SUITABILITY FOR DEVELOPMENT

☐ URBANIZED (OR SUBSTANTIALLY ALTERED)

☐ CLASS A HIGH SUITABILITY

☐ CLASS B MODERATE HIGH SUITABILITY

▦ CLASS C MODERATE SUITABILITY

■ CLASS D LOW SUITABILITY

▨ CLASS E VERY LOW SUITABILITY

■ COMMITTED OPEN SPACE

FIGURE 8-8　Example of electrostatic plot.

We believe this methodology can be applied to national, regional, and local site-screening efforts and to site selection and evaluation throughout the world, under a variety of circumstances and constraints.

We believe, too, that the use of Landsat imagery provides for the creation of much of the needed data even in areas where other kinds of data are not so readily available as they are in Southern California. Landsat can be interpreted to provide land-use and land-cover data and, with other collateral, good natural resource data. Landsat images can also be joined as a mosaic to provide good planimetric base maps, even where topographic map coverage is inadequate and nonexistent. If anything, the methodology is most powerful precisely where existing data resources are the most inadequate, since in these cases the creation of GBISs may represent a far greater step forward in planning than in situations richer in existing data.

We also want to emphasize that projects of this kind create important data resources for future use. While it is common practice to create these GBISs for a single project, we are increasingly finding it possible to integrate these data bases with others and use them in subsequent project efforts. ESRI has devoted considerable effort in recent years to devising ways of updating such data bases effectively and to providing statistical summaries of land-use changes from one survey period to the next.

Additional insights into ways we have in mind for applying this technology to future planning efforts can be gained by examining papers cited in the Bibliography.

REFERENCES

ANTENUCCI, JOHN and JACK DANGERMOND, *Maryland Automated Geographic Information System (MAGI)*, 1974.

DANGERMOND, JACK, *Environmental Planning Study: Guasare/Socuy Micro-Region; State of Zulia, Venezuela*, 1977a. (In several volumes.)

_____, *Land Capability/Suitability Study, Los Angeles County General Plan Revision Program, Final Report*, 1977b.

_____, "A Case Study of the Zulia Regional Planning Study, Describing Work Completed," *Harvard Computer Graphics Week Program*, 1978a.

_____, *Wildland Recreation Study, San Bernardino National Forest*, 1978b.

_____, *Caspian Sea Coast, Ecological Report*, 1978c.

_____, *Environmental Analysis and Mapping: Benghazi Regional Planning Study*, 1978d.

_____, *California Automated Resource Inventory (CARI) System Report*, 1978e.

_____, *PIOS Software System Documentation (Updated)*, 1979.

_____, and H. W. GRINNELL JR., "Land Use Studies at S.C.E.—The Development and Use of a Land Use Oriented Planning Information System," *Proceedings of the 1976 URISA Conference*, 1976.

HYDROLOGIC ENGINEERING CENTER, U. S. Army Corps of Engineers, *Guide Manual for the Creation of Grid Cell Data Banks,* 1978.

MICHEL, RUSSELL J., and KEITH MAW, D. *Exploration into Technical Procedures for Vertical Integration (Draft),* 1979.

APPENDIX

Two figures are included in this appendix: Figure 8-9 is a sketch of the hardware configuration ESRI used for this project; Figure 8-10 is a schematic diagram of the ESRI software system used.

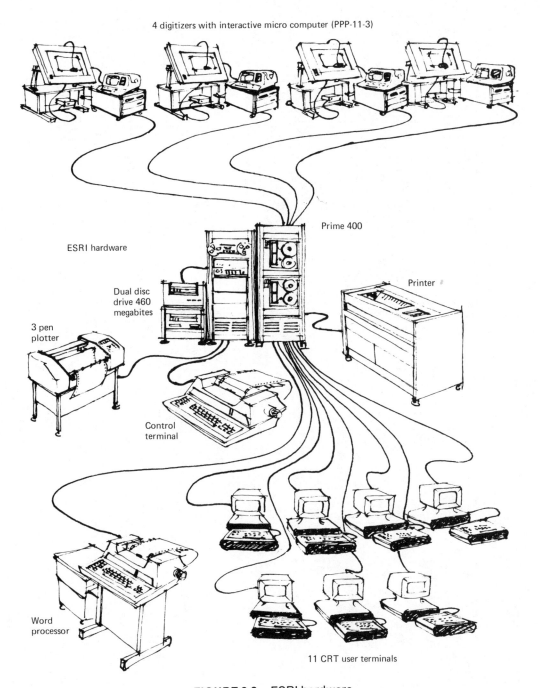

4 digitizers with interactive micro computer (PPP-11-3)

Prime 400

ESRI hardware

Dual disc
drive 460
megabites

Printer

3 pen
plotter

Control
terminal

Word
processor

11 CRT user terminals

FIGURE 8-9 ESRI hardware.

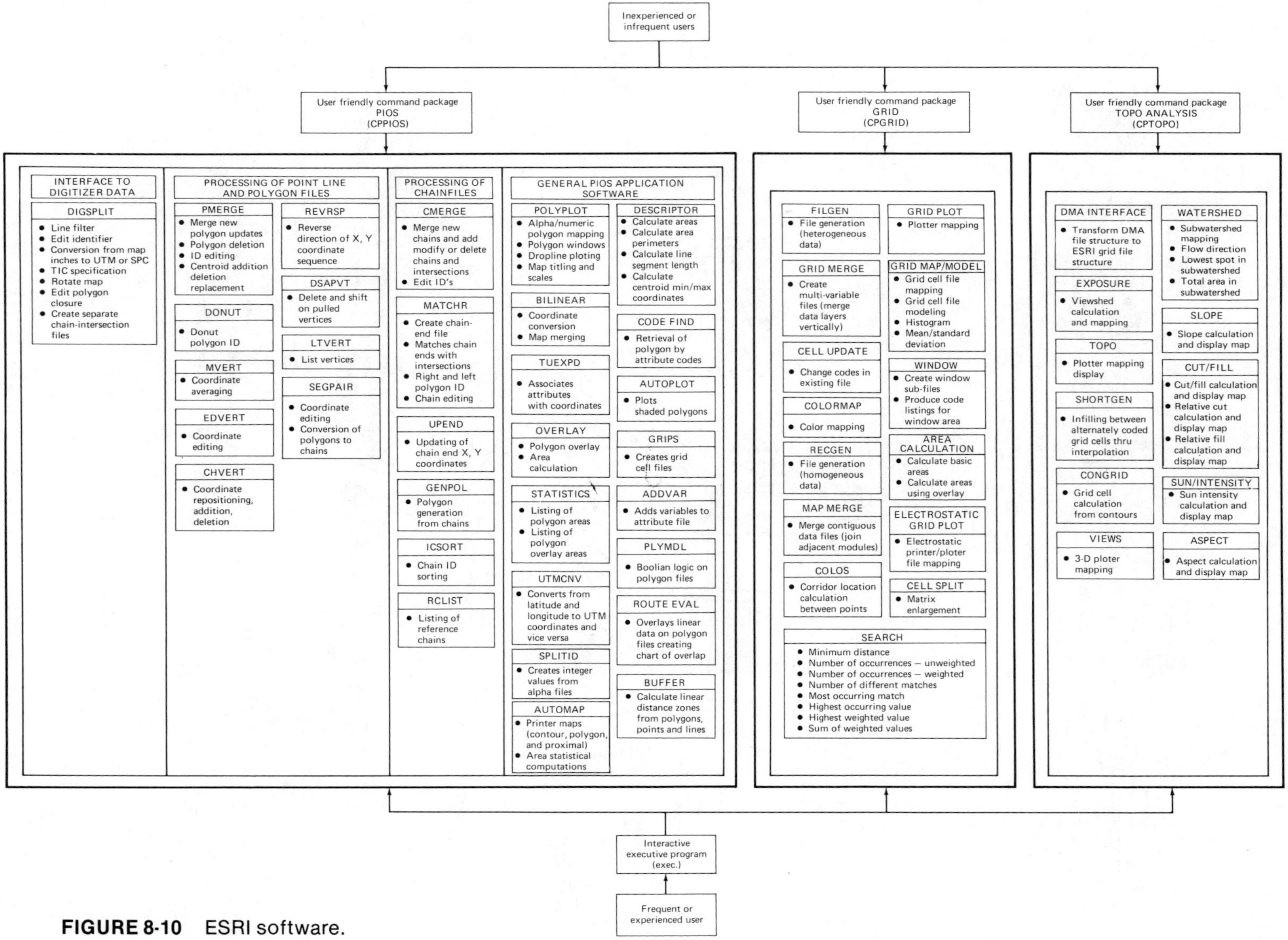

FIGURE 8-10 ESRI software.

Chapter 9

Cartographic Analysis of Deer Habitat Utilization

C. Dana Tomlin

Stephen H. Berwick

Sandra M. Tomlin

PROBLEM

In 1977 the Yale School of Forestry and Environmental Studies initiated a study of the white-tailed deer (*Odocoileus virginianus*) population at the Yale Forest in northeastern Connecticut. The Yale Forest property comprises some 7800 acres located in the towns of Union, Ashford, Eastford, and Woodstock, Connecticut, about 30 miles northeast of Hartford. The area is one of second-growth forest, low hill topography, and distinctively rural New England character.

As one part of the deer population study, standard pellet-group counts were conducted during the spring of 1977 over an area of approximately one square mile. Pellet-group counting is a method of estimating wildlife population density and forage use based on measurement of the periodic accumulation of fecal droppings at sampling sites within a given area. In this case, a defecation rate of 12.7 pellet groups per deer per day was assumed.

Within the study area, five vegetative cover types were sampled to develop estimates of deer utilization. Among these cover types were red pine (*Pinus resinosa*), white pine (*Pinus strobus*), hemlock (*Tsuga canadensis*), mixed hardwoods (predominantly *Acer saccharum* and *Betula allegheniensis*), and open field. Sampling sites were located along transects within each cover type. These were grouped at five sites per transect and five transects per cover type for a total of 125 sites. The first site of each transect was located randomly. Subsequent sites were established at uniform distances along each transect line. At each sampling site, pellet groups were counted over a circular area of 0.01 acre or approximately 24 feet in diameter.

Analysis of the 1977 pellet-group counts found statistically significant differences between cover types and indicated the following habitat preference ratings, expressed as estimates of the number of deer per square mile of each habitat type:

Hemlock	124
White pine	71
Mixed hardwoods	54
Red pine	23
Open field	1

Not yet considered at this point, however (and often overlooked in studies of this sort), were effects due to the spatial nature of data being examined. Among the most important of these were, first, the inherent lack of statistical independence among observations made at neighboring locations, and second, the influence of specific spatial relationships between sampling sites and other locational features such as roads, water bodies, or areas of a particular vegetation type. This second group of spatial effects was recently examined as part of the Yale Forest study and is discussed below in terms of the computer graphic techniques employed.

The stated purpose of this phase of the deer habitat study was to examine, in a quick, flexible, and largely intuitive manner, the relationship between pellet-group counts and certain factors associated with the spatial context of each sampling site. Its more general purpose was, in fact, to demonstrate the speed, flexibility, and intuitive nature of one particular approach to that problem in the form of computer mapping. This effort was to be directed toward a local audience of student foresters generally unfamiliar with digital technology, uncomfortable with involved mathematics, and suspicious of anything not advertised in the L. L. Bean spring catalogue.

METHODOLOGY AND RESULTS

In keeping with these objectives, a decidedly small set of data was examined. Only two maps of the mile-square study area were encoded. The first was simply a collection of point values indicating pellet-group counts for each of the 125 sampling sites. The second was a map of areas characterized by land-cover types and site features, including roads, structures, hemlock stands, red and white pine stands, hardwood areas, areas of mixed hardwood and softwood growth, open fields, and wet lands. This map is shown in Figure 9-1.

Both of these digital maps were derived from conventional maps compiled at a scale of 1:15,840 from field observations and aerial photographs. Pellet-group counts were digitized as z-coordinate values associated with x, y-coordinate loca-

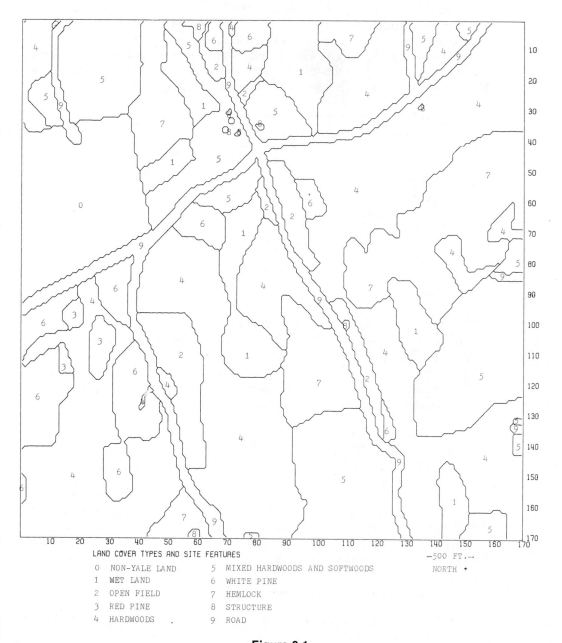

LAND COVER TYPES AND SITE FEATURES

0	NON-YALE LAND	5	MIXED HARDWOODS AND SOFTWOODS
1	WET LAND	6	WHITE PINE
2	OPEN FIELD	7	HEMLOCK
3	RED PINE	8	STRUCTURE
4	HARDWOODS	9	ROAD

—500 FT.—→

NORTH ◆

Figure 9-1

tions. Land-cover types and site features were defined by boundary lines digitized as sequences of *x, y*-coordinate pairs.

These digitized coordinates were then used to create grid maps for subsequent analysis. A grid-cell size approximately 30 feet square was chosen as one that would provide the resolution necessary to distinguish between sampling sites without requiring excessively large amounts of storage space. Each grid map contained 28,900 cells, dimensioned at 170 rows by 170 columns, and each cell was represented as a sixteen-bit integer. In the case of the pellet-count map, each cell containing the center of the sampling site (no cells contained more than one) was assigned the pellet count ($\times$ 100) recorded at that site. All other cells were set to a value of zero. For the land-cover and site-features map, values were assigned as follows:

0   land outside the Yale Forest property

1   wet land

2   open field

3   red pine

4   hardwoods

5   mixed hardwoods and softwoods

6   white pine

7   hemlock

8   structure

9   road

Cells containing boundary lines, and therefore including more than one of the above categories, were assigned to whichever of those categories had the greatest value. The above values were initially assigned with this in mind, such that each cell would be characterized according to its most "important" attribute.

Analyses of the spatial effect of land-cover types and site features on deer pellet group counts generally followed a common procedure involving:

- Transformation of the cover type map to generate a new map of some particular spatial phenomenon
- Examination of pellet-group counts, by cover type, within each region of this new map

Spatial factors such as the size, shape, proximity, and visual exposure of selected site features were examined in this manner, both individually and in weighted combination. In each case, categories of the spatial-factor map, the land-cover map, and the pellet-count map were then compared on an overlay basis to generate cross-tabular statistics.

Among the clearest findings were:

- A mild direct relationship between pellet-group count and local diversity of land-cover types

- A mild inverse relationship between pellet-group count and visual exposure to roads and structures

In light of the lack of spatial distribution among sampling sites and the small number of factors considered, however, the significance of these results was felt to be questionable at best.

Nonetheless, the potential for applying computer graphic techniques in this area was clearly demonstrated.

USE OF COMPUTER GRAPHICS

The intuitive nature of graphics in general and the speed and flexibility of computer graphics in particular were found to be of critical importance to this project. This was true not only in the presentation of results but also in the formulation of the analyses themselves.

All the analyses were performed in an informal and exploratory manner using packaged software in an interactive mode. The user-oriented nature and modular structure of that software proved to be particularly accommodating in this regard. Consider, for example, the following man-machine dialogue:

```
OK, MAP ANALYSIS PACKAGE READY

•

relumber covermap for development/

NO, THERE IS NO OPERATION NAMED "RELUMBER";
    FOR HELP, TYPE "EXPLAIN"

•

renumber covermap for development assigning 0 to 1/
        thru 7 and 1 to 8 thru 9

OK,  "DEVELOPMENT" CREATED BY RENUMBERING "COVERMAP"
    ASSIGNING   0 to     1  =  WET LAND
                THRU    7  =  HEMLOCK
    ASSIGNING   1 to     8  =  STRUCTURE
                THRU    9  =  ROAD

•

renumber covermap assigning 0% to 4, to 5, to 7/
        and 100% to 0 and 200% to 6 and 300%
        to 3 and 600% to 1 thru 2, to 8 thru 9/
        for friction

OK,  "FRICTION" CREATED BY RENUMBERING "COVERMAP"
    ASSIGNING   100 TO 0  =  NON-YALE LAND
    ASSIGNING   600 TO 1  =  WET LAND
                THRU 2  =  OPEN FIELD
    ASSIGNING   300 TO 3  =  RED PINE
    ASSIGNING     0 TO 4  =  HARDWOODS
                THRU 5  =  MIXED GROWTH
```

```
ASSIGNING  200 TO 6  =  WHITE PINE
ASSIGNING    0 TO 7  =  HEMLOCK
ASSIGNING  600 TO 8  =  STRUCTURE
           THRU 9    =  ROAD
```

•

```
spread development thru friction for proximitymap
OK, "PROXIMITYMAP" CREATED BY SPREADING "DEVELOPMENT"
    THRU "FRICTION"
```

•

```
contour proximitymap
```

OK, "PROXIMITYMAP" DISPLAYED AS A CONTOUR PLOT

This is the command-response sequence generated in creating the effective proximity map shown in Figure 9-2. Here, "renumber," "spread," and "contour" are processing operations; "covermap," "development," "friction," and "proximitymap" are user-defined map file names; and "for," "assigning," "to," "thru," and "and" are parts of command-modifying phrases. "Relumber" is detected as a mistake.

All software, hardware, manpower, and funding in support of this project were made available through the Yale School of Forestry and Environmental Studies. Data encoding, analysis, and display capabilities were provided through the use of software developed as part of the Map Analysis Package (Tomlin, 1980). The Map Analysis Package is written in FORTRAN IV and may be used either interactively or in batch mode. At present, the Package employs a grid-cell data structure for all analytic operations. Input data, however, may exist in the form of digitized points, lines, or polygons and output may be produced in the form of line-plotter graphics.

For this study, spatial coordinate data were encoded using a Talos RP648a digitizer and a GT44 graphics terminal linked to a PDP 11/40 processor. These coordinate files were then stored on disk packs accessible to Yale's IBM 370/158 mainframe computer. The 370, operating under IBM's Time Sharing Option (TSO) and accessed through a Hewlett Packard 2648A graphics terminal, was used for all subsequent analyses. Preliminary graphics were generated by a high-speed line printer while final maps were produced using a CalComp 763 drum plotter.

Throughout this phase of the deer habitat study, slave labor was employed wherever possible. Digitizing was done by a first-year graduate student of requisite steady hand and weak mind but without previous experience. The authors called upon similar capabilities in performing the analyses and preparing graphics. The analyses were performed at a total cost of about five CPU minutes.

EXAMPLES

As mentioned earlier, each of the spatial factors examined in this study was measured and expressed as a new map created by cartographic transformation of an existing map showing land-cover types and site features. In one case, for example, the cover-type map was used to generate a map of "effective proximity" to roads and structures. This map is shown in Figure 9-2. Note here that "effective" proximity is clearly not measured in terms of Euclidean distance. Rather, it is defined in terms of units consumable at rates that vary among cover types according to the degree to which those types either support or impede the movement of deer—that is, units analogous to minutes of travel time or dollars of travel cost. In creating this map, it was assumed that areas of greater vegetation density (such as hemlock stands, hardwood stands, and areas of mixed hardwood and softwood growth),

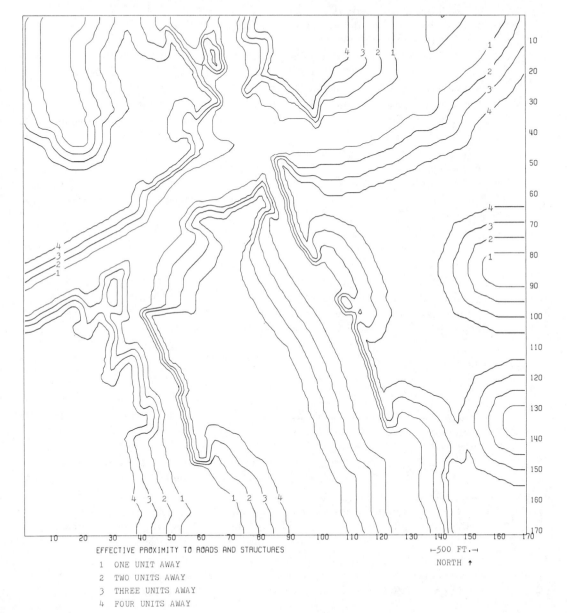

EFFECTIVE PROXIMITY TO ROADS AND STRUCTURES

1   ONE UNIT AWAY
2   TWO UNITS AWAY
3   THREE UNITS AWAY
4   FOUR UNITS AWAY

├─500 FT.─┤

NORTH ↑

Figure 9-2

which generally offered better protection, were for that reason more conducive to deer movement. Open areas (such as wet lands and fields), on the other hand, were regarded as zones of higher "friction" relative to the movement of deer. For this reason the proximity contours shown in Figure 9-2 are closer together in areas crossing wet lands and fields.

An alternative interpretation of "effective proximity" to roads and structures was also considered. Here, it was argued that it is not the movement of deer but the dissipation of noise, activity, and influence of man that should be measured and mapped. In this case, higher rather than lower "friction factors" were applied to areas of greater vegetation density.

Typical of the other factors examined in this manner were spatial effects such as the "local diversity" of cover types, the "narrowness" of forested areas, and the "shape complexity" of individual forest stands. A map of "local cover-type diversity" is shown in Figure 9-3. Here, the value assigned to each grid cell indicates the number of different cover types occurring within a radius of approximately 25 meters around that cell. In creating the "forest narrowness" map, a value was assigned to each forest cell according to the shortest total distance from that cell to two diametrically opposing forest edges. "Shape complexity" values were computed by isolating individual forest stands (contiguous areas of a single cover type), then characterizing each according to the ratio of its perimeter to the square root of its area.

Examples of the graphics produced in this effort are presented in Figures 9-1 through 9-3. All are grid maps reproduced in line-plotter form. Column/row reference numbers are indicated at the bottom and to the right of each map. Figure 9-2 was created by tracing contour lines over the three-dimensional surface represented by effective proximity values. Figures 9-1 and 9-3 were created by tracing boundaries between cells of different values, then rounding off right angles with diagonal lines. Labeling in each case was done by hand.

RETROSPECT

Even in light of the limited scope and informal nature of this project, surprisingly few problems were encountered. By far the most costly and time-consuming aspects of the work were those associated with data encoding. This was largely due to specific problems in dealing with recently installed hardware.

Also somewhat frustrating was the fact that sampling sites were not uniformly spaced over the study area. As mentioned earlier, the pellet-count data used in this study were not originally collected with spatial analysis in mind. While this presented no serious problems in terms of demonstrating the potential for applying computer mapping techniques, it did limit the ability to draw specific conclusions about the deer population in this particular area. The same was true in terms of the small number of independent variables considered. Most conspicuous by its absence was any consideration of topographic relief. Elevation data are now being encoded in hopes of incorporating factors such as slope, aspect, and cool air drainage.

Local reaction to the substantive content of this phase of the deer population study has focused with appropriate skepticism on the informality of the analyses

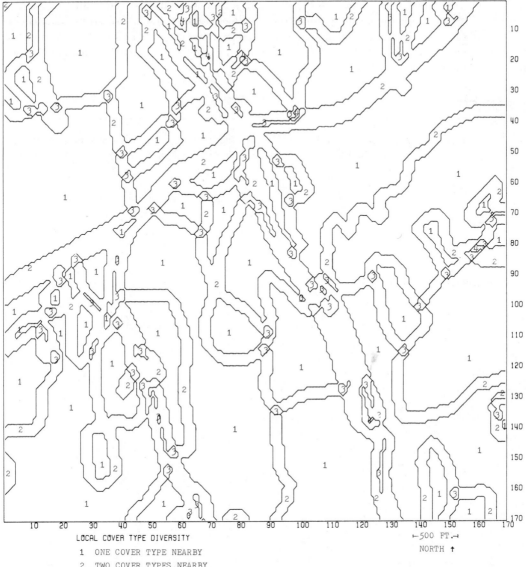

LOCAL COVER TYPE DIVERSITY

1	ONE COVER TYPE NEARBY
2	TWO COVER TYPES NEARBY
3	THREE COVER TYPES NEARBY
4	FOUR COVER TYPES NEARBY

⊢500 FT.⊣

NORTH ↑

Figure 9-3

performed. Reaction to the general approach demonstrated by this work, however, has been very enthusiastic. Particularly encouraging is the variety of projects making use of the Map Analysis Package at the University of Connecticut and at Yale. Favorable reaction to the package has generally focused on its intuitive command language, its range of modeling capabilities, and its organization as a series of independent "building-block" operations.

Most of the data processing capabilities used in this study can be found in many of the increasingly numerous packaged geographic information systems currently available. Experience at Yale and elsewhere suggests that such capabilities, if packaged in a sufficiently generalized manner, can accommodate a surprisingly wide range of applications.

REFERENCE

TOMLIN, C. D, "Digital Cartographic Modeling Techniques in Environmental Planning," Doctoral dissertation in preparation, Yale School of Forestry and Environmental Studies, 1980.

Part III

TWO COMPUTER GRAPHIC CASE STUDIES: FEDERAL AND LOCAL GOVERNMENT

Chapter 10

Graphical Display Maps Foster Regulation Policy

T. K. Gardenier

ABSTRACT

There is growing concern within the federal regulatory system for prioritizing budgetary allocations on the basis of health benefits as related to changes in environmental quality. The recently promulgated Toxic Substances Control Act, for example, calls for evaluating all chemicals as to their health hazard. The evaluations have involved design of clinical protocols for toxicity and exposure estimation, and extrapolations from animal to human risks. Literature searches using multiagency citations of ongoing studies are also being currently conducted, leading to what are called Chemical Hazard Information Profile (CHIP) reports. The President's Public Health Initiative (PHI) project currently underway within the federal government is testing for synergistic and interaction effects of chemical pollutants impacting public health.

The present chapter illustrates the application of the Domestic Information Display System (DIDS) in exploring the relationship between causes of death and environmental pollutant concentrations with the objectives of:

1. Scanning geographical variations to generate hypotheses about environmental determinants of disease
2. Isolating clusters or statistical typologies of disease
3. Pinpointing occupational or genetic synergisms that may be important to consider in disease etiology
4. Identifying highly correlated causes of death to determine the suitability of combining them in epidemiological investigations

RELATED QUANTITATIVE METHODOLOGY

Analysis of the quantitative relationship between environmental pollution and health effects has stressed the use of statistical correlations and factor and cluster analysis. Selected relevant studies in this area will be discussed below with a view to evaluating the methodology for administrative planning purposes.

In recent definitions of "risk" as related to regulatory policy, the concept of "health effect" has often been used. Health effect has recently been defined by Crocker and others (1979) as a dose-response relationship between pollution and mortality rates. Other researchers (Harris, 1974; McDonald and Schwing, 1973; Zeidenberg, Prindle, and Landau, 1961) included multiple hazards in the definition of a health effect and attempted to associate morbidity as well as mortality indices with pollution and demographic variables. The statistical method used for these links was correlation and regression analysis, often applied to generate hypotheses for jointly occurring or possibly causal relationships (Asher, 1976).

Lave and Seskin (1977) used data from a sample of SMSAs relating to socioeconomic variables, total mortality, selected mortality and morbidity rates, and statistical indicators derived from ambient air levels for sulfate and suspended particulates as indicators of air quality. Several climate indicators such as minimum and maximum daily temperature, precipitation, average hourly windspeed, and home heating characteristics such as gas versus electricity and type of heating equipment were also used as possible predictors of specific mortality—for example, mortality from respiratory cancer. In addition to income and race classifications, socioeconomic data used by Lave and Seskin included census figures for percentage of labor force in employed in fields such as agriculture, construction, manufacturing, transportation, and finance. Using the regression coefficients, some statistical association was found between selected mortality rates and air quality and economic indicators. The conclusions have been debated, however, owing to the multicollinearity, or high degree of dependence, among the variables correlated with mortality rates.

A factor-analytic approach was pursued by Lake and others (1977) to identify components of significant characteristic sets (SCS) of demographic and environmental indicators of air and water quality. The statistical "factors" derived in the analyses were then associated with environmental data, thereby reducing the number of comparisons between each possible indicator and a particular pollutant. References to the use of factor analysis as a mathematical technique in these settings may be found in Kim and Mueller (1977).

In neither of the approaches mentioned above has the issue of synergism been handled—that is, the combined effects of different chemicals in the environment. Clinicians and researchers are stressing that synergism may act in the development of some types of disease. In the Symposium and Workshop on Nuclear and Non-Nuclear Energy Systems held by Mitre Corporation (1979), Dr. Richard Bates cited the example for arteriosclerosis, a disease related to diet and stress, but where certain chemical exposures may play a synergistic role.

This rather new trend in thinking creates the demand for a parallel trend in data analysis to generate hypotheses for interaction and synergistic effects. Prospective studies that demand monitoring of the environment and health effects are expensive to conduct. However, retrospective analysis of epidemiological and health data with graphical tools would aid researchers and planners. For example, a geographic scan of areas in the vicinity of power plants, for incidence of one or more types of disease, elicits a quick visual response to the query without demanding large-scale, mathematically sophisticated numerical analysis.

COMPUTER GRAPHICS IN IDENTIFYING STATISTICAL ASSOCIATION

The role of graphics in statistical presentation as well as analysis and hypothesis formulation has been stated succinctly by Schmid (1954). Schmid compared the effect of charts or graphs to presentation in text or tabular form. Some of the advantages of graphical display are:

1. Economy of time, because visual portrayal summarizes the main features of massive data results
2. Appeal to interest and attention, since graphics makes it easier to highlight issues
3. Analytical thinking and hypothesis generation by eliciting otherwise hidden results and relationships

Estimating the association between environmental and health data has required the administrative coordination of large-scale data bases from several sources and the merging of new monitoring information into existing files. For example, air quality and water quality data of interest to the U.S. Environmental Protection Agency include concentration levels of various pollutants obtained through air and water monitors. Data coordination is done at EPA regions throughout the United States and at the headquarters. Health-related data to be discussed in this study included county-level mortality rates from 46 causes of death in the United States averaged over the years 1968–1972 aggregated from the vital statistics tapes of the National Center for Health Statistics by Sauer (1972). The air, water, and health modules were integrated into the computer graphics and analysis system called

UPGRADE (User-Prompted Graphic Data Evaluation System), accessible through the President's Council on Environmental Quality (1977) and accessed through the computer system of the National Institutes of Health. Health-related data are within the module CLIDE (County-Level Integrated Database for Epidemiology) of UP-GRADE and are arranged into four subfiles for white males, white females, black males, and black females.

Statistical analyses of the association within and between health and socio-economic or environmental data modules formerly used the Pearson product moment correlation coefficient or multivariate regression (Lave, 1977; Wallace, 1978). Although useful to statisticians, results of statistical mathematical models developed with multivariate regression, which includes the Pearson coefficients for two variables, have often appeared unduly esoteric for policymakers and administrative planners. Display through the use of maps was thus perceived useful in addition to correlation calculations carried out in 1978 by SAS (Statistical Analysis System).

The Domestic Information Display System (DIDS), developed in prototype form at NASA Goddard Space Flight Center, has provided exceptionally relevant assistance at the U.S. Environmental Protection Agency. The DIDS system represents a collaborative effort by fifteen federal agencies to integrate, display, and evaluate socioeconomic, environmental, and epidemiological data. The data modules discussed under UPGRADE above were also incorporated into this system in order to utilize the color-mapping features of DIDS. The system presents a U.S. map displaying data on state, county, or congressional district level in various colors, singly or in combination. The user may select the basic color combination of interest to him, the variable(s) to be mapped, and any combinations or transformations within variables, as will be discussed below.

Combining variables within the DIDS system is accomplished through the use of a feature called "compositing," initially suggested by Fieser in the Progress Report of the General Capabilities Subcommittee of DIDS (Gardenier, 1979). The compositing or overlaying capability incorporates multiple evaluation criteria to derive a single index, which can then be mapped as a function of another variable. For example, a county-level composite map representing economic distress may be a function of input factors of unemployment rate, educational attainment, per capita income, and dilapidated housing. To analyze the relationship between these variables would involve $N(N - 1)/2$ correlation coefficients; a complete set of maps to be generated for an exploratory relationship would number $3[N(N - 1)]/2$, because one would need individual maps for each variable *and* for their joint distribution. However, the user may choose to add the data from all or some of the indicators, with appropriate weights, if necessary. Then, the user may map the composite as a summary figure to pursue his query.

Mapping applications with DIDS provided fast and efficient feedback to working groups within the U.S. Environmental Protection Agency in policy decisions on such matters as sulfur dioxide emissions from coal-fired power plants, the association between incidence of bladder cancer and water quality, and the prioritizing of budget allocations to areas where high air pollutant levels correspond to high epidemiological risk. A parallel research effort also pinpointed the following sub-groups of data:

1. Clusters of diseases likely to occur together in various populations
2. Clusters of pollution conditions

After such clusters had been identified, relationships were discovered between pollution states, which may be cumulative in effect, and diseases that may be interactive or population specific. Thus the system pinpointed regional areas needing the most policy attention. It also aided in the query for isolating patterns of diseases, as stressed in the symposium conducted by Mitre Corporation (1979).

ILLUSTRATIONS OF GRAPHICAL MAPS FOR ENVIRONMENT AND HEALTH

Within the U.S. Environmental Protection Agency the use of the mapping features of computer graphics has recently given the opportunity to "stop, look, and listen." Maps obtained from data stored within the UPGRADE and DIDS systems have helped administrators involved in risk assessment in selecting focal points for emphasis and in generating possible hypotheses in efforts to link epidemiological, demographic, and environmental indicators.

The first step in this exploration was to identify, extract, and integrate air- and water-related pollution data from STORET and NASQUAN data files with mortality data from various causes of death (Sauer, 1972). Table 10-1 lists the available data modules for which graphical displays were obtained. The data for this particular application were arranged and unitized at the county level, although DIDS also has units at the SMSA and state level.

A sample illustration of mortality data is given in Figure 10-1 which shows age-adjusted mortality from cancer per 1 million population at risk. Three shades—white, grey, and black—have been used to depict the three categories to which the data have been partitioned. DIDS has a default feature of five categories, each representing successive 20th percentiles. The user can select colors of interest for each category from a reference grid.*

Another representation for water quality data using representation for water basin units of the U.S. Geological Survey is shown in Figure 10-2. Four intervals, each representing a quartile and ranging from black to white, are represented for water hardness (mg/liter $CaCO_3$). Using a similar data base, we can divide the data distribution into two categories; Figure 10-3 shows data for dissolved mercury with the same units as in Figure 10-2 but using the lower versus upper 50th percentile. Figures 10-2 and 10-3 have both been obtained using the UPGRADE system discussed earlier.

Recently a new feature has been added to the DIDS system so that the user can determine how many intervals are appropriate for the distribution being scanned.

*All examples here will use black-and-white representation, although the output of the DIDS system is in color.

Table 10-1   HEALTH AND ENVIRONMENTAL DATA MODULES IN MAPS

Mortality Rate (by county)	*Water Quality Data, by county*
White male deaths, age adjusted, 1970	Chromium in Whole Water STORET
Tuberculosis, all forms	#1034 UG/L
Other infective disease	(Maximums all years)
Cancer, buccal cavity, pharynx	(85 percentiles all years)
Cancer of esophagus	
Cancer of stomach	Chromium Dissolved in Water STORET
Cancer of intestine	#1030 UG/L
Cancer of rectum	(Maximums all years)
Cancer of liver	(85 percentiles all years)
Cancer of pancreas	
Other digestive cancer	Chromium in Sus Fr Water STORET
	#1031 UG/L
White female deaths, 1970	(Maximums all years)
Tuberculosis, all forms	(85 percentiles all years)
Other infective disease	
Cancer, buccal cavity, pharynx	*Water quality data, by county, 1975*
Cancer of esophagus	PH annual mean (NASQ)
Cancer of intestine	Total dissolved solids—annual mean
Cancer of rectum	(NASQ)
Cancer of respiratory system	Phosphorus annual mean (NASQ)
Cancer of breast	Nitrate and nitrite and annual mean
Leukemia	(NASQ)
Diabetes	Arsenic annual mean (NASQ)
Alcoholism	Cadmium annual mean (NASQ)
Rheumatic heart disease	Chromium annual mean
Hypertension	Cobalt annual mean (NASQ)
Acute ischemic heart disease	Copper annual mean (NASQ)
Chronic ischemic heart disease	Iron annual mean (NASQ)
Other heart disease	Lead annual mean (NASQ)
Cerebrovascular disease	Manganese annual mean (NASQ)
Arteriosclerosis	Mercury annual mean (NASQ)
Influenza and pneumonia	Selenium annual mean (NASQ)
Chronic respiratory disease	Zinc annual mean (NASQ)
Cirrhosis of liver	Water hardness (NASQ)
Infant mortality	
Cancer of thyroid	*Water quality data, by county, 1976*
Major CU diseases	Total inorganic nitrogen (NASQ)
Cancer, all forms and sites	Total organic nitrogen (NASQ)
	Total nitrogen (NASQ)
Air quality data, by county, 1975	Total fecal coliform bacteria—log
TSP emission density	mean (NASQ)
SO_2 emission density	
CO emission density	Fish killed by pollution, number of reports
HC emission density	(1960–1975)
NOX emission density	Number of fish killed by pollution,
	reported (1960–1975)

Source: NASA *Fast Facts*: Domestic Information Display System, Office of Federal Statistical Policy and Standards, U.S. Department of Commerce, Washington, D.C., 1979.

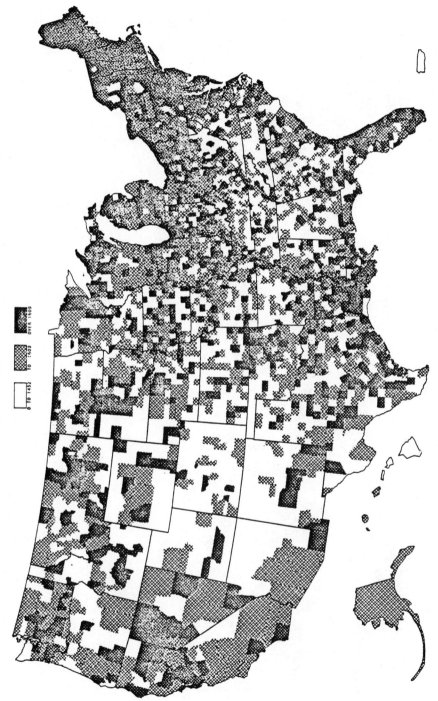

Figure 10-1 Age-adjusted mortality from cancer, all forms and sites (from National Center for Health Statistics, U.S. DHEW) (ICDA 140-209) per 1,000,000 at risk, blacks and whites combined, 1966–1972

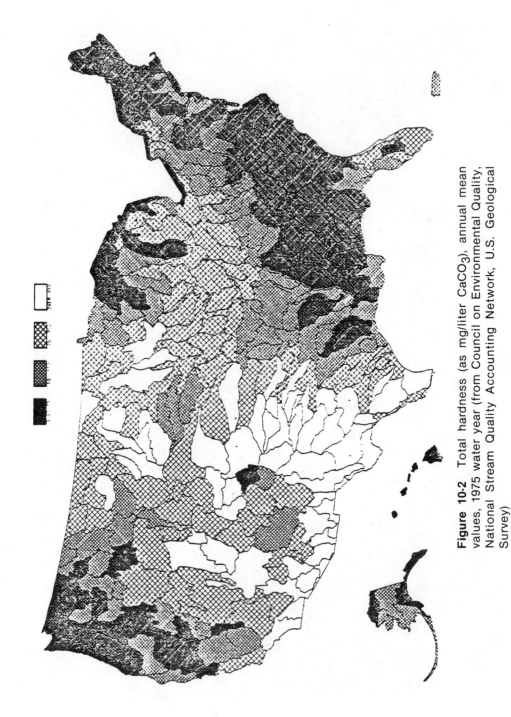

Figure 10-2 Total hardness (as mg/liter $CaCO_3$), annual mean values, 1975 water year (from Council on Environmental Quality, National Stream Quality Accounting Network, U.S. Geological Survey)

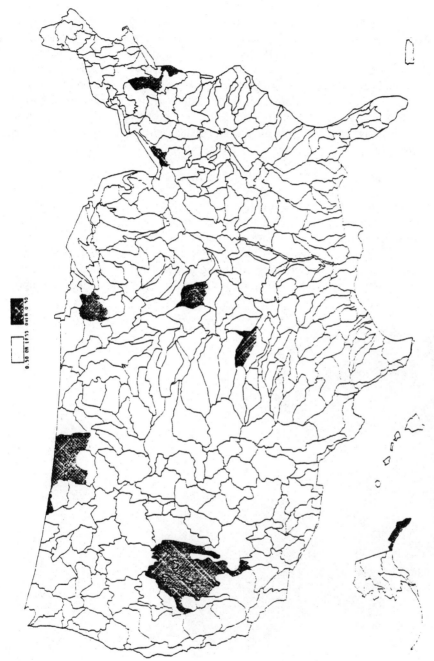

Figure 10-3 Mercury (dissolved), micrograms per liter, annual mean values, 1975 water year (from Council on Environmental Quality, National Stream Quality Accounting Network, U.S. Geological Survey)

Depending upon the shape of the distribution, the user may also choose to vary the intervals for each category rather than use equal percentiles. The histogram is plotted on the CRT (cathode ray tube) screen.

Another feature, the "zoom" capability, enables the user to scan specific regions of interest. For example, data for a given state can be selected for mapping both within the UPGRADE and DIDS systems; within DIDS one may, furthermore, select the option for zoom, then move the horizontal and vertical cursors until a rectangular area is enclosed to be projected to full scale on the CRT. In this way, data for specific counties can be compared visually, since the image is larger. Figure 10-4 shows cancer mortality data similar to those in Figure 10-1, but specifically for the state of Louisiana. Five intervals have been chosen, each representing 20 percentile units. The shading has been achieved by five symbols.

Exploration of Interrelationships through Bivariate Maps

When two variables are scanned together, a "co-relation" is explored, the results of which are usually summarized in a statistical index of correlation. The most often used method of computing this index is through the Pearson product moment correlation coefficient, which ranges from -1.0 to +1.0. While statisticians and experts in mathematical modeling have long depended upon the correlation coefficient, the index often is not as meaningful to administrators and planners. Indeed, data points

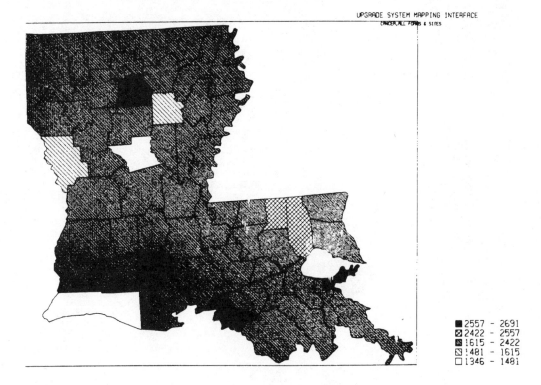

Figure 10-4   Cancer mortality rates for the State of Louisiana

in the extremes can often cause major fluctuations in its value, making comparability across data sets difficult.

A visual scan of the bivariate maps, however, makes it quite feasible to base policy-related decisions on a map of the spatial distribution of two modes of interest. Meyer and others (1975) summarize this pioneering work of the U.S. Bureau of the Census, now also applied within DIDS. Fienberg (1979) quotes the publication of such maps in STATUS, a monthly chartbook published by the U.S. Bureau of the Census during the mid 1970s to display economic and social trends. The specific example given by Fienberg was the relationship between mortality from cardiovascular disease among males age 35–74 and percentage of housing units with 1.01 or more persons per room. Data refer to the average of mortality rates for years 1968–71; housing statistics are for 1970. Three maps are given:

1. A map for death rate, showing four intervals
2. A map for housing, again with four subcategories
3. A bivariate map with 4 × 4 or 16 color categories

It is difficult to appreciate the visual effect of the color graphics available through these charts without seeing a color display. The individual map for death rate used three shades of blue and then yellow for the four categories; the map for housing occupancy used red and two shades of pink, with yellow as the last category. When the two color maps were superimposed through overlaying, the combination of the blue and red backgrounds yielded a pattern of sixteen colors. Purple emerged from the combination of red and blue, green from the combination of yellow and blue, and orange from red and yellow. Thus, yellow corresponded to those counties where mortality rates were low *and* housing occupancy was low, purple to those counties where both mortality and housing occupancy were high; the two remaining corners to those counties that have high death rate and low housing occupancy, and vice versa. Concentration of similar colors in specific areas would mean that geographical variations affected the observations. If the colors were randomly distributed throughout the map, geography would not be considered relevant.

In policy applications of a bivariate map, emphasis upon the locations or areas depicted by the colors in the four corners appeared to be vitally important. In statistical applications, nevertheless, highlighting the diagonal has appeared to be of interest, since these would be the relevant data for a correlation coefficient (Fienberg, 1979; Tukey, 1979; Wainer, 1978). An illustration may be given using the relationship between incidence of pulmonary disorders and concentration of carbon monoxide. A regulatory agency would be most interested in knowing those geographical locations with high concentration of carbon monoxide *and* with high incidence of pulmonary disorders. The impact of regulation for these "high-priority" areas would be to reduce pollutant concentrations in order to minimize health risks. Those areas with low carbon monoxide concentration *and* low incidence of pulmonary disorder would receive low budget priority for pollution control; so would, perhaps, areas where pollution is high but health hazard is low. Thus there is a difference between a statistician's and policy analyst's priorities using information from the same map. While a statistician would tend to look along the *diagonal* of a bivariate grid in order to evaluate whether there *is* a statistical association between, for example, carbon monoxide concentration and pulmonary disorders, a policy analyst would be more apt to scan the areas that represent the corners.

Advantages of Cross and Diamond Defaults

Let us consider two selected indicators of health and pollution, which have been divided into three intervals, thus creating a grid of nine cells, as shown in Figure 10-5. Let us also assume that the intervals within each variable have been selected after careful review of the histograms and any possible adjustments for nonnormality and clinical evaluations of threshold risk. Owing to the uncertainty and unreliability associated with type of underlying statistical distribution, measurement error, and so on, a three-category partition within each of the two variables would appear reasonable, since the middle category would act as a "buffer zone" for uncertainties, and the adjoining two would delineate the high and low observations. Eliminating the middle interval on the two dimensions, as observed in Figure 10-5, creates a cross-diagram. The policymaker would then eliminate the colors within the cross and concentrate on the four colors at the edges. From a color graphics standpoint, this creates the necessity for choice of the most appropriate five colors to represent the choices that emerge from the two-way chart or contingency table.

The upper left and lower right corners represent the "safety" and "danger" zones; the lower left and upper right corners represent cases of contrasting observations—reminiscent of the "false positive" and "false negative" observations in statistical hypothesis testing. Where there is a negative relationship or correlation between the variables, the "safety" and "danger" corners trade places with the "X" corners. Green has been found effective in DIDS applications as a "safety color" and red as a "danger" color, with white to represent the central regions of the cross. Yellow and brown provide good contrast with the blue background of DIDS CRT. The colors seem to maintain their tone when color Xerox is interfaced with DIDS for reproduction.

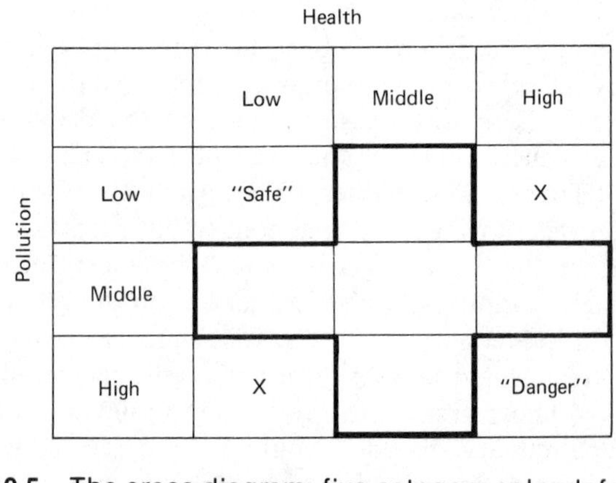

Health

	Low	Middle	High
Low	"Safe"		X
Middle			
High	X		"Danger"

(Pollution — vertical axis label on left)

Figure 10-5 The cross diagram: five-category color default in two-way maps

Figure 10-6 shows a modification of this concept into the diamond shape represented in the CRT to describe the intervals of each class mapped for the variables. On each of the two axes two rather than three classes are chosen, yielding a grid of four cells. An inner box is created to represent a middle "uncertainty" region, perhaps a low priority for policy attention. Initially, if four intervals were chosen for each variable, there would be a grid of sixteen cells; then the innermost square of four cells would create the diamond. In most DIDS applications, white has been chosen for the diamond color.

Let us interpret the map represented in Figure 10-6. The two axes represent population change 1960–1970 versus 1970–1975. Thus, we can visually interpret population growth trends by evaluating the lightest (high population growth throughout 1960–1975) versus darkest (low population growth throughout the inverval). The other two contrasts show regions where population growth slowed down compared with overall national trends and vice versa.

With these features we can evaluate, graphically, relationships between two indices as well as time trends for a specific economic, environmental, or health index.

Possibilities for Future Refinements in Mapping Graphics

Experience with graphical displays of environment and health data suggests some avenues for development in the use of maps to depict variable relationships.

1. Often one is interested in exploring three, four, or more variables simultaneously. Two-way mapping could be extended to the third dimension of DIDS, thereby making a third variable feasible for display. At present, the compositing feature is used to calculate the difference, product, or a weighted function of the variables of interest, then to use these converted values to map singly or in combination with another variable. This very useful feature was incorporated into the DIDS system during 1979.

2. One could utilize the physics of color theory and overlay *several* maps, not only two, to display a three- or multidimensional relation. This would be accomplished by a hardware addition to the system as well as a three-dimensional reference chart for colors displayed on the CRT. Informally the same has been done by taking the hard-copy outputs of DIDS maps, making transparencies, then overlaying the individual transparencies.

3. From a statistical standpoint, there is also interest in submitting the output displayed in bivariate or multivariate maps to statistical tests of significance. This creates the demand to print, on the CRT, a table showing the number of observations in each cell created by the cross-tabulation table in bivariate maps. This table would be as useful as the histogram now incorporated for display of univariate data. One would then be able to apply the many available tests to see if there is a *statistical* relationship (Fleiss, 1973) prior to pinpointing the locations in the four extreme corners of interest. Computer algorithms and programs are available through the Biomedical Computer Programs (BMD) series to analyze not only two, but multidimensional count data through loglinear models (Bishop, 1975; Dixon, 1977).

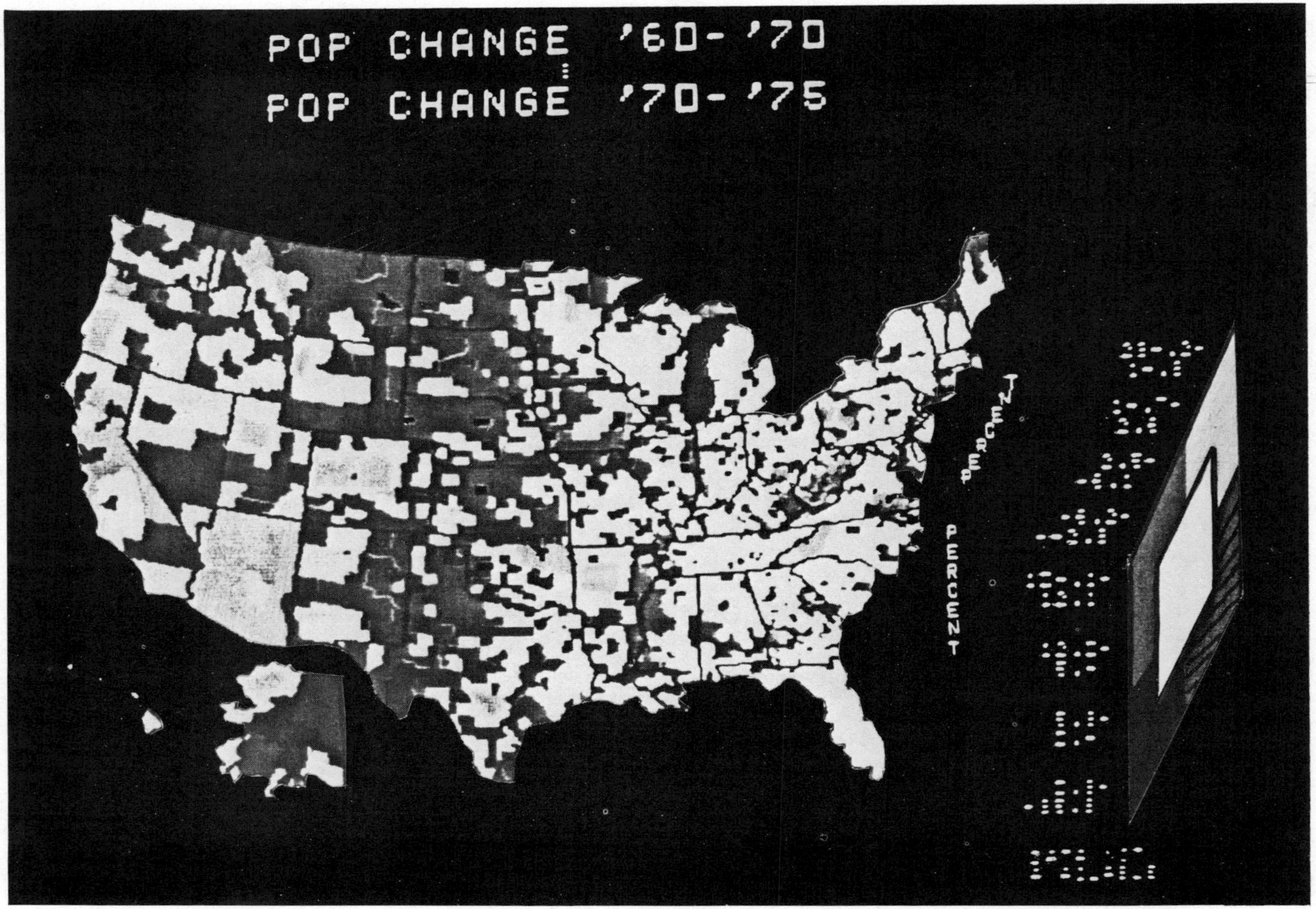

Figure 10-6 Analysis of trends in population change through bivariate maps

```
        OFFICE OF ECONOMIC OPPORTUNITY ... INFORMATION CENTER


             P O V E R T Y    I N D I C A T O R S


  SOCIO-ECONOMIC
     INDICATORS       U N F A V O R A B L E            F A V O R A B L E
                      EXT  SIG    MOD    NORMAL    MOD    SIG   EXT
                      □----□------□--------□----•----□--------□------□---□

MAGNITUDE OF
     POVERTY                                    •IIIIIIIIIIIIIIIIIIIII

SEVERITY OF
     POVERTY                          IIII•

ECONOMIC
     COMPENSATION                   IIIIII•

ECONOMIC ACTIVITY     IIIIIIIIIIIIIIIIIIIIII•

FAMILY RESOURCES      IIIIIIIIIIIIIIIIIII•

EMPLOYMENT
     CONDITIONS                            •IIIIIIIIIIIIIIIIIIIIIIIIII

EDUCATIONAL
     ACHIEVEMENT                     IIIII•

FUNCTIONAL
     ILLITERACY                         •IIIII

ADEQUACY OF
     HEALTH CARE      IIIIIIIIIIIIIIIIIII•

HEALTH STATUS                   NO DATA AVAILABLE

SUFFICIENCY
     OF HOUSING                          •IIIIIIIIIIII

AGRICULTURAL
     PROSPERITY                          •IIIIIII

                      □----□------□--------□----•----□--------□------□---□
                      EXT  SIG    MOD    NORMAL    MOD    SIG   EXT
                      U N F A V O R A B L E            F A V O R A B L E


                         EXT  --  EXTREMELY
                         SIG  --  SIGNIFICANTLY
                         MOD  --  MODERATELY
```

Figure 10-7 Example of possible profiling applications (from U.S. Department of Commerce, National Bureau of Standards (1969).

Some programs for histograms and bivariate plots from the Statistical Analysis System (SAS) have been interfaced with both UPGRADE and DIDS. It is suggested that the BMD P1F–P3F software be interfaced with the outputs to make the results meaningful to statisticians.

4. In many applications of the county-, SMSA-, or state-level data, users have wanted to observe the status of a particular location as compared with national norms on the profile of a number of variables. One may thus envision an added feature to the system similar to that in Figure 10-7 (Smith, 1973), where multiple variables would be plotted as a profile for the location of interest. The user would select the number of variables; there would be an indexing to retrieve the titles of each variable as well as median values for national norms; then percentiles would be plotted for the specific location, showing which aspects and by how much the location is below or above national norms. Value judgments could also be super-imposed, if needed, as shown in the legends "favorable," "unfavorable," and "moderate, significant, extreme."

5. The use of three categories in classifying epidemiological and environmental data has promise for future applications where the policy analyst would have fewer resources to analyze the shape of the specific distribution than to isolate classes of locations with relatively extreme observations. Uses of the trinomial in monitoring data and in profiling has been discussed by the present author in a previous report (Gardenier, 1979). Using three categories for a single variable, thus nine categories for a bivariate chart, enables one to eliminate the middle interval and eliminate the mathematical boundary-value problem that has been of concern to statisticians.

In summary, great strides have been achieved by the application of maps as graphic tools in evaluating the relationship between epidemiological, environmental, and demographic data. The use of color, although its visual effect could not be demonstrated here, adds to the appeal of the maps for the user. Much still needs to be experimented with and implemented in the interpretation of maps, their interface with statistical analysis methods, and the evaluation of multicolor, multivariable maps.

REFERENCES

ASHER, H. B., *Causal Modeling.* Beverly Hills: Sage Publications, 1976.

BISHOP, Y. M. M., S. E. FIENBERG, P. W. HOLLAND, *Discrete Multivariate Analysis: Theory and Practice.* Cambridge, Mass.: MIT Press, 1975.

CROCKER, T. D., W. SCHULZE, S. BEN-DAVID, and A. V. KNEESE, *Methods Development for Assessing Air Pollution Control Benefits,* EPA-600/5-79-001a. Washington, D.C.: Office of Health and Ecological Effects, Environmental Protection Agency, 1979.

DIXON, W. J., M. B. BROWN, *Bio-Medical Computer Programs P Series.* Berkeley: University of California Press, 1977.

FIENBERG, S. E., "Graphical Methods in Statistics," *The American Statistician,* **33,** 165–178 (1979).

FLEISS, J. L., *Statistical Methods for Rates and Proportions.* New York: John Wiley & Sons, 1973.

GARDENIER, T. K., "Profiling for Efficacy in Long-Range Clinical Trials," *Advances in Medical Systems: An Assessment of the Contribution.* Washington, D.C.: Sage Publications, 1979, pp. 95–101.

————, "Progress Report of the General Capabilities Subcommittee, DIDS Analytical Committee," Unpublished. Washington, D.C.: U.S. Environmental Protection Agency, 1979.

GODDARD SPACE FLIGHT CENTER, *Fast Facts,* **1:**2 (December 19, 1978).

HARRIS, R. H., *The Implications of Cancer-Causing Substances in Mississippi River Water.* Washington, D.C.: Technical Report, Environmental Defense Fund, 1974.

HELWIG, J. T., *SAS Introductory Guide.* Raleigh, N.C.: SAS Institute, Inc., 1978.

KIM, J., And C. W. MUELLER, *Factor Analysis: Statistical Methods and Practical Issues.* Beverly Hills: Sage Publications, 1977.

LAKE, E., C. BLAIR, J. HUDSON, and R. TABORS, *Classification of American Cities for Case Study Analysis.* EPA-600/5-77-008a,b. Washington, D.C.: Office of Research and Development, Environmental Protection Agency, 1977.

LAVE, L. B., and E. P. SESKIN, *Air Pollution and Human Health.* Baltimore: Johns Hopkins University Press, 1977.

MCDONALD, G. C., and R. C. SCHWING, "Instabilities of Regression Estimates Relating Air Pollution to Mortality," *Technimetrics,* **15,** 463 (1973).

MEYER, M. A., F. R. BROOME, and R. H. SCHWEITZER, "Color Statistical Mapping," *American Cartographer, 2, 100-117 (1975).*

MITRE CORPORATION, *Symposium/Workshop on Nuclear and Nonnuclear Energy Systems: Risk Assessment and Governmental Decision Making.* McLean, Va.: Mitre Corporation, 1979.

PRESIDENT'S COUNCIL ON ENVIRONMENTAL QUALITY, *The UPGRADE System: User's Overview,* Draft, 1977.

SAUER, H. I., *Geographic Patterns in the Risk of Dying and Associated Factors, U.S. 1968-1972, Final Report.* Contract HRA 230-76-0077. Washington, D.C.:National Center for Health Statistics, DHEW, 1972.

SCHMID, C. F., *Handbook of Graphic Presentation.* New York: Ronald Press, 1954.

SMITH, D. M., *The Geography of Social Well-Being in the United States: An Introduction to Territorial Social Indicators.* New York: McGraw-Hill, 1973.

TUKEY, J. W., "Methodology, and the Statistician's Response for BOTH Accuracy AND Relevance," *Journal of the American Statistical Association,* **74,** 368, 786-793 (1979).

U.S. Department of Commerce, National Bureau of Standards, *Community Profiles*, Office of Economic Opportunity Information Center, Washington, D.C. (1969).

Wainer, H., "An Empirical Inquiry into Two-Variable Color Maps," *First General Conference on Social Graphics,* Leesburg, Va., 1978.

Wallace, L., "Dependence of Mortality Rates on County Population," Unpublished Paper. Washington, D.C.: U.S. Environmental Protection Agency, 1978.

Zeidenberg, L. D., R. A. Prindle, and E. Landau, "The Nashville Air Pollution Study, I. Sulfur Dioxide and Bronchial Asthma," American Review of Respiratory Diseases, **84,** 489 (1961).

Chapter 11

The Influence
of Computer Graphics
on Local Government Productivity

John Michael Hadalski, Jr.

ABSTRACT

As a public administrator trained in management analysis, I am deeply concerned with the efficiency and productivity of public-sector operations in the City of Philadelphia government.

For several years I have been associated with professional engineers, planners, cartographers, photogrammetrists, data-base managers, and surveyors, among others, in two programs that I feel could serve as a basis for further testing on the use of computer graphics as a productive, efficient management tool in local government.

The first project involves a test of technology, systems design, and unit cost development for computer graphics applications in large-scale tax mapping, utility mapping, and digital base mapping involving twelve companies and local governments in Southeastern Pennsylvania. This program, the Regional Mapping and Land Records System (RMLR), was initiated some time ago in the Philadelphia Standard Metropolitan Statistical Area in a 50-square-mile area in Norristown. This area was selected because of varying types of land use, topography, and building density that would be of interest to urban, suburban, and rural planners, plus the sufficiency of first-order monumentation which allowed the aerial photography, photoanalytics, and orthophotography features of the program to be adequately tested.

In addition to being Philadelphia's Steering Committee representative to the RMLR program, I have been directing a program in the city government to ascertain existing mapping and land data retrieval costs and systems for the fifteen city departments that maintain maps and land data. This analysis and the RMLR final reports will determine the city's future direction in digital mapping and data systems.

Additionally, the city is now working closely with the major local utility companies to identify areas where city and utility mapping and land data systems interface, the steps involved in this interaction, and the benefits of computer graphics application to this interaction. At present a portion of Philadelphia's Center City has been identified as the first-place implementation area for the potential benefits of computer graphics technology. The costs for the program in Center City have been budgeted in the city's capital program.

To date, the city and utilities have identified goals and objectives for this program, along with a system model for base-map and overlay features. Specifications for aerial photography have also been completed. As in the RMLR program, it is expected that the base-map development will be cost-shared by the participants, with overlays purchased individually according to the participants' preference.

The City Records Department will also soon be in the process of photographing approximately 5000 tax plats, which are presently on cardboard. As these plats are copied for archival record, deed research will be initiated for land parcel record update. When the new City-Utility computer graphic base map has been created, the researched property lines will be digitized into the data bank.

It is hoped that the lessons of these endeavors will point to a larger transitionary context applicable to local governments generally, regarding the productive capacity of computer graphic technology.

Work of this nature is important, since the foremost concern facing local governments in the United States today arises from increasing demands for services and a shrinking revenue source from which to provide them. The challenges fostered by California's Proposition 13, along with a long tradition of regressive taxation structures, have forced localities to adopt procedures aimed at increasing productivity.

Much of the impetus is due to perceived uncontrollable inflation coupled with unfavorable comparisons of American worker output vis-a-vis those of Western European and Japanese counterparts. The productivity growth rate in the American economy is now about 2 percent per year, while those for the Western European and Japanese economies approximate 3.8 percent and 5.5 percent per year, respectively. This low productivity growth rate will maintain the sad local dilemma of increasing service demands with dwindling revenues.

In this environment, a potential solution lies with incorporating technological innovation into the local government sector to increase work production rates and to indicate to an often unbelieving citizenry that tax dollars can be spent in ways that will maximize local government's service to the community.

In this chapter I will first discuss the identification of areas where computer graphics can have a sizeable benefit for local governments in terms of productivity, using some of the information assembled from the Philadelphia program. The remainder of the chapter will outline the major technological and organizational problems that must be overcome in placing an effective computer graphics system in a local government environment.

MAPPING AND LAND-DATA SYSTEMS IN LOCAL GOVERNMENT, AS PORTRAYED BY THE CITY OF PHILADELPHIA

Land-data systems refer to the geography or to some operational consideration in the locality stemming from geographic identification of facility location, ownership, or other relevant information. In Philadelphia, a number of existing land-data systems are parcel oriented. These parcel systems relate to real estate assessment, the processing of zoning applications, legal opening or striking of city streets from the City Plan, title transfers of property, processing of permits, collecting of taxes, and a host of other functions.

Many of these parcel data systems are computerized. Each department's files are indexed by keys that are peculiar to each agency. This has resulted in an extensive listing of unrelated computer indices for information pertaining to a finite number of parcels. The maintenance of separate parcel files, each with varying updating schedules, causes extensive inaccuracy and lack of integrity when the files must be cross-referenced.

The irony in local government is that these parcel files must be cross-referenced quite often. In the site-acquisition process, for example, the existing title, current land use, last permit issuance date, property and building assessment, violations and lien data would all have to be cross-referenced and researched. The developer would, most likely, know only the address of the property in question.

A recent survey in the city revealed that when the property address is used as the sole retrieval index, it takes over an hour to retrieve deed information, nearly an hour to retrieve mortgage information, a half-hour to retrieve zoning information, and twenty minutes each to obtain tax and lien information from the agencies involved. These times do not include transportation from one agency to another.

There are approximately 750,000 parcels in Philadelphia. When several agencies maintain their own unique parcel files, however, an artificial number of parcels much greater than 750,000 is actually created, with considerable distortion of the facts. For example, two agencies show varying totals for actual parcel numbers in the city. The variance in these totals is 20 percent. This variance for total parcel numbers between the City Records Department, which controls deeds, and the Board of Revision of Taxes causes some slippage in the property descriptions of parcels, which are housed in both agencies. This, in turn, bears directly upon assessment practices, the ability to collect outstanding real estate taxes, and title search costs, since these endeavors require precise identification of the properties in question. Without some graphic capacity to rectify parcels or areas of questionable description or accuracy, this becomes a near impossible task.

As in the case of land-data systems, there are many map varieties in the Philadelphia City Government, each maintained and updated by any one of fifteen city agencies that use maps. This situation results in excessive redundancy, duplication, and lack of coordination. A recent survey found that a single change to the official City Plan may result in 28 separate updates, at an average of 1.70 hours per update. In 1978, a total of 36 confirmed City Plan changes ordained by City Council resulted in 1008 such updates to the Official Street System. This figure does not include separate updates made by each agency for other data unrelated to the street system.

Philadelphia, like other large cities, must have a constant exchange of map information with local utilities whenever construction, reconstruction, or even excavation at a predetermined site is contemplated. This exchange is required because each utility maintains its own maps of its underground plant. Most of these maps are also on various scales, and they usually have only rough approximations of property lines. Therefore, in addition to researching all the various utility lines, construction projects may also require the same property ownership, zoning, and violation searches seen in our site-acquisition example.

Thus, in both the land-data and mapping system the same unproductive forces are at work. Excessive manipulation and absence of coordination allow a finite set of information to become burdensome and cumbersome to both the responsible agencies and the taxpayer.

Conversations with municipal officials from across the nation, at conferences and meetings such as Harvard Computer Graphics Week, lead me to believe that Philadelphia is not alone in this "information proliferation" syndrome.

In order to alleviate this situation, I believe two things are needed. The first is the appropriate harnessing of the relevant computer technology in the areas of computer interactive graphics and data-base management. The second is effective management and planning strategy for the use of this technology.

THE INFLUENCE OF COMPUTER GRAPHICS ON LOCAL GOVERNMENT PRODUCTIVITY

A computer graphics project can greatly benefit local government in the area of tax mapping. Tax maps, or plats, are the foundation of a locality's assessment process, since they provide a visual record of the dimensions of private property parcels. Additionally, the numbering system used to maintain the parcel numbers on tax plats (plan and lot, or block and lot in most cases) provides the basis for locating relevant deed and mortgage information about a parcel at either the County Recorder's or Assessor's office.

Computer interactive graphics allows all the differing alphanumeric land-data information and symbolic map information to be merged into a single system. Therefore, all the associated indices can be tied to the system, along with the graphic capacity to prepare, update, and rectify property-line data.

Using the site-acquisition example given earlier, we see that the title, zoning, land-use, and assessment data can now be gleaned from a central data base because of appropriate cross-indexing. If property lines can also be digitized into the graphic data base, a graphic description of the property can be received in seconds through a graphics terminal with printer auxiliary. This process will obviously increase the productivity of the city agencies concerned and will give them appropriate justification for increasing certain fees for permits, prints, or copies of records.

Additionally, since a single integrated graphic and alphanumeric data base (or some appropriate distributed processing format) would be the basis for this integrated graphics system, the erosion of deed-description data in tax plats would be prevented, since the updating of the data would not be coordinated.

Some professionals engaged in graphic tax map preparation estimate that a given locality's total real estate tax receipts can be increased anywhere from 0.01 to 2.0 percent of the total value of all its assessed real estate through computerized tax mapping and parcel indexing (Kimball, 1979). The exact level of increased receipts seems to depend on the existing level of deed-description slippage from the plats.

In a computer graphics program, an accurate computer plotter can draw lines dozens of inches in length per second, depending upon whether wet ink or ballpoint pen is used and on the speed of the ink moving into the pen vis-à-vis the friction of the ink on the paper. A typical tax plat from the City of Philadelphia could be updated by the plotter in about 45 minutes, after the appropriate research and editing had been completed. A typical draftsman could take several work days just to do the drafting on such a tax plat.

In the tax mapping portion of the Regional Mapping and Land Records Project (RMLR) referred to earlier, the vendor (Vernon Graphics, Inc.) employed a decision rule in their programming, where a deviation of greater than five feet in frontage between the Assessor's file for the pilot area and the plotback of digital planimetric maps would result in the posting of both sets of figures in the parcel data. Through a program of this type, slippage is easy to detect and correct.

I pointed out earlier the redundancy involved in the updating of a city plan. Through a digital graphics system, the updating procedure can be accomplished far faster, since the coordinates of the proposed change can be placed into computer storage. The laborious task of redoing an entire map sheet by hand in order to update a single change in a corner is no longer required. Additionally, if the change is updated at a central agency responsible for the system, or by an agent responsible to the locality, the change is simply updated once for all the agencies concerned.

In the area of capital construction, if a common base map with selected overlays at specified scale can be developed for a locality and cooperating utilities, considerable research and redrafting of utility information at selected sites will be avoided. The design work on major capital construction projects can then be reduced substantially, decreasing final design costs of the project.

An important point to remember is that scale is of no real concern to the computer, as long as the coordinate points are accurately digitized into storage. The computer can recall the utility-line information, for example, at any desired scale, based upon the coordinate values.

In the City of Philadelphia all the various map and land-data information is housed in files of various types and sizes that take up thousands of square feet of office space, at current market value of at least $11 per square foot. The computer will have a significant impact in reducing floor-space costs for filing purposes for this function.

In many counties the capital construction of new facilities may result in the aerial photography and digitizing of many separate sites. In an overall graphics program that includes an accurate photogrammetric base, the need for separate flights and individual digitizing programs will be eliminated, as far as common geography is concerned.

Finally, in an interactive graphics program, there is no need to maintain different types of separate base mapping. The computer has the capacity to overlay parcel descriptions with flood-plain data graphically, or utility data with land-use maps, so that a single hierarchical data base can serve all map needs.

Computer graphics can also be applied to areas unrelated to large-scale mapping. For example, trends analysis and composite statistics laboriously kept by hand or stored in reams of meaningless printouts in areas such as overtime usage, employee safety, crime and fire statistics, health and welfare caseload statistics, and street sanitation output measurements can all be portrayed graphically by means of graph coordinates, or by use of the GBF DIME file.

TECHNOLOGICAL ISSUES IN A LOCAL GRAPHICS PROGRAM

When a locality wants to embark upon a large-scale computer mapping program, one of the first questions it faces is whether or not to fly new aerial photography or to digitize existing mapping. To effectively answer the question, one must identify the key issues, supply quantitative weights to each issue on the basis of either cost data or subjective analysis, and examine the alternatives that the issue analysis fosters. An an example, the decision to fly new aerial photos may be predicated on issues such as:

1. Is existing mapping accurate enough for the needs of the system users?
2. Is it necessary for various local, regional, and utility systems to "fit" into the program?
3. Is more than one type of mapping system contemplated in the overall program, such as tax mapping, utility mapping, flood plain mapping, and so on?
4. Does sufficient ground control exist in order to fly new aerial photos?
5. Can new aerial photos, photoanalytics, and ground control be regarded as necessary features by funding authorities?

6. Are there any other local agencies and utilities interested in such a program?

These questions could then be ranked in the order of importance, with quantitative weights being assigned to each answer. This type of analysis places subjective reasoning in a logical format, to which concentration on local political, organizational, and economic issues affecting the program can then be directed. Analysis of *both* the technological and organizational issues will reduce the many alternatives to a manageable number.

If new aerial photography is chosen as an ingredient in the large-scale interactive graphics mapping program, the question of scale will arise. In the RMLR demonstration, a scale of 1 : 8000 was used for aerial photography in urban and suburban areas. This resulted in compiled urban mapping at the metric scale of 1 : 500 (1 cm = 500 m, or roughly 1 in. = 41.6 ft). The aerial photography yielded an accuracy that was well within National Map Accuracy standards but deviated from absolute accuracy by about 1.5 feet. If more accuracy is desired, an aerial photography scale of 1 : 6000 or even 1 : 4000 can be used. With each larger scale selected, a larger number of models or photographs of an area will be required, since a smaller amount of total area will be on each model.

You will note that the RMLR demonstration used mapping compiled at the metric scale. A locality wishing to embark upon a similar effort should consider pending American metrification in light of whether potential system users, such as repair crew foreman, utility inspectors, and the like, would be willing to use metric-scale maps. This issue assumes further importance if conversion of existing mapping to the new system is contemplated, and in relation to system design considerations such as sheet size and scale.

In cases where aerial photography is required, the issue of orthophotography must be addressed. Aerial photographs are made inaccurate by lens distortion toward the edges of the frame and by the natural curvature of the earth. Orthophotography is a development procedure that removes the distortion.

Orthophotography is a useful tool, but its utility in urban environments has been questioned. Constant development and redevelopment cause photos of urban areas to be out of date relatively quickly. Also, the slant of tall buildings, along with concentrated land use, hides many property lines in photos. In such environments, orthophotos may have limited application in tax mapping, unless accompanied by scissor drafting procedures using existing maps, a very labor-intensive activity that may have limited utility anyway if the existing plats are out of date.

The alternative to orthophotography is called *direct stereo digitization*. Two models from the aerial photography from a given area are placed together on an overlapping basis in an instrument called a stereoscope, and the instrument is adjusted until all distortion is removed from a new singular modular view of the area. This procedure allows for the digitizing of points directly into the computer from plates developed through the stereoscope process. Its drawback is the larger number of models required because of the overlap process. This will bear directly on the overlap used in the actual aerial flight. The benefits of the process appear to be increased accuracy in urban areas, and the ability to digitize already researched property lines directly into the computer, avoiding the scissor drafting process.

A question frequently asked is whether a locality should purchase digitizing equipment and graphics hardware, or utilize a service bureau. The local situation will determine the answer, but there are some helpful analytical measures. One such measure is the research time involved in assembling the last deed of record for each parcel on a plat in a tax-mapping program, along with relevant parcel numbering and assessment data. Service bureaus, or firms, may charge a fee for researching this information to update the plats. By determining the research-time cost charged by service bureaus, analyzing the security risks and manpower costs necessary to provide firms with copies of deeds and plats, and comparing this information to the rental and purchase prices of digitizers, one can determine the tax-mapping parameters clearly. For a program of larger scope, one can also determine the number of changes or updates to the type of mapping system involved, during periodic time intervals, in order to determine the justification for in-house digitizers after initial backlogs have been removed. The staff required to man specified digitizing stations must also be determined. Other factors involved are the expertise of in-house programming staff, and the problems that licensed proprietary software may cause, if a service bureau is used initially, but with conversion to an in-house operation contemplated later.

With regard to tax mapping, a locality should also decide on the extent of graphic capacity. Certain graphic systems allow the user to "window" in on specific parcels, to perform range searches of parcels established within specific search parameters, and to display both assessment data frontage and planimetric plotback frontage where variation exceeds a certain percentage. Other, less expensive systems provide what is essentially automated drafting, along with display of certain information from the computer data base.

The total scope of the effort will need to be defined by analysis of the needs of system users. A model of the system, in terms of design features, significant sections such as aerial photography and digital base mapping, and planning milestones should be constructed before testing and implementation.

If absolute accuracy is not essential in the program, and the type of mapping being envisioned is largely statistical, then local governments have wide leverage in harnessing the technology for a graphics program. For example, many localities can use the GBF DIME file provided by the U.S. Census Bureau, which operates according to polygon retrieval with street intersections as "nodes" or coordinate points, being matched to either existing mapping or new photography. Various identifying cross-indexed data such as addresses and street codes can be placed into the data format by use of an ADMATCH program. The property lines would have to be forced into the street system, unless new coordinate values were substituted into the program from new accurate base mapping. It must be remembered, however, that this methodology is used primarily for statistical mapping, and not for engineering or design work. A requirement for its effectiveness is a GBF DIME file that is as up-to-date as possible.

POLICY AND ORGANIZATION ISSUES IN LOCAL GOVERNMENT COMPUTER GRAPHICS PROJECTS

The most important concern in local government's attempt to provide a productive environment for a computer graphics program lies in the areas of organizational planning, analysis, and user acceptability. The many computer graphics seminars and conferences held in recent years testify irrefutably that the technology works. Problems in implementation of technology arise from deficiencies in planning, cost estimating, budgeting, scheduling, and institutional development.

After appropriate feasibility testing, top management's first step in developing a large-scale computer mapping project is to state clearly and precisely what the goals of the system are to be. In this context, a goal is "a broad statement of intended accomplishments, or a description of a general condition that is deemed desirable. An objective is a specific, well-defined and measurable condition which must be attained, in order to reach a specific goal through a program strategy" (Public Technology, Inc., 1977).

In local government, top management must relate in "people terms." Citizens are interested in police and fire protection, trash collection, and street repair. Therefore, better mapping is not an end in itself, but a means to accomplish the aforementioned goals. The issue facing computer graphics here is one of "technology transfer," or moving the system design off the drawing board and into the local government.

Recent literature suggests that four groups or "estates" must be involved at different points along a continuum in the evolution of research and development projects. A consensus is difficult to reach because of disagreements that arise *within* each group. However, a lack of consensus among the groups may prevent the use of computer technology in a local public-sector environment.

The four estates fall along a continuum represented at one extreme by truth and at the other by power. The first estate is "science," the closest to the truth, since it works with a set of disciplines aimed at the discovery of rational laws.

The next estate consists of "professionals" such as engineers and surveyors. This estate applies scientific findings to societal needs. The first and second estates may be grouped as "technicians" for purposes of discussion.

The third estate is that of "administrators." Administrators possess a circumscribed body of knowledge gleaned from many professions in carrying out their tasks, and they must be guided by concerns related to organizational interests.

Finally, "politicians" comprise the fourth estate. This estate is closest to pure power, and furthest from pure truth, but "politicians are the prime decision-makers in policy innovation. They may not (and usually do not) initiate policy processes, but they eventually legitimatize a course of action," (Lambright and Teich, 1979). I have grouped the third and fourth estates together as "managerial" for purposes of discussion.

In attempting to implement a computer project, all four of these groups or estates will have to be involved in the decision-making process. Competing demands will need to be weighed in order to allocate scarce resources. The decision on implementation may be guided by considerations of politics just as much as by those of technological quality.

Technological innovation may fail because not all of these estates have been fully involved. Management may hold aloof from the scientists because of a lingering view of the scientist as a "solitary scholar in the dingy garret or kitchen laboratory" (Mason, 1979).

For their part, the "technicians" may remain aloof on grounds that "the work of highly specialized professionals can be evaluated only by other highly specialized professionals." The drawback here is that such specialists focus on "internal" technical considerations. Important "external" criteria are usually ignored, such as the impact on social priorities of the proposed research in respect to ongoing existing research programs (Bozeman, 1979).

The phrase "technical conversion" has been coined for this situation, referring to "the process by which human political choices are translated into organizational and technical terms, and resolved in whole or in part through technical decisionmaking, often in forums and in languages that are physically and mentally inaccessible to the public" (Carrol, 1975).

Managers often feel intimidated by technological considerations, since they will be forced to participate in forums where they do not understand the language or the objectives. At the same time, the professionals involved with many technologies lack the political or management linkages needed to implement a large-scale project.

When goals, objectives, and issues are clearly and "correctly" addressed in terms of the local environment and the four estates have been engaged, a constituency needed for the system is ready to be cultivated. Any program, to be successful, must have a constituent base present from all four estates.

As a result of managerial or professional entrenchment, or incorrectly perceived goals, objectives, and issues, the constituent base may be split between the technical and managerial estates. If the project is confined to the technical estates, it will then be subject to political and administrative manipulation.

Conversely, a project having adequate political and managerial support can be rendered totally ineffective if the participation of the "users," such as engineers and planners, is not willingly forthcoming.

In order to build the appropriate constituency, two factors are essential. They are "integrative" project coordination, and the willingness of project staff to engage in advocacy-adversary relationships.

Integrative management was described by Gerald Gordon and his colleagues and students in addressing the question of leadership in technological projects. According to Gordon, the two most desirable types of project management are *high differentiators* and *high remote associators.*

High differentiators "have the ability to make, as well as appreciate, fine distinctions or differentiations between people, objects and institutions." High remote associators "have the ability to tie diverse, dissimilar and disparate things together in highly meaningful ways" (Mitroff, 1979).

Gordon combined high and low values of these two dimensions, which resulted in four problem-solving styles in technological management.

1. High Differentiators (Di) and High Remote Associators (Ra)—
   INTEGRATORS
2. Low (Di) and High (Ra)—PROBLEM SOLVERS
3. High (Di) and Low (Ra)—PROBLEM RECOGNIZERS
4. Low (Di) and Low (Ra)—DOERS

In this listing, "Doers" has replaced Gordon's original noun, "Technicians," in order to avoid confusion with Lambright and Teich's use of "technicians" in their work on the four estates involved in scientific management.

Integrators have the ability to objectively relate previously unformulated problems *and* to solve them. Problem solvers are unable to relate new problems but can solve those already indicated. Problem recognizers can perceive and relate new problems but lack the skills necessary to solve them. Finally, doers must be closely directed or supervised (Mitroff, 1979).

If these notions are correct, than an organizational design can be established for governmental technological projects, but only if "the key role of the integrator should be placed in key informational and policy positions, so that (he) can encourage the kind of problem solving flexibility that is characteristic of innovative technology assessment. . . .Apparently, the ability to make high differentiations, to tolerate a goodly amount of openendedness in the solution of problems, and to avoid premature closure is vitally critical in the effective management of problem solving" (Mitroff, 1979).

Therefore, project staff should have appropriate technical training, the ability to relate that training to diverse issues and to *move from* the technology when necessary in order to relate to members of the managerial estates.

Advocacy-adversary relationships with elements within the estates and the local bureaucracy *will* take place, whether or not they are expected or even desired. The extent to which project management handles the relationships will, in the long run, determine the magnitude of the constituency that has been cultivated, the degree of consensus reached among the estates on the technological innovation, and the final success or failure of the program.

In my experience, the technical estates function on concepts, laws, technology, empirical data, evidence, and jargon. The administrative estate functions on procedure, and the political estate functions on the art of politics. Any new system innovation, particularly one that requires considerable expense and conversion, will require the project staff to adopt the various roles to its modus operandi. In other words, one must recognize "The narrow rationality of scientific decision-making and the intrinsic limitations of scientific tools. To get to the 'truth' the assessor will have to rely not only on models and algorithms, but on the advocacy and adversary process" (Majone, 1978).

Following is a listing developed by Richard O. Mason, Associate Professor of Management and Information Systems, and Chairman of the Public and Not-For-Profit Management Program at the University of California, Los Angeles. Dr. Mason developed this listing in association with Dr. Vaughn Blankenship and Dr. Fred Betz, both of the National Science Foundation.

Keeping in mind the concepts advanced in this chapter on policy and organizational issues, local project coordinators may be able to begin empirical analysis of their own computer graphics ideas, using the criteria developed from this listing. The complete listing reads as follows:

1. *Ideation.* Creating the basic ideas with respect to problem formulation and research objectives. Basic managerial questions include:
   (a) Who forms the ideas?
   (b) What constitues a good idea, one worth pursuing?
   (c) How are priorities set?

2. *Planning and design.* Formulating hypotheses or refined research questions and the specifications of a series of tasks necessary to complete the research. Basic managerial questions include:
   (a) What concepts and theory are to be used?
   (b) How is data to be collected?
   (c) What resources are required to accomplish the research?
   (d) How will the work be done?

3. *Resource acquisition (financing and staffing).* Obtaining or providing the resources for carrying out the plan and design, the most "generalized" resources being "capital" in the form of dollars and equipment, "labor" in the form of human skills/motivations, and "information" in the form of data and the results of past studies. Basic managerial questions include:
   (a) Who supplies the resources or finances them?
   (b) How is a "price" or "cost" for the research determined?
   (c) What are the criteria for deciding whether or not to fund or support the research?
   (d) What factors affect the motivation of the researcher?

4. *Organizing.* Selecting human resources, establishing expectations, objectives, communication, division of labor. Basic managerial questions include:
   (a) What is the nature of the division of labor? How are research tasks assigned to people?
   (b) How are task objectives set?
   (c) What modes of communication are used?
   (d) How are research activities related to the surrounding organizational environment?
   (e) How are research activities related to the "funder," the supporter of the research, or the source of the resources?
   (f) What new managerial skills does the scientific investigator require?

5. *Producing.* Applying the resources to the resources tasks according to plan. This involves integration of resources and coordination of interdependencies, management of incentives, quality control over output. Basic managerial questions include:
   (a) How is the work done?
   (b) How is the work supervised?
   (c) What is the nature of the work environment?

6. *Output/utilization/evaluation/feedback.* Relating the scientific conclusions obtained to the original intentions (goals, plans) of the investigator(s) and communicating them to (a) the project's financial sponsor, (b) the scientific peer group, (c) potential direct users of the results, and (d) the public. Basic managerial questions include:
   (a) Who are the potential "users" of the research?
   (b) How are the results communicated to them?
   (c) How are the results to be evaluated? (Mason, 1979)

CONCLUSION: THE FUTURE OF COMPUTER GRAPHICS IN LOCAL GOVERNMENT

This chapter has been devoted largely to the management science of designing and implementing a computer graphics program in local government. The technology discussed here can be used effectively in statistical mapping, tax mapping, contour mapping, flood plain mapping, and to some extent in utility mapping. The computer graphic concepts explored in this paper aid in the accurate location of specific facilities or in connoting specific geographic conditions.

Future developments may emphasize the use of computer graphics for plans and schematic drawings in local government. Accurate data management techniques, coupled with raster type graphic terminals, will allow for great accuracy. A wide selection of "menus" of range and parameter searches will allow the engineer and designer to graphically display various conditions in his design work.

The introduction of colored graphics terminals will allow systems people to graphically portray more types of hierarchical data on the terminal, thereby increasing the decision-making potential of graphics.

The day is also imminent when a merging of the fields of computer graphics and computer micrographics will take place. In this sense, hard-copy large-scale maps produced from computer plotters can be microfilmed and placed in a COM (computer-operated microfilm) system for later retrieval. Hard-copy maps may someday be obsolete in local government, replaced by graphic terminals, COM aperture card systems, and portable microfilm readers.

Finally, I believe we shall see a continued relationship between large-scale mapping and the federal government's GBF DIME file. The large-scale local computer mapping project can be made accurate to the parcel location. The intersecting of the parcel coordinates at the parcel center, known as the parcel centroid, along with street centerline data, can be merged into the GBF DIME file data. This will serve to increase the accuracy of the maps produced through use of the DIME file. This is important for localities that use existing coordinates from the federal government's Metropolitan Map Series for local services, or that even use blow-ups of such maps for tax-map purposes. The combination of large-scale controlled mapping with GBF DIME can serve to increase the accuracy of these blow-ups, making their use much more feasible.

In the future, the greatest need for research will probably be in the realm of planning and analysis. To this extent, further research is needed into event and activity prediction for PERT (project evaluation review technique) as applicable to local graphics programs, as well as research into decision-tree systems analysis and budgetary and cost-effectiveness analysis. This research will serve to alleviate the difficult organizational, structural, and institutional problems impeding the technology transfer of computer graphics into local government, where it will be able to contribute to an efficient and productive operating environment.

REFERENCES

ANDERSON, ROBERT H., and NORMAN Z. SHAPIRO, *Design Considerations for Computer-Based Interactive Map Display Systems,* A Report Prepared for Defense Advanced Research Projects Agency. Santa Monica: Rand Corporation, 1979.

BOZEMAN, BARRY, " 'Straight Arrow Policy' and Its Dangers," *Public Administration Review,* **39,** 116–121 (March–April 1979).

CARROL, JAMES D., "Science, Knowledge and Choice: The Future as Post-Industrial Administration," *Public Administration Review,* **35,** 578–581 (November–December 1975).

EMERY, HENRY A., "Information Ecology," *Automated Mapping Chronicle,* **2,** 1–4 (February 1979).

GORDON, GERALD, and EDWARD V. MORSE, "Creative Potential and Organizational Structure," *Academy of Management Journal,* **12,** 37–49 (1969).

HADALSKI, JOHN M., "A Management Perspective of Computer Graphics in Local Government," *Presented at Harvard Computer Graphics Week, 1979,* Cambridge, Mass.

KANTER, JEROME, *Management-Oriented Management Information Systems.* Englewood Cliffs, N.J.: Prentice-Hall, Inc. 1977.

KIMBALL, JOHN, L. Robert Kimball and Associates, Interview, September 19, 1979.

LAMBRIGHT, W. HENRY, and ALBERT H. TEICH, "Policy Innovation in Federal R & D: The Case of Energy," *Public Administration Review,* **39,** 140–148 (March–April 1979).

MAJONE, GIANDOMENICO, "Technology Assessment in a Dialectic Key," *Public Administration Review,* **38,** 52–58 (January–February 1978).

MASON, RICHARD O., "The Role of Management in Science," *Public Administration Review,* **39,** 112–116 (March–April 1979).

MITROFF, IAN I., "On Managing Holistically or Is the Management of Science Becoming More Important than the Philosophy of Science?" *Public Administration Review,* **39,** 129–133 (March–April 1979).

NATIONAL LEAGUE OF CITIES, "GBF/DIME, Dollars and Sense," *Nation's Cities,* November 1975, pp. 22–36.

PAYNE, WALTER C., "Evaluation of Horizontal Control Monumentation, Philadelphia Region, Southeastern Pennsylvania," Philadelphia, 1978. (Mimeographed.)

PRICE, DON K., *The Scientific Estates.* Cambridge, Mass.: Harvard University Press, 1965.

PUBLIC TECHNOLOGY, INC., *Land Management: A Management Report for State and Local Government.* Washington, D.C.: National Science Foundation, 1977.

Part IV

ANALYTICAL CAPABILITIES
OF GEOGRAPHIC
INFORMATION SYSTEMS

Chapter **12**

Computer-Aided Siting
of Coal-Fired Power Plants:
A Case Study

Dennis R. Smith
John H. Robinson

ABSTRACT

This chapter describes aspects of a study to identify fifteen sites on which construction and operation of a coal-fired electric generating station would be environmentally and economically feasible. The study area covered 52,500 square miles in two states. Dames & Moore's Geographic Information Management System (GIMS™) was used as a computer aid in the site-selection process.

Computer-Aided Siting

In recent years many attempts have been made to use computers, especially computer mapping systems, as an aid in the power plant siting process. These applications, primarily in the regional analysis portion of a comprehensive areawide siting study, have met with mixed success for several reasons:

1. The analyses performed at the regional level were seen as very simple tasks that could be handled adequately with manual overlay techniques.

2. Most strategies for regional analysis (or screening) that were based on computer mapping used the suitability mapping approach where environmental, cost, and socioeconomic issues (on criteria) were combined using a weighted overlay system to form a final composite map of suitability. This approach, while not entirely dependent on computer mapping technology, was developed parallel with the use of computer mapping and is most easily applied with a computer. The approach was criticized because it attempted to combine several dissimilar types of issues using abstract utility scales, which are said to be unreliable as a measurement of judgment. Because the suitability mapping research was conducted using computer mapping techniques, the usefulness of these techniques was called into question.

3. The analyses performed were primarily coincident analyses—that is, several factors were overlaid at one point (or grid cell) without consideration of the spatial relationship of that point or grid cell to surrounding features.

These problems and others have led to further development of the applications of computer aids in spatial analysis. In fact, several major utilities have fully embraced the idea of computer-based geographic data management systems and are currently building computerized data files for their service areas that include a wide range of land-use, environmental, and demographic data.

Of major importance in the continued development of computer aids for siting is the development of spatial-analysis techniques that lead to the creation of improved information for decision making at the regional level of analysis (where regional is used to define the screening of a large area such as a service territory to identify those areas containing factors that lead to the identification of sites). In this regard, Dames & Moore has developed several new techniques as alternatives to the single composite overlay suitability approach (which considers all issues at the same time). These new techniques have been successfully tested in several siting projects and are now included among the standard approaches that Dames & Moore uses in its site-selection work.

Case Study Background

Late in 1977, Dames & Moore was hired by a group of utilities to perform a site-selection study for a coal-fired power plant. The main objective was to prepare a "site bank" of at least fifteen environmentally and economically viable sites, dispersed within or adjacent to the client's service territory, ranked, and publicly defendable. Other objectives included

1. A siting report that would be suitable for inclusion in an environmental impact study.

2. Development of an effective siting methodology for future client use

3. A client staff trained in the siting methodology and

4. Installation of software compatible with the client's data processing system

for cost-effective changes in the data base and for additional computer-assisted siting.

SITING METHODOLOGY AND TECHNIQUE

Most current methodologies attempt to facilitate multiobjective decision making. Siting studies today are concerned not only with engineering and economic factors but also with environmental issues. The objective of the methodology is to organize the data into a manageable set of interrelationships, such that all persons and groups concerned with the siting study will be provided with the appropriate level of information to make decisions.

Site Suitability Model

The siting process evaluated the entire candidate area on economic and environmental factors. Areas that indicated lower cost and least environmental sensitivities and that fell outside the regional restriction screen were identified as potential siting areas, from which specific sites were selected for the "site bank."

Certain environmental criteria were applied at the beginning of the study to exclude large regions from the study area. These exclusionary considerations included dedicated lands such as parks and forests, urban areas, and designated wetland areas. After the exclusionary screen was applied, the areas that remained were designated as eligible siting areas. A site suitability model was then used to identify areas that were most suitable from an environmental perspective. Next, a cost analysis was applied to identify areas that were both environmentally suitable and least costly. The general form of the suitability model used to evaluate the environmental criteria is shown in Figure 12-1.

GIMS—Geographic Information Management System

To perform the application of the site suitability model, as described above, Dames & Moore's GIMS was employed. This system was used for encoding all geographic data required for the analysis into a computerized data base, performing all the required manipulations of these data to evaluate environmental sensitivity, cost, and derating impacts, and displaying the results.

Technically speaking, GIMS is a state-of-the-art geographic information management system. Operated most commonly on Control Data Corporation hardware, GIMS has also been installed on an IBM 370-168, a Univax 1108, and a Digital Equipment Corporation PDP 11/45. The software consists of about 10,000 statements in ANSI standard Fortran, and there is a high level of user documentation. The system is usually operated in batch mode, although there is an interactive version. Digitized input data are in the form of point, linear, chain/identifier (or polygon), isoline, and associated attributed tables. Data are stored in their absolute geographic form (actual X, Y, Z information) and can be generalized into a cell format to facilitate spatial modeling (cells). Analysis can be performed in both absolute and generalized formats, and hard copy output is produced on the line printer or plotter.

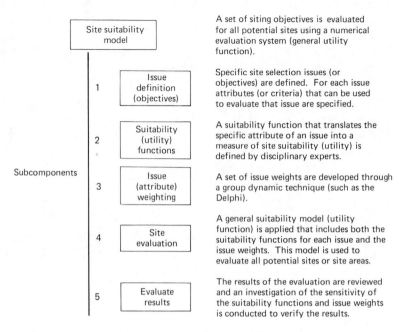

	Site suitability model	A set of siting objectives is evaluated for all potential sites using a numerical evaluation system (general utility function).
1	Issue definition (objectives)	Specific site selection issues (or objectives) are defined. For each issue attributes (or criteria) that can be used to evaluate that issue are specified.
2	Suitability (utility) functions	A suitability function that translates the specific attribute of an issue into a measure of site suitability (utility) is defined by disciplinary experts.
3	Issue (attribute) weighting	A set of issue weights are developed through a group dynamic technique (such as the Delphi).
4	Site evaluation	A general suitability model (utility function) is applied that includes both the suitability functions for each issue and the issue weights. This model is used to evaluate all potential sites or site areas.
5	Evaluate results	The results of the evaluation are reviewed and an investigation of the sensitivity of the suitability functions and issue weights is conducted to verify the results.

Subcomponents

Figure 12-1   Site suitability model

SITE-SELECTION CRITERIA

Of the many issues that might be used as determinants for plant siting, initial discussion established two major classes: economic and environmental. Throughout the initial phases of the data management program, significant adjustments to the approaches were made. The original economic issue was the availability of cooling water; through discussion and interviews, this was expanded to include transmission, fuel supply, and air quality factors. Environmental issues were more stable, focusing on agricultural soil, recreation, and stream sensitivities. A third major issue, power plant derating, was also developed and later combined with the cost factors. Overall, the three major issues (environmental sensitivity, cost of construction and operation, power plant derating) were generated utilizing thirteen supportive issues based on 50 intermediate operations performed on an original list of twelve source maps. The flow of information for this modeling is described later in the chapter and illustrated with a data-structure diagram.

Environmental Sensitivity

Three environmental issues were addressed: prime agricultural soils, stream sensitivity, and recreation potential. These issues are subjective in nature, and their evaluation was expressed on a 1–5 interval weighting scale. The agricultural soil sensitivity issue was derived from a map depicting seven soil classifications in the study area. The nominal labels identifying the soils were translated into the interval evaluation scale. Stream sensitivity was evaluated by applying an interval weight to all stream segments. The economic modeling of cooling water determined which stream segments would be utilized as supply sources, and then each segment's environmental rating was applied to the potential site. For the recreation sensitivity issue, a map was used depicting counties over the two-state study area. Each county was evaluated from a recreation perspective and assigned a nominal rating indicating its recreation potential.

These three environmental issues were then combined into a total environmental rating of each cell, with each issue assigned an equal weight in the combination operation. An alternative to the assumption of equality is to assign the issues variable weights that represent differing levels of importance. These weights usually are assigned from a ratio scale and represent the relative importance of each issue to the others.

After the rating scales and weights are applied and a final environmental sensitivity map is formed, this map is reviewed to understand the reasons for the resulting spatial pattern of suitability. Of primary importance is the determination of the fractional contribution that each issue makes to the final composite suitability map. This contribution is more complex than the simple use of the weight as a measure of contribution.

One of the first characteristics considered for each map is the geographic variation of the values across it. The extent of the variations for each map is measured by the standard deviation for the map's parameter. The standard deviations on the three environmental sensitivity maps are as follows:

	SD	MEAN
Soil sensitivity	1.65	2.01
Recreational sensitivity	0.69	1.89
Water sensitivity	0.58	2.13

The correlations between the variations of any pair of maps are represented by the correlation coefficient, which is a number between -1 and $+1$. The $+1$ indicates the variables always vary together in the same scalar direction; the -1 indicates that the variables always vary in the opposite scalar direction. A value of zero indicates that the variations are in phase for half of the area and out of phase for half of the area in a way that approximates independent variation.

CORRELATION COEFFICIENTS

	Soil Sensitivity	Recreation Sensitivity	Water Sensitivity
Soil Sensitivity	1.00	-0.14	0.13
Recreational Sensitivity	-0.14	1.00	0.71
Water Sensitivity	0.13	0.71	1.00

With the correlations between all possible combinations of issue maps taken two at a time, the contribution of each issue to the composite suitability variance can be calculated. This is the sum of the variance and covariances (product of correlation coefficient and standard deviations) for each issue. The covariances and contributions are shown in the following table.

COVARIANCES AND CONTRIBUTIONS

	Soil Sensitivity	Recreation Sensitivity	Water Sensitivity	Issue Contribution
Soil Sensitivity	2.72	− 0.16	0.12	2.68
Recreation Sensitivity	− 0.16	0.48	0.28	0.60
Water Sensitivity	0.12	0.28	0.34	0.74
			Total suitability variance	4.02

The individual issue contribution in fractional form can now be calculated by dividing the individual issue contribution by the suitability variance. These results are shown in the following table:

FRACTIONAL CONTRIBUTIONS

Soil sensitivity	0.67
Recreation sensitivity	0.15
Water sensitivity	0.18

These individual issue contributions expressed in fractional form can be viewed as the sensitivity of the composite map to changes in the weights of the individual issue maps. For this reason, they can be referred to as the *entire map sensitivity*.

Cost of Construction and Operation

The cost model used to estimate the plant cost in constant dollars included all major components of a power plant, both capital and operating costs. The general form of the model is

$$P_{(i,j)} = (a_1x_1 + a_2x_2 + a_3x_3 + a_4x_4 + a_5x_5 + a_6x_6)Z$$

where
$P_{(i,j)}$ = present value in 1989 dollars of a plant at location i,j
a_n = number of cost units of factor x_n at location i,j
x_1 = capital cost of plant
x_2 = operation and maintenance cost of plant
x_3 = delivered fuel cost at plant
x_4 = capital, operation, and maintenance cost of transmission
x_5 = capital, operation, and maintenance cost of cooling
x_6 = derating cost for scrubber-operation, pumping, and transmission losses
Z = present-value discount factor.

Of the total set of factors considered, four economic issues were addressed as site variable costs: air quality control, cooling water, fuel transportation, and transmission connection. Costs were broken into two categories: capital costs and operating-maintenance cost. For the purpose of comparison, all costs were expressed in millions of 1989 dollars, allowing for the aggregation of one-time and series costs. Additionally, operating overhead was considered in the form of a derating to reflect variable consumption of energy induced by site-dependent factors. These derating issues are explained in the next section. The final cost maps were expressed in 1989 dollars per megawatt of output (present-value revenue requirement) after derating was considered.

The air quality costs were based on zones of four unique air quality designations. The estimated capital cost for scrubbers was obtained by the direct translation of the various elements into their respective required cost. Operating and maintenance costs were likewise developed by a similar translation.

The capital cost of the cooling supply system was based on the impoundment or procurement cost of the water source and the cost of construction of the water-supply pipeline. The water source costs were geographically depicted as linear elements indicating streams, rivers, shorelines of lakes, bays, and the Atlantic Ocean. The cost of pipeline construction was based on the distance calculated from each water source to each site, with consideration given to the intervening topography. In estimating the minimum cooling cost for each cell, the source cost, pipe length, and pumping head were simultaneously optimized.

The capital cost of fuel transportation was evaluated by determining the cost of railroad spur construction to all potential sites from the existing four-railroad network. From the existing rail networks, the length of new spur construction was computed. This length was determined in conjunction with the elevation map, which depicts the elevation rise from one cell to another. Where grades exceeded 3 percent, additional spur length was incurred to reduce the grade to a maximum of 3 percent. The analysis showed increased rail construction cost in areas of varying terrain.

The operational cost for transporation of fuel is based on the total distance traveled from the mine along the existing rail network and the new spur lines. The mine is located in the southwestern part of the study area adjacent to rail network 1. The minimum distance outward from the mine was calculated for each cell along rail network 1, and where closed loops existed, the shortest distance was determined. At the transfer points from rail network 1 to the other three rail systems, a distance penalty was incurred equal to 60 miles (roughly equivalent to the cost penalty of a unit train transfer). The aggregate distances were then computed outward along each of these three additional systems. The resultant map depicts the minimum distance along existing rail networks from the mine, with the incurred equivalent economic penalty for rail system transfers. The fuel-transportation model is explained in more detail in a later section.

The capital cost of tying into the existing transmission system was evaluated by assigning a predetermined upgrade cost for each segment of the existing network. The existing transmission system consists of both 345-kV and 500-kV lines. Parallel analyses were undertaken on both line capacities with the objective of providing a connection to the transmission system at the least capital cost.

All the economic issues were combined to develop a minimum-cost map. It is interesting to report that when evaluated, the above-mentioned site-dependent issues varied by as much as 35 percent of the basic plant costs (construction and fuel costs). The site-dependent variables in the fuel-transportation issue alone varied by over $700 million.

Power Plant Derating

For clarification purposes, the gross electrical output of the generator in the power plant to be sited is expected to be 690 megawatts (MW). Lighting, conveyors, pumps, space heating, electrostatic precipitator, and plant auxiliaries require approximately 40 MW, which leaves approximately 650 MW. Minimum level of sulfur scrubbers is expected to account for 39 MW, thus leaving approximately 611 MW. The 611 MW will be further reduced by three site-dependent factors: derating for an increase in the requirement of scrubber operation, derating for pumping of cooling water, and transmission-line losses.

The derating for operation of scrubbers was obtained by a direct translation of the various air quality zones into their revenue requirement costs. Each air quality zone depicted a unique air quality designation and its associated control requirement. The derating for pumping of cooling water was based upon the water sources and the vertical distance from the source to each potential site. Pumping head costs were incurred only on upslopes and no recovery of head was accounted for on downslopes. Since the sources represented both fresh and salt water, different head costs were utilized based on differing required volumes. The transmission-line losses were established by a direct translation of the efficiency factors assigned to each segment of the existing transmission system.

The three derating maps were used to establish the deliverable output of the power plant. The deratings for pumping cooling water and for operating scrubbers were subtracted from the net output of the plant to determine the megawatts available for transmission at each site. These megawatts were further reduced by variable transmission-system efficiencies, which ranged from 89 to 99 percent. The resulting map depicts the deliverable plant output based on the above site-dependent factors with the deliverable output ranging from 530 to 608 MW from a plant generator nominally rated at 690 MW.

SITE-SELECTION ANALYSIS

The site selection analysis is performed by addressing the desired major issues, by utilizing the operational capabilities of GIMS, and by applying data management techniques. All these are directed at achieving the siting objectives of the project. The flow of information through this analysis is graphically depicted in the data-structure diagram (Figure 12-2). Certain operations to be performed on the data can be classed as spatial analysis models. These models are concerned not only with the coincident data within a cell but also with the data and their relationship and distances to other cells in the study area. The overall site suitability of a cell is finally determined by combining the multiobjective issues in a composite overlay and sequentially ranking all cells.

Information Flow

Figure 12-2 is a data-structure diagram depicting the flow of data and information through the project. The project's overall objective is depicted by the composite suitability map on the far right. Prior to this composite map are the major issues of

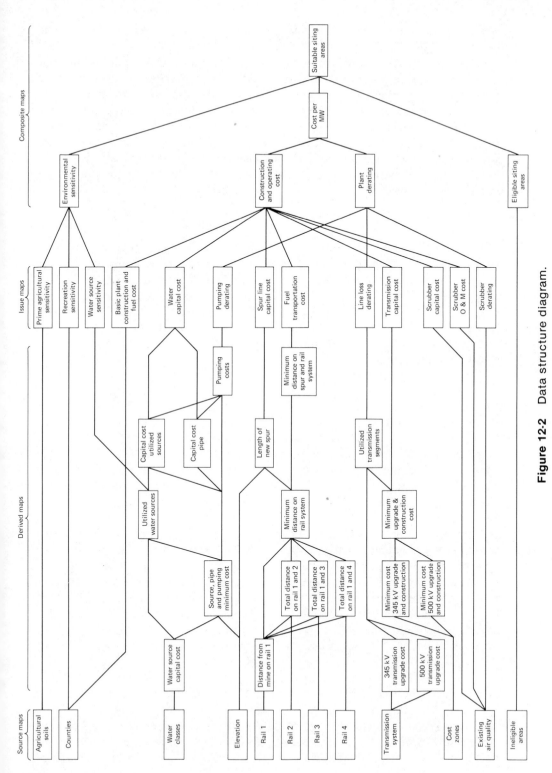

Figure 12-2 Data structure diagram.

concern in the project, specifically environmental sensitivity, economic factors, and derating factors. These major issues were developed from thirteen supportive issues, which in turn were developed from over 50 manipulations of the source data using GIMS analytic functions. The data-structure diagram shown here is a generalization of the actual working data-structure diagram. All the information generated throughout the diagram was based on the geographic source data maps, depicted on the far left of the diagram. Throughout the diagram, other unit factors are included, such as costs of spur line construction per mile, fuel transportation per mile, construction of cooling water pipe, pumping head, and scrubbers. These factors are used to calibrate particular generic models that peform operations on the various maps in the data base.

Spatial Analysis

Many of the operations performed on the data base by GIMS are concerned with the coincident data in each cell. In this type of operation a transformation is applied to every cell in the study area. The other operations performed were spatial analysis functions, which required information not only about the data in each specific cell but also about the data adjacent to the cell and the data elsewhere on the map. Spatial calculations may also require the distances to other select data; these distances may be affected by intervening impedance factors such as slope or elevation change.

To explain the spatial analysis performed for this siting study, the following discussion details the development of the capital costs and operating costs of the fuel-transportation issues. As the data-structure diagram (Figure 12-2) indicates, the fuel-transportation cost consists of two issues: Spur-Line Capital Cost and Fuel-Transportation Cost. These two issues are developed from five source maps: four railroad maps and the elevation map. The analysis also required the input of certain constants or locational factors, such as location of mine; cost per mile for fuel transport; cost for transfer to another railroad; location of transfer points; maximum grade for construction of new spurs; and cost per mile for construction of new spur.

Figure 12-3 presents a display of one portion of the study area that will be used to graphically explain the analysis. Map A is a composite of all the railroad lines, the location of the mine, and the location of the transfer points. A distance operation is performed along the rails using the mine as the seed or starting cell, and a transfer penalty of twenty additional miles is imposed at each transfer point. The result of this operation is Map B, whose cells contain equivalent distances from the mine along existing rails. This equivalent distance will be multiplied later by a cost-per-mile factor, but for functional purposes the maps will remain, for now, in units of distance. Map B will be left as is for a moment.

The next set of maps (Figure 12-4) begins with Map C, which is a spur-line seed map formed by a composite of all four rails. The seed map is input to a grade operation that uses the elevation map (not shown) for impedence factors. The grade model works its way out from the seed cells to all adjacent cells. The model uses the change in elevation and the horizontal distance between adjacent cells, and it determines the grade. If the grade is allowable, 3 percent or less, the new cell is given

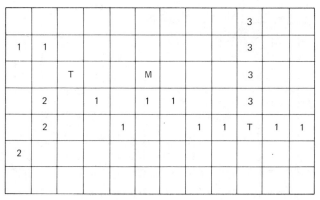

Map A: Railroad composite

									3		
1	1								3		
		T			M				3		
	2		1		1	1			3		
	2			1			1	1	T	1	1
2											

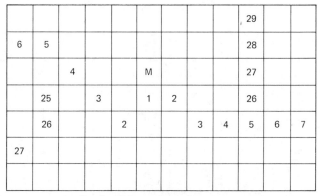

Map B: Minimum distance on rail system

									29		
6	5								28		
		4			M				27		
	25		3		1	2			26		
	26			2			3	4	5	6	7
27											

1 = Railroad one   2 = Railroad two   3 = Railroad three
M = Mine   T = Transfer point

Figure 12-3

a value equal to the distance traveled from the seeds. If the grade is more than 3 percent, then additional distance is incurred and accumulated to reduce the grade to 3 percent. The result of this operation is Map D, whose cells contain lengths for new spur lines. Note that the lower left corner contains values that increment at a high rate as they move away from the seeds. The reason is the topography, which was steep or rugged in this area, and the spur lines incurred a greater length in order to maintain a maximum 3 percent grade.

The distances of new spur lines on Map D are readily multiplied by the unit cost per mile of constructing new spurs to produce Map E, Spur Line Capital Cost, an issue map.

The information has now been developed that will permit the calculation of total distance from the mine to each site and thus of the cost of fuel transport to each site. To perform this operation the data are utilized from Map B, Minimum Distance on Rail System, and from Map D, Length of New Spur.

If a site is away from an existing rail line, the total distance from the mine is an

Map C: Spur line seed

								0			
0	0							0			
		0			M			0			
	0		0		0	0		0			
	0			0			0	0	0	0	0
0											

Map D: Length of new spur

1	1	2	3	4	4	3	2	1	0	1	2
0	0	1	2	3	3	2	2	1	0	1	2
1	1	0	1	2	M	1	2	1	0	1	2
1	0	1	0	1	0	0	1	1	0	1	1
1	0	2	4	0	1	1	0	0	0	0	0
0	2	7	5	4	3	2	1	1	1	1	1
1	4	8	9	8	5	6	2	2	2	2	2

Map E: Spur line capital cost

10	10	20	30	40	40	30	20	10	0	10	20
0	0	10	20	30	30	20	20	10	0	10	20
10	10	0	10	20	M	10	20	10	0	10	20
10	0	10	0	10	0	0	10	10	0	10	10
10	0	10	40	0	10	10	0	0	0	0	0
0	20	70	57	40	30	20	10	10	10	10	10
10	40	80	90	80	50	60	20	20	20	20	20

Figure 12-4

addition of the length of spur and the distance along the existing rail lines to the spur. Before performing this addition, we must determine what point along the existing rail line was used as the seed to generate the spur length to this site.

This determination is performed with a spread operation, which functions on the same logic as the grade operation. Instead of accumulating distances from the seeds, however, the operation spreads the unique value of the seed, which in this case is the distance along existing rail lines. A new map, Map F, Spread of Distance along Rail Lines, is generated and added to Map D, Length of New Spur, to determine the total distance from the mine, Map G. This map is multiplied by the cost per mile of fuel transport to produce Map H, Fuel-Transportation Cost, an issue map (see Figure 12-5).

This type of data manipulation exemplifies spatial-analysis applications that GIMS was developed to solve.

Composite Overlay

To develop the three major issues and the final suitability map from the thirteen supportive issues, five composite operations were performed. The first combined with the seven economic issues into one composite cost issue. The second combined the three supportive derating issues into the one composite delivered plant-output issue. The third combined the three sensitivity issues into the one composite environmental sensitivity issue.

The next operation performed was the evaluation of the dollar cost per megawatt. This map was generated by dividing the minimum-cost composite issue by the delivered plant output issue for each site. This resultant map depicts the desired economic measure of dollars per megawatt, which ranged in value from 8.10 to 9.90 million revenue requirement dollars per megawatt delivered, with a mean value of 8.88 million per megawatt, all expressed in 1989 dollars.

The last composite operation was used to combine the Cost Per Megawatt Map with Composite Environmental Sensitivity Map. This combination was performed by using a matrix evaluation, which simultaneously focused on the least environmental sensitivity values and the lowest cost values. This final composite suitability siting map contains a ranked value at every potential site. The best ranking sites are those that require the least cost and would impact the environment the least.

CONCLUSIONS

The use of GIMS to support the siting approach yielded significant data for the site-selection process itself and benefited the project in several ways.

Case Study Results

The results of the total-cost analysis show that in the aggregate, the total life cycle cost of the power plant in 1989 dollars could range from 4.25 to 6.1 billion. The variation among all possible siting locations was approximately 35 percent of the

6	5	4	3	1	2	29	29	29	29	29	29
6	5	4	3	1	1	2	28	28	28	28	28
6	4	4	3	1	M	2	2	27	27	27	7
6	25	3	3	1	1	2	2	4	26	6	7
26	26	26	3	2	1	2	3	4	5	6	7
27	27	3	3	2	1	2	3	4	5	6	7
27	27	3	3	2	1	2	3	4	5	6	7

Map F: Spread of distance along rail lines

7	6	6	6	5	6	32	31	30	29	30	31
6	5	5	5	4	4	4	30	29	28	29	30
6	5	4	4	3	M	3	4	28	27	28	9
7	25	4	3	2	1	2	3	5	26	7	8
27	26	28	7	2	2	3	3	4	5	6	7
27	29	10	8	6	4	4	4	5	6	7	8
28	31	11	12	10	6	8	5	6	7	8	9

Map G: Minimum distance on spur and rail system

21	18	18	18	15	18	96	93	90	87	90	93
18	15	15	15	12	12	12	90	87	84	87	96
18	15	12	12	9	M	9	12	84	81	84	27
21	75	12	9	6	3	6	9	15	78	21	24
81	78	84	21	6	6	9	9	12	15	18	21
81	87	30	24	18	12	12	12	15	18	21	24
84	93	33	36	30	18	24	15	18	21	24	27

Map H: Fuel transportation cost

Figure 12-5

base cost (4.25 billion). Stated in dollars per megawatt of output, the costs ranged from 8.8 to 9.1 million.

When costs were combined with the assessment of environmental sensitivity, several regions within the siting area were found to be within the 90th percentile for both cost and environmental sensitivity. From these subregional areas the potential power plant locations were selected.

Summary of the Siting Method

The use of GIMS as a data management and analysis tool provides several benefits that are not just theoretically attractive but enhance the actual results of the study. These benefits include:

1. A comprehensive cost surface of total plant costs was developed early in the siting study—a task that could not have been completed to the same level of detail and geographic coverage manually or by other methods of estimation.

2. An areawide analysis of both costs and environmental sensitivity was created, providing a more meaningful comparison of these two major considerations within a total regional context. This, in turn, supports the goal of finding the best sites available from a larger region based on a balanced consideration of both cost and environmental impacts.

3. Evaluation of total plant costs on a regional basis can determine if the differences in cost are significant as compared to the non-site-related (or variable) portion of plant costs. The cost of building and operating a plant is a major consideration, but if the cost does not vary significantly from site to site, it may not be important in site selection. The analysis shows that the range of cost was, in fact, significant.

In addition, the use of the spatial analysis approach provides typical benefits associated with the use of a rigorous methodology, such as a clear trace of the analysis/decision process, clarity of approach, and the flexibility to repeat any portion of the analysis with little time or effort.

Finally, this case study demonstrates the importance of extending the typical application of computerized data management systems to include sophisticated spatial (or locational) analysis. Such application, where significantly greater information is generated, compellingly demonstrates the value of the systems.

Chapter **13**

Mapping Congestion Patterns on Urban Highway Networks

J. B. Schneider

DESCRIPTION OF THE PROBLEM

A major function of the transportation planner in a metropolitan area is to find ways to reduce or eliminate congestion in the urban highway network. This chapter shows how computer graphics can be used to map congestion in various parts of the urban highway network at various times of the day. Such displays are needed because the relief of congestion is one of the major tasks of the Transportation Systems Management (TSM) programs currently required in all large urban areas. These programs are designed to formulate and apply non-capital-intensive actions to increase the utilization of existing facilities. Implementing these actions involves changing present ways of managing traffic, and so we want to be sure that the combined impacts of the various elements of a TSM program will produce the intended, desired effects. Since improvements in one congested location often move

202

the congestion to another location, any TSM program should strive to obtain an areawide definition of the "problem" and to view its policies and solutions in an areawide context (Remak, 1976).

An example of the kind of congestion-relief planning process we have in mind is shown in Figure 13-1. Our question is: What kind of display system could most effectively support the conduct of this type of process?

Displays could support various aspects of the process, as indicated in Figure 13-1. First, they could help the planner define the problem by allowing the easy mapping of various indices of congestion. Second, they could help the planner interpret the results of simulation models designed to predict the impact of various TSM actions. Third, they could assist the interpretation of field data gathered in "before and after" studies associated with small-scale, short-term experiments designed to test various TSM concepts in various settings. Fourth, they could be helpful in a similar way in the evaluation of the impacts of TSM actions that were devised with the aid of simulation models and then implemented.

To design a single data display system that would serve satisfactorily all these requirements would not be easy and might be impossible. However, we have tried to identify the common elements of all these tasks and to design a display system that will serve many of them now and that can be evolved over time to be more comprehensive in its capabilities.

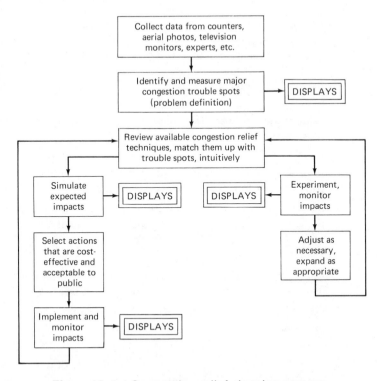

Figure 13-1 Congestion-relief planning process

Congestion is neither defined nor measured easily. It is necessarily a constructed variable in that it cannot be directly observed. Differing definitions for congestion have been proposed by several authors. Wingo (1959) suggests that congestion simply means traffic conditions that substantially reduce average speeds on the roadway. Rothrock (1954) suggests that congestion is an absence of the complete freedom of movement of the vehicles of which the traffic stream is composed. He further states that congestion actually begins whenever there is any impedance to such free movement, however slight. In another article, Rothrock and Keefer (1954) state that congestion may be simply expressed by a statement that traffic congestion consists of too many vehicles occupying space in a lane of highway for too long a time. Finally, Hall and George (1959) infer that congestion means more time lost in traveling from trip origin to destination, greater delays in the movement of persons and goods, and increased opportunities to be involved in a collision. The measurement of congestion, based on these general definitions, would be quite impossible.

More recently, methods have been developed for defining congestion in terms of the basic properties of the traffic capacity of a roadway, namely time and the space it provides. Density of travel, volume of travel, travel time, and other similar characteristics of traffic flow are some of these properties. Measuring these characteristics and what influences them on congested facilities as well as comparing these variables against theoretical or practical operating capacities have provided useful results.

Some definitions useful to this discussion are given below. These definitions have been taken largely from Pignataro (1973). Congestion indices are normally derived from these basic elements.

Density. The number of vehicles per mile on the traveled roadway at a given instant.

Volume. The number of vehicles passing a given point during a specific period.

Possible capacity. The maximum number of vehicles that can pass a given point in a lane of roadway during one hour under prevailing roadway and traffic conditions (also referred to as the *steady-state capacity*).

Practical capacity. The maximum number of vehicles that can pass a given point on a lane of roadway during one hour under the prevailing roadway and traffic conditions, without unreasonable delay or restriction to the driver's freedom to maneuver.

Design capacity. The practical capacity or lesser value determined for use in designing the highway to accommodate the design volume.

Speed. The rate of movement of a vehicle, generally expressed in kilometers per hour.

Operating speed. The highest overall speed, exclusive of stops, at which a driver can travel on a given highway under prevailing conditions, without at any time exceeding the design speed.

Practical speed. The average speed of vehicles that pass a given point on a lane of roadway under prevailing roadway and traffic conditions, where unreasonable delay or restrictions do not exist.

Design speed. A speed determined for design as related to the physical features of a highway that might influence vehicle operation. It is the maximum safe speed that can be maintained over a specified section of highway when conditions are so favorable that the design features of the highway govern.

These elements can be combined in various ways to produce congestion measures or indices. Our review of the literature indicates that there is no universally preferred congestion index in use today, but that a variety of measures should be examined in the study of congestion patterns in a large urban area. It is not our purpose to select any particular measure—only to design a system that can accept and display a variety of measures to suit the purposes of particular analyses.

METHODOLOGICAL APPROACH

Our examination of the literature indicates that there are three main sources of data on the elements that can be combined in various ways to create congestion indices. One of these is the stimulation model that has been designed to replicate or forecast the flow of vehicles on a street or urban freeway network. Examples of these simulation models are the NETSIM model developed by the Federal Highway Administration (Kubel, 1978; Labrum, 1978) and the freeway simulation model, FREQ6PE, developed by Professor Adolf May and others at the University of California in Berkeley (Jovanis, 1978; May, 1978).

These models generate a large volume of data in the form of measures of effectiveness (MOEs). Some of the MOEs can be used to create congestion indices, which can then be displayed in ways that will help the user comprehend the results of the simulation. These models are well suited to the policy analysis or testing task, which is aimed at defining the probable impacts of alternative TSM strategies. Until recently, simulation models of this type have not included the capability of creating displays from their output. However, two graphics systems developed recently at the University of Washington do provide such a capability (Schneider, 1979).

A second source of data is the set of passive monitoring systems installed and operating in many urban areas. Examples are loop detectors, television monitors, aerial photography, and other sensing or counting devices. The data available from these systems are usually heavy in volume but very narrow in terms of the range of activity monitored. For example, a loop detector installed in the pavement gives only a presence-absence indication directly whenever a vehicle passes through its magnetic field. The speed of the vehicle can be inferred by assuming a certain vehicle length. From several detectors, one can infer a little information about the flow of vehicles on a roadway, but the gaps in this information field are quite substantial. Other existing monitoring systems have similar strengths and weaknesses.

A third data source can be described as an active monitoring system. These are the automatic vehicle detector (AVM) systems that are beginning to be used in a variety of cities in a variety of ways. For example, some transit agencies are equipping their bus fleet with AVMs so they can keep track of how well the buses are maintaining their schedules. The dispatching of police cars is another type of application that seems to have potential (O'Conner, 1978). Clearly, one could use the AVM data to track vehicles as they move through a congested network. By comparing their actual position with where they would be under free-flow conditions, one could create a rough measure of the level of congestion on any particular route at various times of the day, week, or season.

Some applications of computer graphics have utilized data from these sources. In Toronto, a graphics system has been developed to display data from loop detectors that have been installed on a freeway segment in that city (Tsai, 1978). The system has been designed to serve freeway management objectives rather than to define and evaluate freeway congestion patterns, but it could be modified to do so without much difficulty. Too few loop detectors are available, however, to permit the display of an areawide picture.

The Michigan Department of Transportation is currently involved in a project that will include the installation of about 3000 loop detectors in nearly all sections of the Detroit freeway system. They plan to display several performance indicators, in color, using data obtained from these loops every twenty seconds. Data will be available from each one-third mile segment of the freeway system, on a real-time basis.

In Dallas, the Hazeltine Corporation has developed a computer-aided dispatching system (CADS) that involves the use of AVM equipment installed in 700 police cars (O'Conner, 1978). A dispatcher can see the location of all active cars and can use this information in assigning cars to calls on a real-time basis (the location update period is two seconds). Multicolored maps are displayed and may be call-centered, patrol-element centered, or cursor-centered. Clearly, a similar system could be used to study the pattern of congestion as it evolves over time in an urban area.

Overall, it appears that data are available from several sources, and several systems for acquiring them have been developed. We now discuss the design of a computer graphics system for displaying these data in a format useful for policy analysis.

ROLE OF COMPUTER GRAPHICS

In general, several dimensions must be considered when displaying congestion data. The dimensions include: what data to display, what means to display them, what scale to use, and whether to treat the data as a discrete or continuous occurrence. Research in the area of data presentation by Hughes (1975), Robinson and Sale (1978), and Muehrcke (1974, 1976), points out that no unified theory exists to help determine what data display technique is best for any given application. In most cases, no one display will be satisfactory to all observers. This suggests that any automated congestion display system should provide flexibility in the design of the displays. If the system is designed to accommodate various data transformations and a variety of symbols, it should be able to generate alternative displays of congestion data in a relatively quick and inexpensive manner. Experimentation with these displays should suggest which ones are most appropriate for satisfying the needs of a particular audience. To help us select capabilities to include in a congestion display system (CDS), a brief review of previous work is helpful.

To obtain a general understanding of display techniques that could be used by CDS to illustrate congestion patterns, several previous examples were reviewed. No examples that were designed to show congestion levels directly were found. Most displays showed only the traditional travel-volume or travel-demand information for the peak period. In order to assess the utility of each display technique examined, several display criteria were established. These criteria, adapted from earlier work by Letendre (1976), are as follows:

Resolution and grain. What level of detail or grossness is the display technique capable of illustrating?

Path accuracy. How well does the display technique reproduce actual routes traveled?

Scale variability. Can the display technique handle sparse or dense data values at large or small scales?

Range of intensity. Can a wide range of values (loadings, trips) be displayed together without distortion or loss?

Orientation. Does the display technique permit easy identification of features other than routes such as employment facilities or other traffic generators?

Aggregation. Does the display technique permit data to be aggregated or the collective overlap of data in several directions to be considered as a whole?

Ease of preparation. Is the display technique elaborate or simple, costly or inexpensive to prepare?

Visual interpretation. Is the display technique readily comprehensible by a wide range of observers?

Much of the early work in illustrating travel flows was performed by regional planning agencies and highway departments in the period 1950–1965. Line illustration techniques were used most often to represent travel flows from one point to another. Two types of maps have been commonly used, the desire-line map and the bandwidth map. To construct such maps, one simply draws straight lines or bands between origin-destination pairs. While these maps are easy to prepare, path accuracy is poor and visual interpretation is difficult, particularly when a large number of lines or bands overlap. The congestion pattern can be inferred from such a map only in very general terms.

Bandwidth maps are often preferred to desire-line maps. In these maps, path accuracy is good and visual interpretation is relatively easy, but again, congestion levels can only be generally inferred. Some studies have used a simplified network called a "spider" network. These displays have reasonably good path accuracy and good visual clarity. Resolution, grain, orientation, and ease of preparation are good, but scale variability and range of intensity are limited. Again, congestion levels can only be inferred in general terms, and different people can be expected to come to somewhat different conclusions in this respect.

Computer-drawn bandwidth maps of a section of an urban network have been produced in Basel, Switzerland (Riepl, 1978). These displays have the same good and bad features as hand-drawn maps but are so detailed that many people find them difficult to interpret. Automating the removal of overlapped lines and shading would probably resolve this problem to some extent. Practicing professionals would, of course, have less difficulty working this type of map than would lay persons.

Bandwidth maps have also been used to display volume-to-capacity ratios. This technique typically involves the use of two colors. For example, if the volume is greater than the capacity, a red band is added to the band that shows the capacity of the facility. One need only look for the red bands to find out where congestion may be a problem. These data displays normally represent some specific time period and therefore give no indication of how the congestion pattern evolves over time and space. Some good examples of these types of maps may be found in a publication of the Metropolitan Washington Council of Governments (MWCOG, 1976). The selection of an appropriate scale that will minimize overlap is a very difficult task in constructing such maps.

Color coding could be used to represent the same information conveyed by the width of the band in these maps. This would ease the overlap problem but would introduce another set of problems having to do with the selection of colors and problems of color perception by various individuals. While this idea deserves some exploration, we will not examine it here.

Overall, we found little previous work of direct utility to our task in the literature. We then decided to ask a group of graphic art students at the University of Washington to design alternative ways to display congestion indices. Space limitations do not allow the presentation of these results, but some were most helpful to the design of the CDS and will be noted later.

Let us now consider the specifics of the design of a CDS. CDS was designed as an interactive graphic program that utilizes Tektronix PLOT-10 software and Terminal Control System Language capable of displaying a variety of traffic congestion indices on an urban street or freeway network. A major objective in the system's development was to provide a rapid means of displaying congestion data sequentially, so that the change in the level and location of congestion over time would be visible to a viewer.

CDS was designed to accept actual or simulated congestion data such as traffic volumes, volume-to-capacity ratios, speed of traffic, and actual-speed-to-speed-limit ratios. It could also be used to display congestion data derived from simulation models of various types.

It is useful to display congestion over time for several reasons. A sequence of displays enables the viewer to visualize the complex interactions among congested areas in an urban area on a holistic basis. This is a phenomenon no one has had an opportunity to see before. Presenting congestion information in this way should enhance the viewer's comprehension about why and where congestion occurs.

Seeing the big picture and seeing it over time may lead the viewer to formulate studies or actions that could be undertaken to alleviate the congestion problem. This holistic overview may also enable viewers to approach and evaluate their congestion-reduction strategies in a more organized, short-range, and efficient manner.

Besides the viewing of data collected in the field, this system was designed for use in the study of the impacts various TSM actions might have on existing congestion conditions. Alternative transportation policies such as staggered work hours, car pooling, preferential treatment, and others can be simulated to see what impact they may have on existing conditions. Research is now underway to find ways to simulate the effect of introducing such policies. It is believed that the study and comparison of these policy alternatives, using a congestion display system, should enable the viewer to better understand what would happen if these policies were adopted, singly or in combination with each other.

CDS is composed of three integral parts: a control-language processor, a matrix-manipulation program, and a display-processor program. Figure 13-2 illustrates the environment of the system. Communication with the user is conducted through the control-language processor. The command structure of the control-language processor is explained in the next section. Commands within this processor can be directed toward either the matrix-manipulation program or the display-processor program. Input to the system originates with the matrix-manipulation program.

The matrix-manipulation program permits actual field or simulated data to be input to the program. Each discrete time interval is represented as a single-column vector of an m-by-n input matrix. Each element of the column vector represents a separate link of the highway network. A row of the matrix contains information about how the level of congestion on a network link changes over time. Figure 13-3 illustrates this concept.

Normal matrix operations can be conducted on the columns of the matrix. These operations include: scaling, adding, exchanging, and multiplying columns. Creating, changing, or displaying column contents or individual column elements is also permitted. These operations allow the congestion data to be easily manipulated

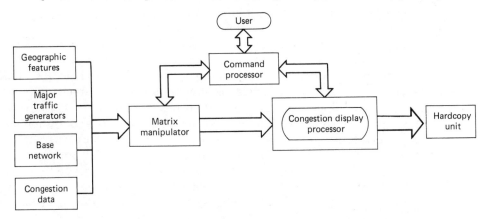

Figure 13-2 Congestion display system overview

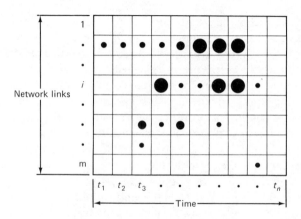

Figure 13-3   Congestion data input matrix

into a form suitable for the congestion display processor program. Moreover, these features are particularly important when simulated congestion data are being formulated.

Several interpolating routines are also incorporated into the matrix-manipulation program. These routines allow time-interval congestion data to be sampled and smoothed between sampling points. This smoothing is needed so that the information presented to the congestion display processor is incrementally continuous enough to not distract the eye when it is drawn in a sequential fashion.

The congestion display processor is a small graphics program that draws base networks, prominent geographic reference points (e.g., political boundaries, small towns, bodies of water), major traffic generators, and various link congestion symbologies on Tektronix equipment. This program works in a manner similar to a video tape player.

Information is read serially by column from the matrix developed by the matrix-manipulation program. Congestion information contained in this column vector is then drawn on the screen. Relative scaling is used to convert numeric information contained in the vector into different symbolic levels of congestion. Each column of the matrix is passed to the display processor and drawn successively until the columns of the matrix are exhausted or until the program is requested to stop.

Normally each column of congestion action is drawn as a separate picture. Base network or prominent geographic features may be included or omitted as desired by the user. This single picture represents one frame of congestion animation. The display processor functions to draw several frames of congestion action in a rapid sequence. This enables the viewer to see how congestion builds up and diffuses throughout the network. Symbol, scale, and shade changes serve to add to this effect. Single-frame forward or reverse as well as fast-frame forward and reverse are options of the program. The display processor may also be requested to repeatedly cycle through a series of several columns of the congestion matrix. This feature permits the viewer to intensely review a complicated section of congestion action over and over again.

Presently, considerable time passes between the drawing of one congestion display frame and the next. This is a characteristic of the transmission rate of the data (1200 BAUD) and the capability of Tektronix storage tube equipment. To use the CDS in an operational setting, a video camera or high-speed microfilm plotter in tandem with a 16mm camera could be used to capture each frame of the congestion display processor output. This video tape or film would then be played back at normal speed to obtain a fully animated effect.

Control of CDS is accomplished through the use of flexible command-language statements. Each command is composed of a verb and optional arguments. Each command either operates on the matrix-manipulation or display-processor program. Commands can be combined to form complete sets of viewing or matrix-manipulation instructions. Sets of commands may be saved on mass storage. These commands are later executed in proper sequence by stepping a pointer through the instruction set. Commands may also be issued interactively one at a time through the terminal.

In general, a few simple commands initiate the display of congestion data. A user may choose to view one display, a series of displays, or time intervals selected from the congestion matrix in some arbitrary order. These displays may be drawn on the screen in forward or backward time sequence. In addition, automatic sequencing or manual control of each display frame is available through the SET PAUSE command. Normally each column vector is drawn as a separate display-frame picture. Displays can be overlaid if the user wants to better understand how congestion is changing in relative terms during a short period. Several congestion symbologies may be chosen as options by the user. Symbol size may be made to vary in accordance with congestion. Symbol shading may also be used to differentiate congestion levels. The CAPTURE command may be used to direct-display processor output to hard-copy units.

An alternative to generating a display frame each time it is needed is to generate each display frame only once, then capture and store it till requested as a binary file on an external storage device. Saving display frames in this way should reduce significantly the time it takes to redraw these images, yielding considerable cost savings. This feature is particularly useful when a repetitious sequence of display frames is being viewed several times.

A multi-level sequential linked-list approach has been used to accommodate the data structure of CDS. The Houston metropolitan area freeway network (Figure 13-4) has been selected as a test network for this system. All the urban freeways were partitioned into segments, a segment being a section of the freeway lying between intersection points of two or more major freeways. Segments were divided into regularly spaced subsegments.

In the data structure each segment is composed of a list of the *(x,y)* coordinates that define the subsegments. A unique name is associated with the segment as well as a set of pointers that distinguish the coordinates contained in the segment from those contained in the entire system. A second level of data structure is used to group segments together as unique freeways. Freeways are defined as segments having a unique name and having pointers to a list of segment names comprising the freeway. Finally, a third level of structure similar to the first two is used to group freeways into a network.

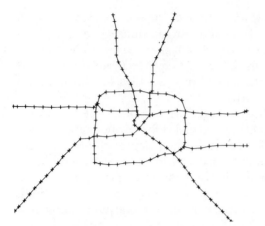
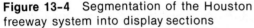

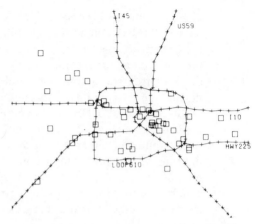

Figure 13-4 Segmentation of the Houston freeway system into display sections

Figure 13-5 Data structure of congestion display system

Figure 13-5, which represents this overall structure, should serve to clarify this notion. Segments S1, S2, and through Sn are defined as a set of (x,y) coordinates. In this diagram, freeways F1 and F2 are composed of segments S1, S2, S3 and S4, S5, S6, respectively. The name "NETWORK" encompasses the freeway segments F1 and F2. CDS maintains internal pointers for moving from segment to segment when required.

This name-oriented structure has several advantages. A single segment or freeway may be extracted, displayed, and examined when the whole network is not of interest. Several networks may be accommodated, or different forms of the same network may be defined and used to display congestion data. A possible disadvantage arises when the network contains many intersections. For example, a city street network coded up in the segment convention related above would require many more names than are useful. In this case, the convention could be dropped. A street may be considered to be identical to a segment without creating conflict in pointer structure. The only real requirement is that each segment be a continuous (connected) sequence of sequential coordinate pairs.

Links are the basic components for displaying the congestion data. Congestion symbology may be drawn to the left, right, or on the links as desired by the user. Each segment contains a series of equally spaced links, numbered in the order in which they are input. Each segment has a count of the number of links associated with it.

In order to extract a particular link from the segment coordinate list, we first search the global segment name table contained in the system. Once the desired link count is found, a simple computation involving the link number and coordinate pointers of the segment will yield the coordinates of the link in question.

Congestion values are associated with the links through the congestion matrix. The organization of this matrix has been given earlier.

Provision is made within CDS to accommodate nonnetwork data points. It is assumed helpful to have the coordinates of major trip generators (shopping centers,

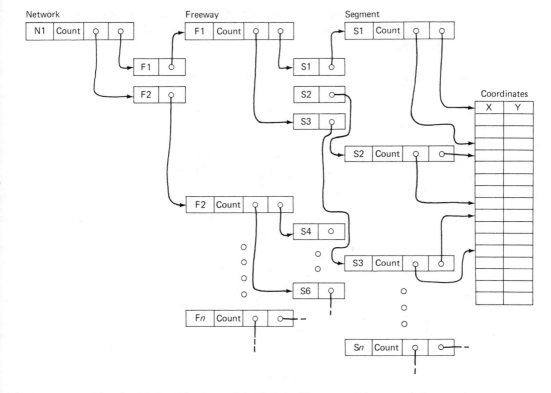

Figure 13-6 Display of major traffic generators and freeway names

offices, parks, major employers) and their identifying labels available for display to relate sites of this type to arising congestion (see Figure 13-6). Labels for these sites are contained in an additional list within the system. Pointers are maintained for locating these sites in conjunction with their coordinates. Also included as non-network data are political boundaries, identifying landmarks, and topographic features that may aid the user in orienting himself to the display. These features may be incorporated into a named set. Thus, the name "NETWORK" may include shoreline features and a city boundary in addition to the network itself.

CDS maintains an *m*-by-*n* matrix for the purpose of relating time-series congestion data to each link in the congestion data matrix. Each column of this matrix represents the status of each link for one time interval. A row represents the change in congestion level over time for one link. CDS contains a matrix-manipulation program to operate on the elements of this matrix.

Congestion data are usually input into CDS in raw form. The congestion data most commonly available are for traffic volumes in fifteen-minute intervals. Interval speed data from traffic-delay studies may also be available as input, although information of this type is less common in large quantities. Several commands exist within the matrix-manipulation program to convert these raw data into a form suitable for viewing. These commands allow normal sorts of matrix transformations to be performed on the data, including scaling, addition, subtraction, multiplication, and division. It is envisioned that these commands would be used, for example, to convert actual traffic volumes into volume-to-capacity ratios, or actual speed to actual-speed-to-speed-limit ratios.

Choosing the proper symbology for representing congestion on links is a difficult problem. No one technique has been found to be totally satisfying. Questions about human perception have been raised but not solved. To what extent can the human eye differentiate between objects of different shapes, sizes, and shadings? Psychological investigation has cast some light on the problem, but guidelines for practical application do not exist. As a result, we have done some experimentation with different symbologies to see which come closest to meeting the requirements we have set for the congestion display system.

CDS is designed to allow the user to draw several different symbols. CDS may also be adapted easily to draw other symbols that appear promising, using interchangeable program software. Different symbol shading options can also be made available in this manner. At present, CDS allows points, lines, triangles, squares, and hexagons as well as size change and shading of these symbols to be used for representing congestion indices. Symbols may be offset to the left or right or placed on links as desired by the user. Symbols are placed midway on the links. Except for size and shape changes, the symbols remain stationary. No great loss is anticipated in the perception of the moving pattern of congestion by the use of this technique. Any diminution in effect is more than compensated for by simplified programming.

Output from CDS may be directed toward either Tektronix-compatible terminals or hard-copy units, such as CalComp plotters. Eventually, it is hoped that the output from this system may be used on high-speed plotting devices such as computer output microfilm. This should enable film records of congestion displays to be easily created. While the cost of such sophisticated equipment remains high, studies in other areas, most notably atmospheric and biomedical research, have shown that problems similar in scale to a congestion pattern canot be fully comprehended without the aid of visual representation. A service bureau could be established where the cost of filming congestion patterns for several cities could be shared. As additional congestion monitoring equipment continues to be placed in the field, the likelihood grows that something like this will become cost-effective.

EXAMPLES OF DISPLAYS FROM THE CDS

In this section we present some displays derived from some of the initial testing of the CDS. Our objectives were only to test the various capabilities of the system, since time constraints did not permit the design and implementation of a series of systematic experiments. Some recommendations for further work of this type are given later.

A major objective in the design of the CDS was to develop the ability to produce low-cost displays, using off-the-shelf hardware and software. Low cost was considered important because a large number of displays are needed in order to incorporate the time dimensions adequately. The displays that follow cost 40 to 50 cents each to compute and plot on the CRT. At present, no information is available on how this unit cost could vary with the size and complexity of the network. It is also estimated that improvements in the efficiency of the CDS program could reduce these unit computing and plotting costs to 10 to 15 cents per display.

In the first set of displays, squares and arrows are used to represent congestion levels on each link in the freeway system. Figure 13-7 uses nonoffset squares to display a hypothetical data set that was designed to represent increasing levels of congestion. Numerous viewers have commented that the squares do not communicate very well, and these displays are included primarily to make this point.

Arrow symbols communicate much more effectively. Figure 13-8 shows the value of offsetting the symbols. The data are the same for both the displays of Figure 13-8, but the lower display with offset symbols is obviously much easier to comprehend.

The overlap between arrows in some locations still is distracting to the eye and should be removed, perhaps with some type of hidden-line removal technique.

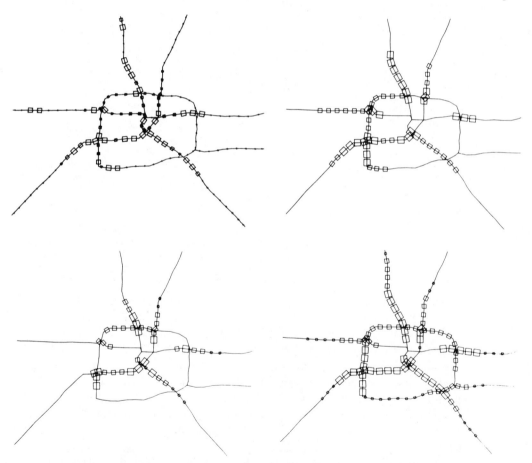

Figure 13-7 Sequence of nonoffset square displays showing increasing levels of congestion

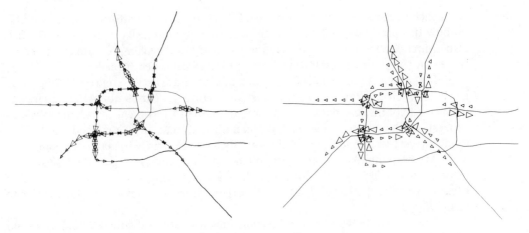

Figure 13-8 Comparison of arrow displays, nonoffset and offset, for identical congestion

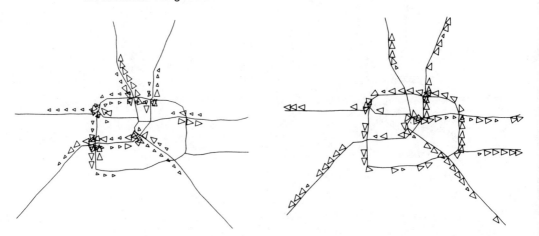

Figure 13-9 Sequential displays with offset arrows

Figure 13-9 shows two offset arrow displays that were designed to illustrate an increased level of congestion. A lower data-value limit was used to remove very small arrows in the lower display to increase its visual clarity.

Figure 13-10 shows a sequence of shaded, nonoffset arrows designed to illustrate an increasing level of congestion. These hypothetical data were designed to show a sequence where minor trouble spots grow into major trouble spots. The pattern remains quite stable but grows in intensity over time. One exception is the lack of a congestion problem in the lowest frame at the upper interchange on the western side of the network. This type of unexpected result could lead to the discovery of some unusual and interesting situations.

Figures 13-11 and 13-12 contain two sets of four congestion displays depicting the morning and evening rush periods on the Houston freeway system. The data are hypothetical and represent some judgments about the level of congestion on this

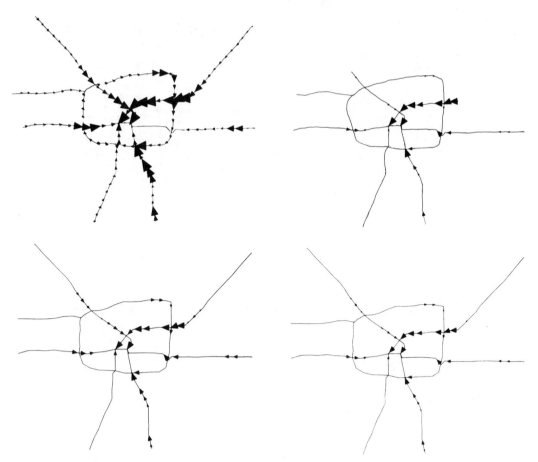

Figure 13-10 Sequence of shaded, nonoffset arrow displays showing increasing levels of congestion

freeway system at different times of the day. The "accordian" display technique used: regularly spaced bars are drawn perpendicular to each link, and the level of congestion is varied by changing the spacing (or density) of these bars. This technique has good visual properties, in the opinion of several viewers, and enables the continuous nature of congestion to be displayed effectively. No directional information is provided, although one can specify, for example, that "only travel inbound to the downtown" is being displayed. A close examination of Figure 13-11 shows the convergence-caused build-up of congestion on the freeways around the downtown. One can also see that the western sections of the two north freeways have the worst congestion problem during the morning peak period.

Figure 13-12 presents four sequential displays of hypothetical evening rush-hour travel. One can easily see the central area emptying out over time and can see that the level of congestion on the outer loop freeways persists a bit longer than on the radial freeways.

Clearly, these examples are too few to allow us to draw any firm conclusions

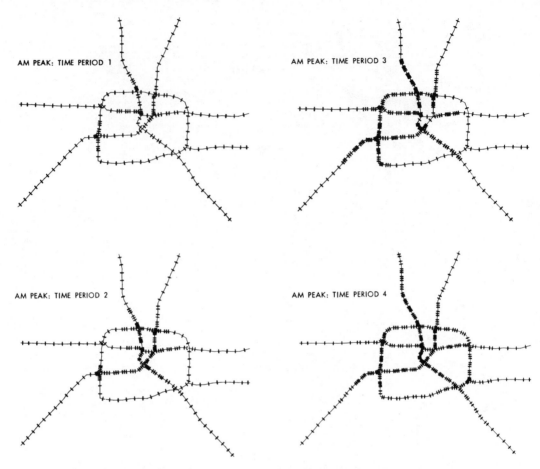

Figure 13-11 Displays of hypothetical congestion data for the Houston freeway system, morning peak period

about the utility of this display technique. They have been well received by a number of viewers and are easily and inexpensively produced by the CDS.

Color can also be used to represent congestion levels on a link-by-link basis. The present version of the CDS does not have a color display capability, but without too much difficulty it could be modified to produce its displays on a color graphics terminal. A major problem with color displays is selecting a compatible set of colors that will produce the desired visual effects.

Recent work by Krebs and Wolf (1979) provides helpful information on the appropriate use of color in creating displays of complex patterns and of their changes over time. The production of such displays is well within the capability of existing computer graphics technology, but major questions remain about how to create colored displays that can be comprehended effectively by a wide variety of people for sustained periods.

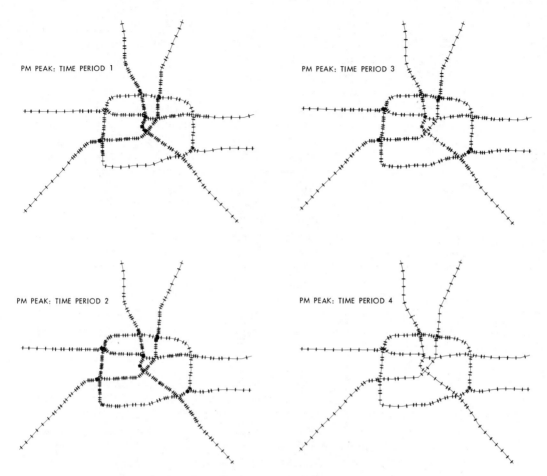

PM PEAK: TIME PERIOD 1

PM PEAK: TIME PERIOD 3

PM PEAK: TIME PERIOD 2

PM PEAK: TIME PERIOD 4

Figure 13-12 Displays of hypothetical congestion data for the Houston freeway system, evening peak period

NEXT STEPS

The utility of applying computer graphics techniques in the study of congestion patterns has as yet been explored only in a limited way. The feasibility of using computer graphics to display congestion data at a reasonable cost has been demonstrated, and the displays themselves have been well received by a limited number of viewers, responding in an informal manner. A program has been developed that, with some additional work, could be evolved into a production-level software system that could be widely applied. A few new display techniques have been tested in a very limited manner and most of them seem reasonably promising. The role of color in such displays has been explored a little, but it is far from clear whether and how color should be used in creating congestion displays. Although animation has not been attempted, the CDS could be used to produce the many displays needed for an animation of the evolving congestion pattern, should that be an objective.

The time required to generate a display containing approximately 150 links and 25 to 30 reference points of congestion information with CDS was about two CPU seconds. The cost for this computing at interactive rates was 20 cents per second. Drawing the information on the screen after the calculations were completed took about 30 seconds. The cost of transmitting this information at 1200 baud was about 5 cents per display. Therefore, the overall cost of each display (of the Houston network) was about 45 cents. The costs of dealing with additional links and congestion reference points probably would increase linearly with the number of links and points, rather than as the square of their number, owing to the simplicity of CDS. Display costs would also increase linearly as more information was displayed.

Displays could be animated with the present equipment, but the process would be cumbersome. A person would have to shoot a picture and trigger the next display approximately every 40 seconds. A better approach would be to develop a series of displays on magnetic tape and then plot or film them in rapid succession using a computer output microfilm (COM) device. The software development effort to interface CDS with this type of equipment would require about five half-time months of qualified programmer time.

Based on the issues investigated in this study, the following suggestions are in order:

1. While its contribution to the study of evolving congestion patterns in an urban area could not be directly assessed with actual data, it seems clear that computer graphics could help traffic engineers and transportation planners interpret and validate the operation of purely numeric models such as signal-optimization models or freeway ramp-control simulation models. Computer graphics may also help in detection of errors in input data and in checking that simulation algorithms are working properly.

2. Many different types of display techniques are needed to illustrate congestion information. No one display can do the entire job. In general, symbol displays are more useful for identifying general patterns, while numeric displays are needed to study congestion in detail, once the general congestion trouble spots have been identified.

3. As far as monitoring equipment goes, loop detectors that measure both volume and occupancy would provide the most useful information to a congestion display system in the short term. Later, when AVM systems are improved to the point where they are less expensive and are available to private passenger vehicles in quantity, displaying the information from these systems may become useful for monitoring congestion, real-time traffic control, and diversion strategies.

4. The most useful displays will probably be those that are easiest to comprehend. Interval separation on the basis of gray-scale shading has not proven that effective. Interval separation on the basis of size has also presented its

problems, particularly when the distance between symbols of similar size is large. The use of numeric displays when the numeric information is illustrated is limited, and the use of color coding as a separation technique is probably a better way to proceed.

5. Much experimentation is needed in order to develop a better understanding of the relationships between human perception capabilities and display types. This work should involve the participation of psychologists and cartographers as well as those familiar with traffic-congestion problems. Displays that cannot be readily comprehended will be of little use. It must be remembered, however, that humans can learn to deal with patterns that initially appear too complex to be comprehended. One should not underestimate this human capacity for learning.

The work reported in this chapter is only a first brief look at a very large problem. It does represent a firm foundation upon which further efforts can be based. Eventually, we believe that this approach could provide the transportation profession with important new tools for helping them comprehend the urban transportation problem.

ACKNOWLEDGEMENTS

Charles Inglebritson and Allan Sari, students in the Department of Civil Engineering, contributed substantially to the formulation and development of this paper.

This work was supported by a grant from the Research and Training Program in Urban Transportation of the Urban Mass Transportation Administration of the U.S. Department of Transportation. The results and views expressed are the independent products of University research and are not necessarily concurred in by the sponsoring agency.

REFERENCES

HALL, D., and J. GEORGE, "Travel-Time—An Effective Measurement of Congestion and Level of Service," *Proc. HRB,* **38,** 511–529 (1959).

HUGHES, A., "The Nature and Classification of Cartographic Data," paper presented at Annual Technical Symposium of British Cartographic Society, Swansea, September 12–14, 1975.

JOVANIS, PAUL, WAI-KI YIP, and ADOLF D. MAY, *FREQ6PE—A Freeway Priority Entry Control Simulation Model,* Research Report UCB-ITS-RR-78-9, Institute for Transportation Studies, University of California at Berkeley, November 1978, 516 pp.

KREBS, M. J., and D. J. WOLF, "Design Principles for the Use of Color in Displays," *Proceedings of the Society for Information Display,* **20:**1, 10–15 (First Quarter, 1979).

KUBEL, LESLIE, and others, "What Network Simulation (NETSIM) Can Do for the Traffic Engineer," *Public Roads,* **41:**4, 162–168 (March 1978).

LABRUM, WILLARD D., and others, "Analyzing Intersection Performance with NETSIM," *Public Roads,* **42:**1, 24–29 (June 1978).

LETENDRE, G., "Survey of Methods of Illustrating Urban Travel," paper presented at Annual TRB Meeting, Session 30, Graphics and Interactive Techniques, Washington, D.C., January 1976.

MAY, A. D., *The Role of Operational Planning Models in Transportation Systems Management,* Research Report UCB-ITS-RR-78-11, Institute for Transportation Studies, University of California at Berkeley, December 1978, 22 pp.

METROPOLITAN WASHINGTON COUNCIL OF GOVERNMENTS, *Testing of Transportation Plan Alternatives,* May 1976.

MUEHRCKE, P., "Concepts of Scaling from the Map Reader's Point of View," *American Cartographer, 3(2),* pp. 121–141, 1976.

_____, "Map Reading and Abuse," *Journal of Geography,* **73:**5, 11–23 (1974).

O'CONNER, J. F., *Computer Map Generation in an Automatic Vehicle Monitoring System.* Greenlawn, N.Y.: Hazeltine Corporation: 1978.

PIGNATARO, L. J., *Traffic Engineering—Theory and Practice.* Englewood Cliffs, N.J.: Prentice-Hall, 1973.

REMAK, R., and S. ROSENBLOOM, "Peak Period Traffic Congestion Options for Current Programs," National Cooperative Highway Research Program, Report 169, 1976.

RIEPL, R. J., and C. D. GEHNER, "Interactive Graphics in Europe: Three Computer-Aided Transportation Tools," *Computer Graphics,* **1:**13, 18–25 (December 1978).

ROBINSON, A. H., and R. D. SALE, *The Elements of Cartography,* 4th ed. New York: Wiley, 1978.

ROTHROCK, C. A., "Urban Congestion Index Principles," *HRB Bulletin 156,* pp. 26–34, 1954.

_____, and L. A., KEEFER, "Measurement of Urban Traffic Congestion," *HRB Bulletin 156,* pp. 1-13, 1954.

SCHNEIDER, JERRY B., DAVID M. COMBS, and TYLER C. FOLSOM, *NETGRAF: A Computer Graphics Aid to the Operation and Interpretation of NETSIM, A Traffic Simulation Model, Part 1: Overview and Experimental Results,* Research Report No. 79–3 (DOT-RC-82021-RR79-3), Urban Transportation Program, Departments of Civil Engineering and Urban Planning, University of Washington, Seattle, WA 98195, September 1979, 45 pp.

_____, CHRISTINA L. JETTE, and BRIAN T. LEWIS, *FREGRAF: A Computer Graphics Aid to the Operation and Interpretation of FREQ6PE, A Freeway Simulation Model, Part 1: Overview and Experimental Results,* Research Report No. 79-6 (DOT-RC-82021-RR79-6), Urban Transportation Program, Departments of Civil Engineering and Urban Planning, University of Washington, Seattle, WA 98195, September 1979, 45 pp.

Tsai, J., H. K. Chan, and E. R. Case, "Computer Graphics Applications in Freeway Traffic Surveillance and Control System," Research and Development Division, Ministry of Transportation and Communications, Toronto, Ontario, Canada, August 1978.

Wingo, R., "Measurement of Congestion in Transportation Systems," *HRB Bulletin 221*, pp. 1–39, 1959.

The Princeton Railroad Network Model: Application of Computer Graphics in the Analysis of a Changing Railroad Industry*

Alain L. Kornhauser

Mark Hornung

Yehonathan Hazony

Jerome M. Lutin

ABSTRACT

With the bankruptcy of Penn Central, the passage of legislation that led to the creation of Conrail, the formation of many new mergers (including Burlington Northern + Frisco, CXS, Norfolk Southern, and the Pacific Rail System), and the passage of the 1980 Staggers Rail Act, which begins to deregulate the railroad industry, the United States has entered an era of major changes to one of its largest transportation industries. Mergers, abandonments, bankruptcies, directed service, controlled transfer, and rate deregulation are but a few of the descriptors that are part of this new metamorphic stage. Each of these elements affects the shippers who

*Presented at 1979 Harvard Computer Graphics Week, Cambridge, Massachusetts, July 1979.

utilize the railroad industry, and each therefore affects the distribution of traffic within that system. Competitive balances are being changed both within the industry and with respect to other modes.

Princeton University's Transportation Program has been leading an effort to develop analytical tools that can assist in the formulation and evaluation of the various railroad restructuring proposals. The models use a link-node description of the U.S. railroad system complete with various link and node characteristics as developed by the Federal Railroad Administration. Using the Carload Waybill Sample as the descriptor of historical traffic distribution, various models of shipper route choice behavior have been developed. These models have been assembled to form the so-called Princeton Railroad Network Model and Graphic Information System and are being used to forecast the value and the change in distribution of railroad traffic as a result of various restructuring and regulatory reform proposals. Interactive computer graphics have been used extensively in (1) the transformation of the restructuring proposals into machine-readable form, (2) the confirmation process in which the analytical procedures are validated, (3) the presentation of results for evaluation and consequent modification, approval, or rejection of the restructuring proposal, and (4) the general acceptance of the model by decision makers who would be "turned off" by stacks of computer printout but can easily relate the graphic displays to their long experience and knowledge of the railroad industry.

This chapter describes very briefly some capabilities of Princeton's Railroad Network Model but focuses more on some of its applications and on the uses of interactive computer graphics. We consider here the importance of graphics for the presentation of data on railroad accidents and the density of hazardous-material traffic, the evaluation of the impact of mergers on the distribution of railroad traffic, the concept of participatory value and how it can be used to derive controlled-transfer and directed-service orders, the concept of opportunity cost and its influence on railroads to participate in either controlled-transfer or directed-service proceedings, and the use of the model to define potentially better routing choices by shippers. Examples of current interest to the railroad industry are cited, as well as ways in which the railroad industry and government regulators can use the model to aid in their evaluation of restructuring proposals.

MAJOR ELEMENTS OF THE PRINCETON RAILROAD NETWORK MODEL

The Princeton Railroad Network Model has four major elements: (1) the link-node network and its associated characteristics, (2) historical records of railroad traffic and accidents, (3) efficient minimum-path finding and traffic-assignment algorithms, and models of shipper and railroad routing behavior, and (4) a battery of interactive graphic techniques for displaying railroad input and output data. All these elements are presently implemented on Princeton University's computer facilities, which include an IBM 360/91 and a 370/158 VM with various peripheral devices, including Tektronix 4013 and 4015 terminals for interactive use and a Calcomp 936 plotter for multicolor batch-mode graphics.

The original version of the link-node network of the U.S. railroad system was digitized by IBM Federal Systems Division under contract to the Federal Railroad Administration (Federal Systems Division, 1975). The network itself has been corrected and updated by Princeton University, and it presently consists of 16,373 nodes (termed "Net 3 nodes") and 17,874 links. The entire link-node network together with state boundaries is displayed in Figure 14-1. Attributes for each of the nodes and links presently contained in vector files are listed in Table 14.1

With respect to the nodes, the coordinate attributes are essential to the use of the network graphic displays. In addition, the list of freight and passenger stations encompassed by each node allows for the assignment of freight and passenger data to the network. The other attributes of yard facilities, TOFC ramps, names, and county and state locations describe the various railroad functions occurring at particular nodes as well as providing a means for displaying geographic subsets of the network. Additional statistics defining the types and volume of traffic generated by each railroad have been generated for each node by using the traffic data base described in the next section. Characteristics of historical (1975, 1976, 1977) accidents occurring in the vicinity of each node are also available.

The link attributes include the end nodes of each link (termed A-node, B-node), the distance represented by the link, the railroad owning the link, the railroads having traffic rights, the links classification code according to section 503 of the Quad-R Act (U.S. DOT, 1977), the average population density, the maximum speed limit, and the grade, curvature, signal system, and number of tracks on the mainline links. Through the use of historical traffic data and various uses of the traffic-assignment algorithm, various measures of traffic volume by direction (A to B and B to A) have been and can be generated. These include carload volume, tonnage by commodity, car type, and interchange characteristics. For example, the number of tank cars, class A explosives, coal, Southern Railway owned cars, cars interlined with the Rock Island, and cars destined from/to Chicago can be or have been generated. Using bandwidth graphic display techniques, any of these link attributes can be drawn by the computer.

DEMAND DATA—CARLOAD WAYBILL STATISTICS

Under terms of ICC Order 49 C.F.R. Sec. 1244, line haul railroads having operating revenues of greater than $3 million are required to submit a sample of audited waybills to FRA. Each year's sample represents slightly less than 1 percent of the year's carload movements (between 175,000 and 200,000 carloads per year for 1973 through 1977). Each waybill contains fundamental data identifying the shipment, such as number of cars, net tons, commodity, car type, car owner and number, total revenue and fundamental route data including origin, origin railroad, destination, destination railroad, and, since 1973, each overhead railroad and interline junction. The fundamental route data base has been enhanced by researchers at Princeton University (see Strong, 1978, chap. 7), to (1) reconstruct a great deal of the defaulted

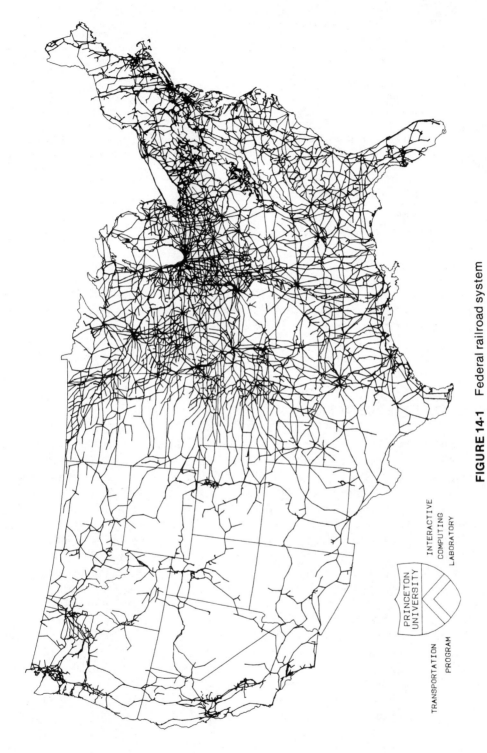

INTERACTIVE COMPUTING LABORATORY

PRINCETON UNIVERSITY

TRANSPORTATION PROGRAM

FIGURE 14-1 Federal railroad system

Table 14-1   LINK AND NODE ATTRIBUTES OF RAILROAD NETWORK

Link Attributes	Node Attributes
A-node	x,y coordinates
B-node	Name, state, county
Distance in tenths of mile	SPLC (Standard Point Location Code)
"503" Line Code	FSAC (Freight Station Accounting Code)
Owning railroad	Rule 260 junction abbreviation (where applicable)
Trackage-rights railroads	TOFC ramp indicator (where applicable)
Average population density	Yard indicator and characteristics (where applicable)
Speed class (proprietary)	
Signal system (only "A" mainlines)	
Grade (only "A" mainlines)	
Curvature (only "A" mainlines)	
Number of tracks (only "A" mainlines)	

junction codes, (2) include "net 3" numbers that facilitate the use of the data in conjunction with the network data base, (3) estimate mileage for each railroad segment of the route, and (4) find the impedance of each route segment equal to the sum of the impedance over each link comprising the route (the impedance of a link is equal to its distance times its 503 mainline/branchline code). The impedance, distance, and number of interline junctions provide surrogate measures for the quality of the waybill's route.

FRA ACCIDENT/INCIDENT FILE

Under its mandate to regulate safety on the U. S. railroad system, the FRA requires each railroad to submit monthly reports of all accidents involving casualties and equipment or property damage. These data are placed on computer tape and used to produce annual tabulations and summaries (U.S. DOT, 1976). The Office of Standards and Procedures of the FRA Associate Administrator for Safety initiated a program to prepare more detailed analyses of these accident reports. One of the highest priorities was identification of areas having a higher incidence of accidents and especially accidents involving hazardous materials. To obtain a quick impression of the geographical distribution of accidents, the Reports and Analysis Division of the Office of Standards and Procedures turned to the use of interactive computer graphics to prepare maps of geo-coded rail accidents. Each accident record for 1975, 1976, and 1977 has been encoded with the net 3 node number in the vicinity of the accident (Lutin, 1978). This encoding has enabled the appending of the accident data to the coordinate attributes of each node, thus permitting cartographic displays of accidents in conjunction with political boundaries, railroad networks, and link traffic volumes.

Figure 14-2 is an example of a series of such maps produced for the Transportation System Center of DOT. Accidents at nodes are indicated by open

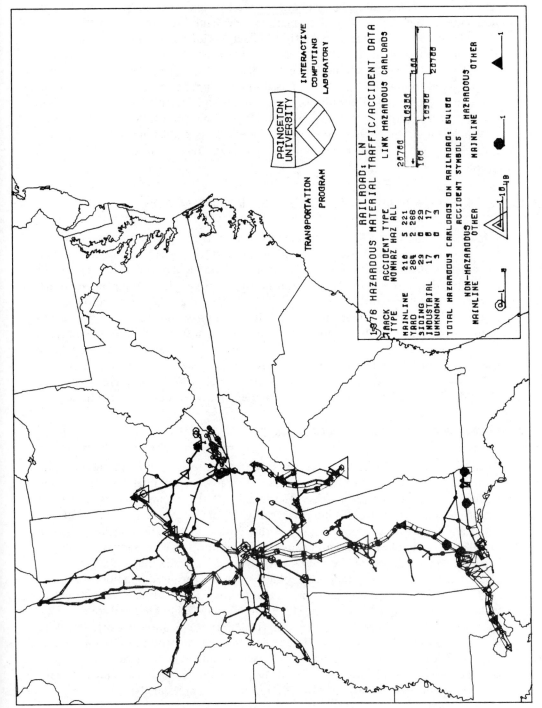

FIGURE 14-2 Accident occurrence and flow of hazardous materials

polygons of two types: octagons for mainline accidents, triangles for yard, siding, and industrial accidents. The symbols are proportional in area to the number of accidents at the node. Hazardous-material accidents are shown similarly, using shaded symbols to distinguish them from regular accidents. The maps also show the flow of hazardous materials, assigned to network links using the algorithm described in the next section. These are displayed as rectangles whose width is proportional to the number of carloads. Flow by direction is indicated, in that, as one looks along a link, the width of the rectangle to the right shows the volume in the forward direction. Plots were made in four colors on a CalComp 936 plotter, in which state boundaries were shown in blue, network links and accident sites in black, hazardous-material accident sites in red, and flows of hazardous materials in green.

MODELS OF SHIPPER AND RAILROAD ROUTING BEHAVIOR

For efficient analysis of historical and forecasted traffic patterns, once we are armed with railroad network characteristics and historic traffic patterns, we need a method for assignment of traffic to links. The historical traffic data provide locations of where traffic got on and off each railroad but no specific routing instructions. Forecasts of future traffic usually specify only the origin and destination of the traffic and no routing information, and it is left to us to forecast the railroads and routes used. Two models developed at Princeton reconstruct the specific link-node sequence between any two points on the U.S. railroad system. These models, the intracarrier route model (Strong, 1978; Kornhauser, 1979; Kornhauser and Still, 1978) and the quanta-net intercarrier route model (Kornhauser, Hornung, and Caudill, 1979), are based on observed shipper and railroad routing behavior.

INTRACARRIER ROUTE-GENERATION MODEL

According to ICC rules the shipper specifies the origin, originating railroad, destination, destination railroad, overhead railroads, and all interrailroad junction points; the railroad, however, selects the actual path the shipment will take between its on-railroad/off-railroad (shipper-specified) points. While each railroad has elaborate blocking and scheduling plans, the result is that traffic tends to flow over mainlines. A simple minimum-impedance algorithm has been shown to provide accurate reconstruction of the routes actually used. A validation of the algorithm-generated route utilizing computer graphic displays is nearing completion.

An example of the minimum-impedance trees that railroads were asked to validate is presented in Figure 14-3. These trees displayed the computed route from a specified node to all other nodes of a particular railroad. Railroad officials were thus able to easily validate the accuracy of the routing algorithm, using only visual inspection of the routes generated and their intimate knowledge of their own railroad operation. Through the use of graphics, non-computer-oriented persons were able to understand and validate the output of a complex analytical process.

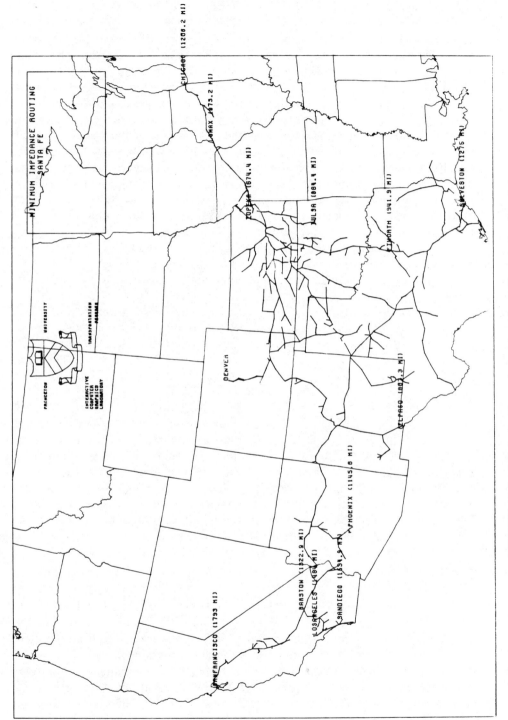

FIGURE 14-3 Minimum-impedance tree from Denver to all points on the Santa Fe Railroad

Optimum intercarrier routes can be generated from a specified origin location on an origin railroad to a specified destination on a destination railroad. This is accomplished through the application of our standard minimum pathfinding algorithm on a modified railroad network. In this modified network each node and link is unique to a specified railroad. Physical nodes where traffic can be interchanged between two railroads are thus transformed into two separate nodes, and a junction link is created to interconnect these points. This renumbered network is termed the Quanta-Network. By assigning very high impedances comparable to, say, 300 A-mainline miles, the optimum routes generated tend to involve the fewest interchanges between railroads. This conforms to historical shipper route-selection behavior. Conceptually, this renumbering of the U.S. railroad system places each railroad on a separate plane or quanta-level, with junction links allowing traffic to flow from one level to another, as depicted in Figure 14-4. In this figure the networks of the Missouri Pacific and Southern Pacific Railroads have been drawn in perspective with the interchange points identified by the vertical links.

Figure 14-5 depicts an actual optimum route generated by the minimum-impedance pathfinding algorithm applied to the Quanta-Network for an Atlanta origination on the Southern Railway System to a Denver destination on the DRGW. The optimum route is shown (in red on the original) to be on Southern to Memphis, where the traffic is interchanged to the MoPac, which takes the shipment to Fort Collins, where it is interchanged to the DRGW for delivery to Denver. The route conforms to one used historically. The graphic display of the route has been essential to the validation and acceptance of this intercarrier route-generation model. This model can generate the route between any two points in the U.S. railway system that minimizes any objective that can be represented as a summation of available link attributes. This includes minimum distance routes; mainline/branchline weighted shortest route; minimum population exposure; minimum accident exposure and minimum risk (valuable for finding alternate routes for hazardous materials); minimum positive grade; and minimum time (if speed-limit data are made available). For the same O-D pair each of these various optimum roles can be generated, and comparison is accomplished best through the simultaneous graphic display of each of the generated routes.

TRAFFIC ASSIGNMENT

The traffic-assignment algorithm uses the minimum-impedance algorithm to route each record of the traffic data base and accumulate traffic-volume statistics on each link of each computed route (the algorithm itself sequences through the traffic data in such a way as to minimize the number of times that a minimum-path tree must be generated). By segmenting the traffic data in certain ways, one can generate various traffic-volume statistics—for example, total carloads, total tons, total carloads of grain, total carloads of hazardous materials (as shown in Figure 14-2), or total TOFC traffic, as shown in Figure 14-6. This figure was generated by assembling the

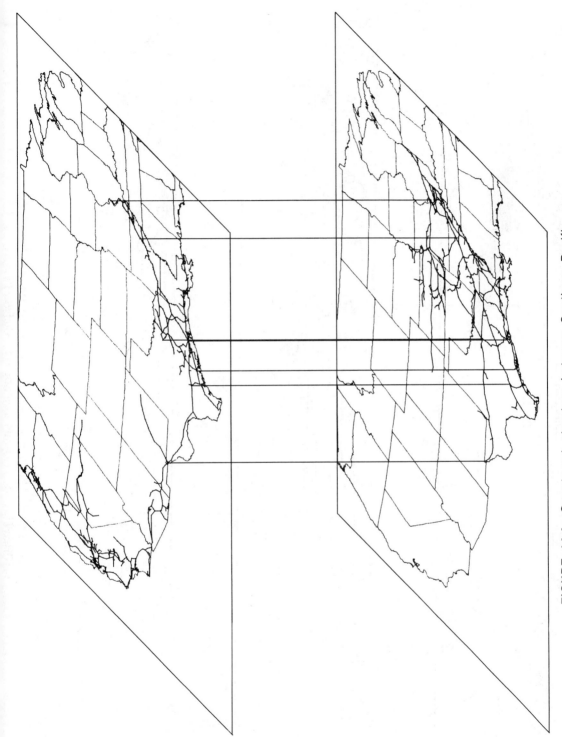

FIGURE 14-4 Quanta-net structure between Southern Pacific (top) and Missouri Pacific (MoPac) (bottom)

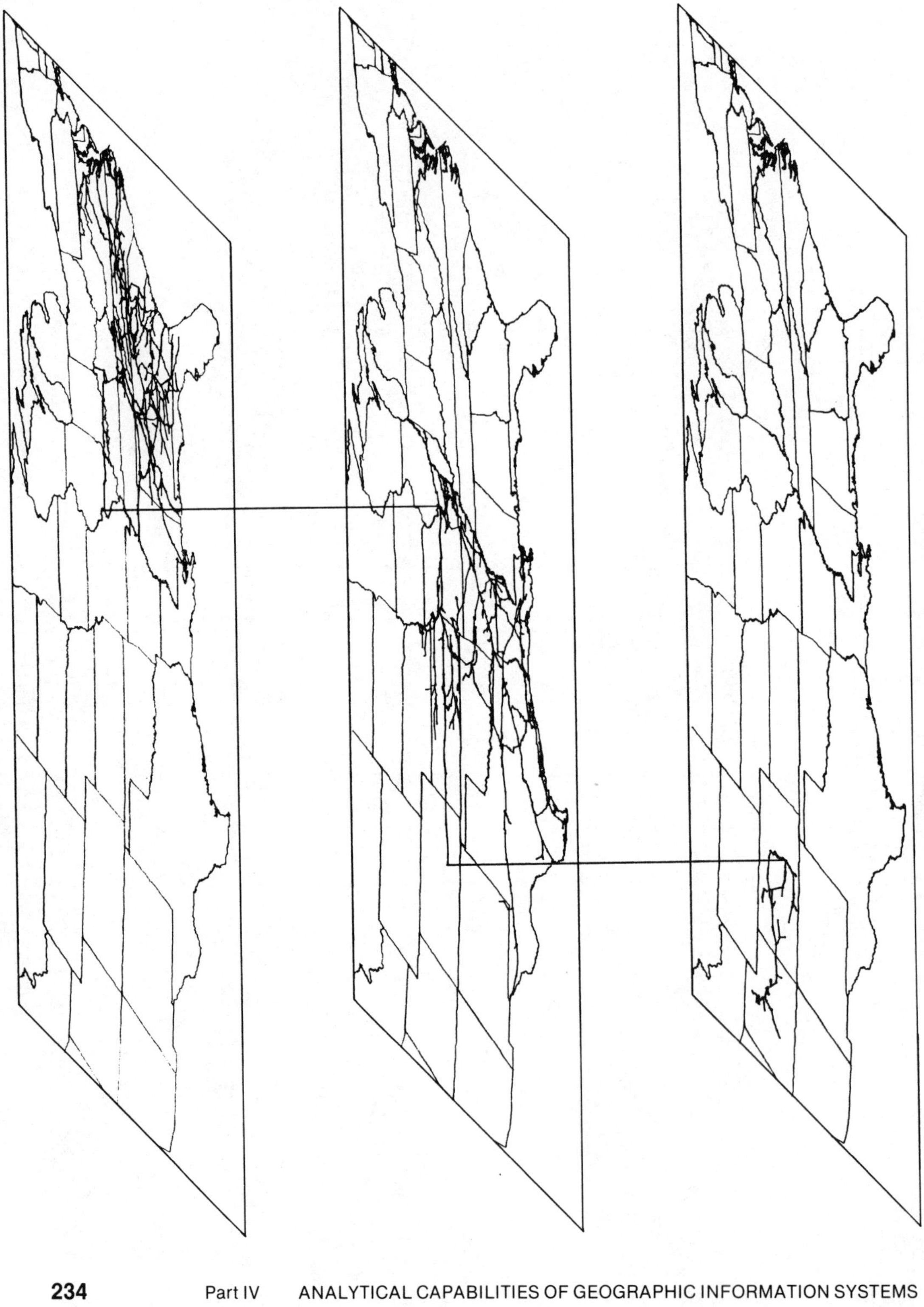

FIGURE 14-5 Minimum-impedance quanta-net route from Denver on DRGW (bottom) to Atlanta on Southern Railway (top)

FIGURE 14-6 1976 estimated carload volumes—TOFC

1976 TOFC traffic volumes assigned to each link of each railroad. Only those links that handle at least an average 30 carloads of TOFC traffic a day were displayed. The matching of the network data, traffic data, routing model, and computer graphics combine to provide direct information on the relative volume of TOFC traffic across the nation as well as the relative directionality of that traffic flow. Such a view of TOFC traffic or, for that matter, any other traffic has not previously been available.

PARTICIPATORY VALUE

More ingenious segmentations of railroad traffic, their assignment to the network, and their display leads to powerful tools for objective network synthesis and analysis. At present several U.S. railroads are bankrupt or supported by federal subsidies. It has been suggested that various pieces of these railroads should be either "sold" to or operated by solvent railroads. A central question is which pieces fit best with which railroad. One objective way to suggest such a dismemberment (controlled transfer or directed service) to a target railroad is to determine the affinity between various neighboring railroads and each link of the target. This may be done through the concepts of participatory value and opportunity costs (Hornung and Kornhauser, 1979).

Participatory value is simply the revenue on the target railroad of the traffic interlined with an acquirer. It can be accumulated for each link, by direction, of the target railroad for each potential acquirer by simply assigning the target's revenue share over the target's portion of the route for all traffic interlined with each acquirer. The accumulation and display of such statistics for each railroad provides direction as to which pieces of the target railroad are most directly valuable to which potential acquiring railroad. For each link of the target railroad the participatory value of each acquiring railroad is known. These can then be ranked and displayed on the target railroad, as in Figure 14-7. In this figure the width of the boxes is proportional to the Southern Pacific's participatory value on each link of the Rock Island by direction. The combination of band widths and colors provides ready information on the relative value of various segments of the Rock Island to the SP, as well as the value of those segments of SP relative to all other railroads. Generation of similar maps for each other potential acquirer yields ready quantitative information on which to base various dismemberment scenarios.

OPPORTUNITY COST

While participatory value is a measure of which pieces of the target railroad are valuable to an acquiring railroad, *opportunity cost* is a means of measuring the extent to which various segments of the acquiring railroad are dependent on the cooperation of the target railroad. This measure is obtained by assigning the acquirer portion of the revenue from acquirer-target interline traffic on the acquiring railroad. The accumulation of these data yields the relative dependence on each link of the acquiring railroad upon traffic interlined with the target.

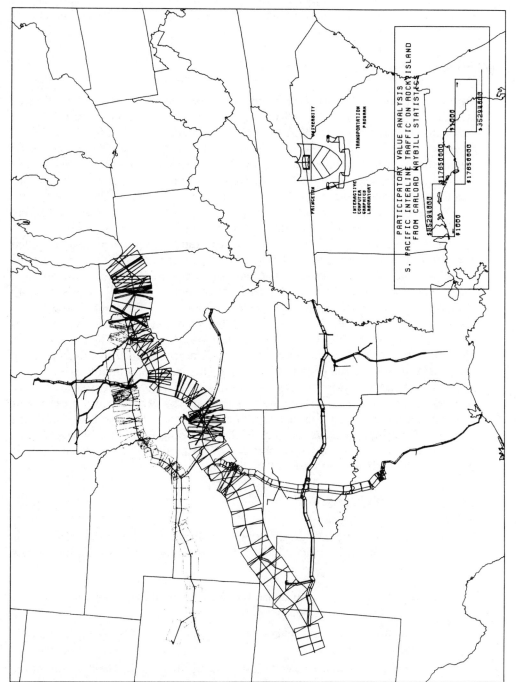

Inside the figure:

PRINCETON

UNIVERSITY

INTERACTIVE
COMPUTER
GRAPHICS
LABORATORY

TRANSPORTATION
PROGRAM

PARTICIPATORY VALUE ANALYSIS
S. PACIFIC INTERLINE TRAFFIC ON ROCK ISLAND
FROM CARLOAD WAYBILL STATISTICS

$85294000 $17650000 $1000   .3529400

$85294000 $1000 $17650000

FIGURE 14-7 Participatory-value analysis—Southern Pacific
interline traffic on Rock Island

Figure 14-8 is a computer drawn map of the "opportunity costs," in terms of revenue, to the SP of Rock Island interchanged traffic. The map explicitly depicts the relative dependence of various segments of the SP upon Rock Island interchange traffic.

ELEMENTARY TRAFFIC DIVERSION

Based on historical traffic records, market classifications, and specification of railroads to be merged, the elemetary traffic-diversion model estimates the redistribution of railroad traffic among the reconfigured railroad [6]. By assigning "before" and "after" merger traffic flows, the differential impact on traffic distribution can be estimated and displayed using computer graphics. The displays are vital to the presentation of the relative impact of the merger over the various segments of each railroad as well as between railroads. These traffic increases/decreases indicate where new capital programs may be needed and where traffic protective conditions should be issued.

The elementary traffic-diversion model is valid only for simple and limited network restructures, such as the Chessie-Family Lines merger. This is because the model assumes that all future traffic patterns are a redistribution over existing traffic patterns and newly formed single-carrier routes. For the analysis of more widespread restructurings, such as controlled transfer of the Rock Island or the simultaneous impact of the BN-Frisco, Sou-N&W, and Chessie-Family Lines mergers, shippers will be faced with entirely new routing options. These new options can be forecasted by the quanta-net route-choice model that forms the crux of the advanced traffic-diversion model (Kornhauser, Hornung, and Caudill, 1979).

In both traffic-diversion models, the traffic-diversion coefficients are user selected. Thus, the models can be used to simulate the two advocacy positions of merging and the impacted railroads as well as the various shades in between, which could be of interest to the regulator, the ICC. The various positions can be analyzed, and graphics can form an essential part of explicit presentations of the differences obtained from each point of view.

ADVANTAGES OF GRAPHICS

Examples have been given of the use of graphic displays of the various elements of the Princeton Railroad Network Model. The graphics add elegance to the analysis by:

1. Giving the analyst confidence that he has conducted the vast amount of "number-crunching" properly

2. Allowing the decision maker to learn the essential results of the analysis almost instanteously

3. Adding enjoyment to the work of both the analyst and the decision maker so that (a) they will tend to interact and discuss the results more

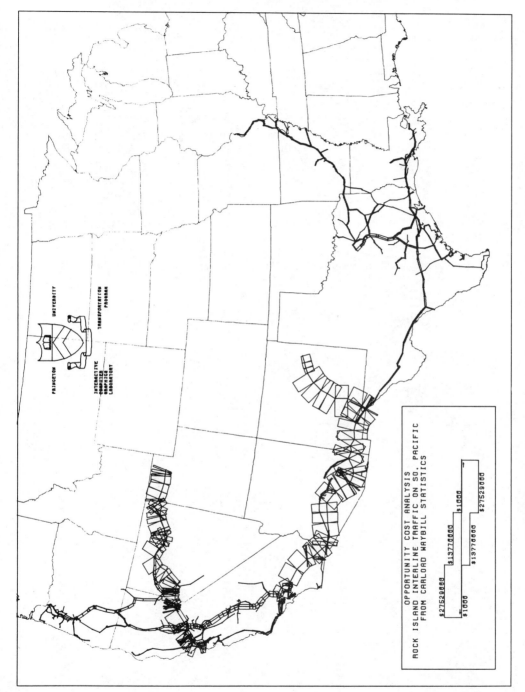

FIGURE 14-8 Opportunity-cost analysis—Rock Island interline traffic on Southern Pacific.

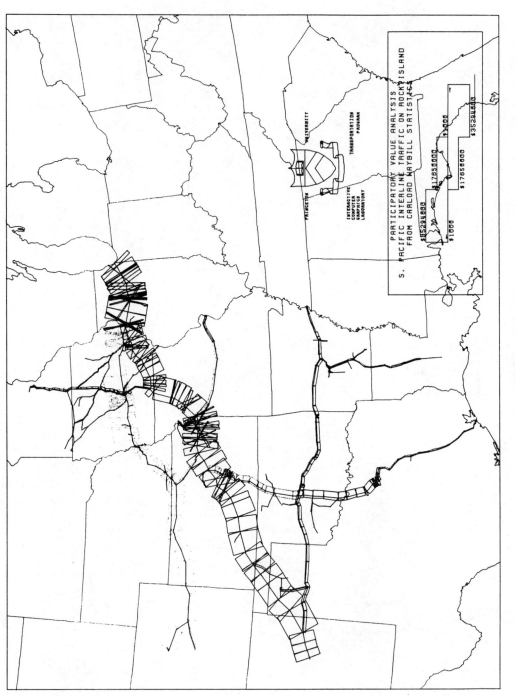

PARTICIPATORY VALUE ANALYSIS
S. PACIFIC INTERLINE TRAFFIC ON ROCK ISLAND
FROM CARLOAD WAYBILL STATISTICS

$35294800

$17650000

$1000

INTERACTIVE
COMPUTER
GRAPHICS
LABORATORY

TRANSPORTATION
PROGRAM

PRINCETON
UNIVERSITY

FIGURE 14-9

thoroughly, and (b) much of the drudgery of analysis will be removed and the productivity of the analyst greatly enhanced. The graphics simply make analysis much more fun.

REFERENCES

FEDERAL SYSTEMS DIVISION, IBM, "Federal Railroad Administration Network Model User's Manual." Gaithersburg, Md.: International Business Machines Corporation, May 1975.

HORNUNG, M., and A.L. KORNHAUSER, "An Analytic Model for Railroad Network Restructuring," Transportation Program Research Report 79-TR-11, Princeton University, June 1979.

KORNHAUSER, A.L., "Elementary Theory of Traffic Diversions: A Tool for Analysis of Reconstructed Railroad Networks," Presented at 1979 Transportation Research Board Conference, Washington, D.C., January 1979. *Transportation Research Record,* no. 721, 1979.

_____, and S.E. STILL, "Analysis of the Flow of Freight Traffic on the U.S. Railroad System for the Year 1974." Washington, D.C.: Rail Services Planning Office, Interstate Commerce Commission, June 1978.

_____, M. HORNUNG and R. CAUDILL "Theory for Estimating Traffic Diversions on a Vastly Restructured U.S. Railroad System," *Transportation Research Record*, no. 758, 1980.

LUTIN, JEROME M., "Railroad Accident Network Data for 1976," final report, Federal Railroad Administration, Gellman Research Associates, Inc., Jenkintown, Pa., 1978.

STRONG, S., "Network Models for Planning Rail System Structure and Operations," Ph.D. Dissertation, Transportation Program, Princeton University, 1978.

U.S. DEPARTMENT OF TRANSPORTATION, "Final Standards, Classification and Designation of Lines of Class I Railroads in the United States," Vol. II, a report by the Secretary of Transportation, June 30, 1977.

U.S. DEPARTMENT OF TRANSPORTATION, "FRA Guide for Preparing Accident/Incident Reports," Washington, D.C.: Federal Railroad Administration, U. S. Department of Transportation, 1976.

Index

A

Address-matching software, 56-57
ADMATCH (or Address Matching System), 56-57
Aerial photography, 176-77
Air pollution, problem of, 4
Air pollution health-risk model, 3-13
    carbon monoxide exposure, effects on
        stable angina pectoris patients in, 7-11
    methodology for, 4-7
American Society of Planning Officials, 30, 31
American Telephone & Telegraph Company (AT&T), Equal Employment Opportunity Commission action against, 93-95

Anderson, E., 8
Anderson, J. R., 40
Angina pectoris patients, carbon monoxide exposure effects on, 7-11
APL language, 37-38
Argos system, 18
Aronow, W. S., 8
Asher, H. B., 154
Automatic vehicle detector (AVM) systems, 206, 220

B

Bailey, R. G., 114
Bandwidth maps, 207-8

Barr, A. J., 106
Base file, geographic, 56
Bashshur, R., 53
Bates, Richard, 155
Bell, R. R., 53
Benkovitz, C. M., 107, 108
Betz, Fred, 181
Biomedical Computer Programs (BMD),
165
Bishop, Y. M. M., 165
Bivariate maps, in Domestic Information
Display System (DIDS), 162-64
Blake, George, 90
Blankenship, Vaughn, 181
Boundaries, methods of defining, 57-58
Boyle, Ray, 46
Bozeman, Barry, 180
Burgess, R. L., 104

C

Calkins, H. W., 32, 33, 49, 53
Carbon monoxide exposure effects, in air
pollution health-risk model, 7-11
Carroll, James D., 180
Caudill, R., 230, 238
Census, U.S. Bureau of the, 163
address-matching software developed by,
56
data of, 58
Character-printed maps, 57
Charleston County Planning Office, 37, 38
Chart books, for program managers, 96
Charts, choice of, 96-97
Chrisman, N. R., 53
Cleveland, Ohio, 53
CLIDE (County-Level Integrated Database
for Epidemiology), 103, 156
Coal, air pollution impact of expanded use
of, 108-12
Coastal mapping program in South
Carolina. See South Carolina, geo-
graphical information system in
COLORMAP computer software, 134
Color maps, 134
Computer graphics:
growth of, 88-91
in policymaking, 87-101
statistical association and, 155-57

Computer mapping. See Maps
Congestion display system (CDS), 207-20
bandwidth maps and, 207-8
commands in, 211-14
control-language processor of, 209
cost of displays in, 214-15
design of, 208-9
display criteria for, 207
display-processor program of, 210-11
examples of displays from, 214-18
links in, 212-14
matrix-manipulation program of, 209-10
nonnetwork data points in, 212-13
Congestion patterns, mapping, 202-21
congestion display system for. See
Congestion display system (CDS)
definitions of congestion, 204
description of the problem, 202-5
display techniques, 206-7
future of, 219-21
sources of data relevant to, 205-6
Cookie-cutter software, in water quality
management program, 20
Coordinate system grid, 56
Council on Environmental Quality, Air
Pollution Health-Risk Model of. See
Air pollution health-risk model
County-Level Integrated Database for
Epidemiology (CLIDE), 103, 156
Crocker, T. D., 154
Cross-diagrams, 164
CRT copy maps, 57, 59, 63

D

Damage function, 5
Dames, 187-89
Dangermond, Jack, 124
Data-base:
of Geoecology Data Base, 104-6
of Regional Environmental Assessment
Program (REAP), 71-73
Data-base management system (DBMS), of
Regional Environmental Assessment
Program, 72
Data exchange standards, 108
Davis, R. M., 109
Decision making. See Regional Environ-
mental Assessment Program

Deer habitat utilization, cartographic
analysis, 141-50
  computer graphics, 145-46
  methodology and results, 142-45
Derating, power-plant, 194
Diamond defaults, 165
Digitizing equipment, 177-78
DIME (Dual-Independent-Map-Encoding), 56
Direct stereo digitization, 177-78
Dispatching system, computer-aided
(CADS), 206
Dixon, W. J., 165
Domestic Information Display System
(DIDS), 154-67
  bivariate maps in, 162-64
  compositing feature of, 156
  cross and diamond defaults in, 164-65
  zoom capability of, 162
Drug Abuse Prevention, Special Action
Office for, 92
Dual-Independent-Map-Encoding (DIME),
56
Dueker, Kenneth, 32, 33, 35
Dwyer, J. L., 21

E

Ecoregions, 114
Eddy, E., 53
Electrostatic plotter maps, 134
Energy, Department of (DOE), 113-16
Environmental pollution. See Pollution,
health effects of
Environmental Protection Agency, U.S., 4,
155-57
Environmental Sciences Division (ESD) of
Oak Ridge National Laboratory,
108-9
Environmental sensitivity, siting of coal-
fired power plants and, 190-92
Environmental Systems Research Institute
(ESRI), 40, 44
  new town selection by. See New towns,
  selection of sites for
Equal Employment Opportunity Com-
mission (EEOC) action against AT&T,
93-95
ESRI (Environmental Systems Research
Institute), 40, 44
EZMAP program, 107

F

Factor-analytic approach to health effects
of pollutants, 154-55
Features. See Geographic features,
methods of defining
Federal Communications Commission
(FCC): Equal Employment Opportunity
Commission action against AT&T and,
93-95
Federal Railroad Administration (FRA), 226, 228
Ferrari, R. L., 5
Fienberg, S. E., 163
Fleiss, J. L., 165
Freeway congestion patterns. See
Congestion patterns, mapping

G

GAP language, Regional Environmental
Assessment Program and, 78
Gardenier, T. K., 156, 167
GBF DIME file, 178, 183
GBIS (Geographically Based Information
System), new town site selection and,
132-33
Geoecology Data Base, 103-16
  applications of, 108-16
    air pollution, impacts, 108-12
    natural vegetation and land use, 112-13
    wilderness-area evaluation, 113-15
  computer system of, 106-7
  data-base design and contents, 104-6
  data resources of, 107-8
  data sets of, 105
Geographical Information Retrieval and
Analysis System (GIRAS), 38, 40, 44
Geographical information systems (GIS):
  demand for, 30-31
  ideal model of, 32-34
  of New York City, 53, 56
  of South Carolina, 31-44
    Coastal Zone Management Act, 31-32
    computer graphics and automated geo-
    graphical data handling, 37-38
    design stage, 33-34
    examples of outputs from, 38-44
    first stage of development, 34-35
    ideal model, 32-34
    second stage of development, 34-37
    state-level approaches to, 44-50

Geographic base file, 56
Geographic features, methods of defining, 57-58
Geological Survey, U.S. (U.S.G.S.): South Carolina coastal mapping program and, 38, 40
George, J., 204
GIMS (Geographical Information Management System), 187-201
GIRAS (Geographical Information Retrieval and Analysis System), 38, 40, 44
Goff, F. G., 103
Gordon, Gerald, 180-81
Graphic tablet, in Tennessee Tech Mapping System, 60
Grid-cell format, data conversion to, 124
GRIDS system, 40
GRIPS (Grid Information from Polygon System), 124
Guinn, C., 46

H

Haak, E., 10
Hall, D., 204
Harris, R. H., 154
Haywood, 172
Health effect:
   definition of, 154
   of pollution, 154-55. *See also* Domestic Information Display System
Hearle, E., 54
Highway networks, congestion in. *See* Congestion patterns, mapping
Histogram support charts, 63
Hornung, M., 230, 236, 238
Hughes, A., 206
Hughes (senator), 92
Hydrologic Engineering Center, 124

I

IGU Commission on Geographical Data Sensing and Processing, 48
Integrated Terrain Unit Mapping (ITUM) approach, 124
Interlaboratory Working Group for Data Exchange (IWGDE), 107, 108, 116

J

Johnson, A. W., 68
Jones, D. K., 16
Jones, K. H., 5, 8, 11
Jovanis, Paul, 205

K

Keefer, L. A., 204
Kennedy, M., 34, 46, 53
Kern, L. H., 104
Keyword searches, in Regional Environmental Assessment Program, 73
Kim, J., 155
Kimball, John, 175
Klopatek, J. M., 112-14
Kongsberg 5000 Flatbed Plotter, 38
Kornhauser, A. L., 230, 236, 238
Krebs, M. J., 218
Kubel, Leslie, 205
Kuper, 172

L

Labrum, Willard D., 205
Lake, E., 154
Lambright, W. Henry, 179
Landau, E., 154
Land-data systems, 173-74
Landsat data, for Water Quality Management Program, 17-25
Land use, Geoecology Data Base and, 112-13
Lave, L. B., 154, 156
Legal Services Corporation (LSC), 96-97
Letendre, G., 207
Lindblom, Charles E., 35
Line-drawn maps, 57
Link-node network of the U.S. railroad system, 226
Local government, computer graphics in, 171-84
   future of, 183-84
   mapping and land-data systems, 173-74
   policy and organization issues, 179-83
   productivity and, 174-76
   technological issues, 176-77
Lutin, Jerome M., 228

M

McDonald, G. C., 154
Majone, Giandomenico, 181
Maps (mapping):
  application of, 64-65
  bandwidth, 207-8
  centralized state system of, 27
  character-printed, 57
  color, 134
  decision steps in, 53-54
  electrostatic plotter, 134
  line-drawn, 57
  multicolor, 63
  outline, 57
  overlay, 63
  plotter, 63
  policy analysis. *See* Policy making,
    computer mapping and
Marble, D. F., 33, 53
Mason, R., 54, 180, 181
May, Adolf, 205
Metropolitan Washington Council of
  Governments (MWCOG), 208
Metzner, C., 53
Meyer, M. A., 163
Meyers, C. R., 34, 53
Michigan Department of Transportation,
  206
Mills, R. F., 18
Minnesota Land Management Information
  System, 48
Mitre Corporation, 155, 157
Mitroff, Ian I., 180, 181
Moore, 187-89
Morbidity rates, pollution and, 154. *See
  also* Domestic Information Display
  System
Morris, S. C., 107
Muehrcke, P., 206
Mueller, C. W., 155
Multicolor mapping, 63

N

National Ambient Air Quality Standards
  (NAAQS), 4, 5
National Conference of State Legislatures,
  48

Natural vegetation, Geoecology Data Base
  and, 112-13
New Jersey. *See* Water Quality Management
  Program
New towns, selection of sites for, 119-39
  automation of maps and data, 124
  computer modeling, 125
  data collection, image acquisition, and
    base-map creation, 122, 124
  data integration and mapping, 124
  detailed site analyses, 127
  examples of graphics produced, 134-35
  further analysis of candidate areas for
    new towns, 126-27
  general outline of the process of regional
    analysis for, 122
  grid-cell format, conversion of data to,
    124
  image interpretation, 124
  resources required, 127, 132
  role of computer graphics in solving the
    problem, 132-33
  selection the region studied, 121-22
New York City, geographic information
  system of, 53, 56
Nordstrand, E., 48
North Dakota, 66-67. *See also* Regional
  Environmental Assessment Program
Novak, K. M., 107

O

Oak Ridge National Laboratory (ORNL),
  107
  Environmental Sciences Division (ESD) of,
    108-9
  Geoecology Data Base developed at. *See*
    Geoecology Data Base
O'Conner, J. F., 206
Olson, R. J., 103, 106
Orthophotography, 177
Outline maps, 57
Overlay mapping, 63

P

Parcel data systems, 173
Peck, L. J., 107
Pen plotters, 57

Peucker, T. K., 53
Philadelphia, 171-76
PIC (Polygon-Intersection-Chain) system, 124
Pignataro, L. J., 204
PIOS system, 44
Plotter maps, 63, 134
Plotters, 57
Policy making (policy analysis):
   character-printed maps and line-drawn
      maps, 57
   combining features and data, 57-58
   computer graphics in, 87-101
     action plan for a computer graphics
       project, 97, 100-101
     chart books for program managers, 96
     choosing the right charts, 96-97
     Equal Employment Opportunity
       Commission action against AT&T, 93-95
     principal role of graphics, 95-96
     Special Action Office for Drug Abuse
       Prevention, 92
   computer mapping and, 52-65
     address-matching software, 56-57
   data files, 54, 56
   decision steps in, 53-54
   selecting and specifying the data, 58
   Tennessee Tech Mapping System, 58-65
Pollution, health effects of, 154-55. *See also*
     Air pollution health-risk model;
     Domestic Information Display System
Polygon-Intersection-Chain (PIC) system,
   124
Power plants. *See* Site selection—for coal-
     fired power plants
President's Council on Environmental
     Quality, 156
Princeton Railroad Network Model, 225-41
   carload waybill statistics and, 226, 228
   elements of, 225
   FRA accident/incident file and, 228, 230
   intercarrier (Quanta-Network) route-
     generation model, 232
   intracarrier route-generation model, 230
   link-node network of the U.S. railroad
     system, 226
   opportunity cost and, 236, 238
   participatory value and, 236
   shipper and railroad routing behavior
     and, 230
   traffic-assignment algorithm and, 232,
     236

Prindle, R. A., 154
Printer maps, 135
Productivity, local government, 174-76
Program analysis. *See* Policy making
Programmers, dependence on, 90
Public Technology, Inc., 179

Q

Quad-R Act, 226
Quanta-Network, 232
Query language, in Regional Environmental
     Assessment Program

R

Railroad industry, 224-25. *See also*
     Princeton Railroad Network Model
Ramapriyan, H. K., 17
Regional Environmental Assessment
     Program, 67-83
   BROWSE, functions of, 73-76
   computer system of, 69-70
   data-base management system of, 72
   data base of, 71-73
   design of, 68
   example of analysis using, 79-81
   as a focal point for information, 70
   functional definition of, 70
   high-level command language (GAP) of,
     78
   MAP functions of, 77-78
   master monitor of, 79
   program definition of, 68
   QUERY in, 76-77
   as a set of tools, 79
   software of, 78-79
   Technical Task Forces (TTFs) of, 68-70
   titles in, 72-73
   top-down and bottom-up design of, 70-71
   User Specifications Teams (RUSTEAMS)
     of, 68-70
Regional Mapping and Land Records
     System (RMLR), 172
Remak, R., 203
Riepl, R. J., 208
Roadless Area and Evaluation Program,
     U.S. Forest Service (RARE-II),
     112-13

Robinette, A., 48
Robinson, A. H., 206
Rothrock, C. A., 204

S

Sale, R. D., 206
Sauer, H. I., 155
Savas, E. S., 53
Scale, for aerial photography, 177
Schmid, C. F., 155
Schneider, Jerry B., 205
Schwing, R. C., 154
Seskin, E. P., 154
Shading densities, in Tennessee Tech
    Mapping System, 60, 63
Shannon, G., 53
Shostack, K., 53
Shriner, C. R., 107
Site selection:
    for coal-fired power plants, 187-201
        background, 188
        composite operations, 199
        cost of construction and operation, 192
        criteria for site selection, 190-94
        data-structure diagram, 194-96
        derating, 194
        environmental sensitivity, 190-94
        methodology and technique, 189-90
        site-selection analysis, 194-99
        spatial analysis, 196-99
    for new towns. See New towns, selection
        of sites for
Smith, D. M., 53, 167
Socioeconomic variables, health effects of
    pollution and, 154
South Carolina, geographical information
    system in, 31-44
    Coastal Zone Management Act, 31-32
    computer graphics and automated
        geographical data handling, 37-38
    design stage, 33-34
    examples of outputs from the
        geographical system, 38-44
    first stage of development, 34-35
    ideal model, 32-34
    second stage of development, 34-37
South Carolina, State Mapping Advisory
    Committee of, 49-50
South Carolina, University of, 37

South Carolina Coastal Zone Management
    Act (1977), 31-32
South Carolina Coastal Zone Planning and
    Management Council, 31-32, 37
Spatial analysis, in siting study for coal-
    fired power plants, 196-99
Standard Metropolitan Statistical Areas
    (SMSAs), 6
Statistical Analysis System (SAS), 106-7
Statistical association, role of graphics in,
    155-57
Still, S. E., 230
Strand, R. H., 106
Strong, S., 230
Sulfur dioxide, impact of increased levels of,
    109
SYMAP, 7, 107

T

Talcott, R., 35
Tax maps (plats), 174-75, 178
Teich, Albert H., 179
Tennessee Tech Mapping System, 58-65
    data selection in, 63
    hardware and peripherals used in, 61
    implications of, 64-65
    mapping options offered by, 61-63
    method of, 59-60
    problems encountered by, 64
    shading densities in, 60, 63
    software routines of, 60
Titles, in Regional Environmental
    Assessment Program, 72-73
Tomlin, C. Dana, 146
Tomlinson, R. F., 32, 48, 49, 53
Traffic-assignment algorithm, 232, 236
Transportation Systems Management (TSM)
    programs, 202-3
Tsai, J., 206
Tukey, J. W., 163

U

UPGRADE (User-Prompted Graphic Data
    Evaluation) System, 103, 156, 157, 162
Upper Cumberland Development Region.
    See Tennessee Tech Mapping System

Urban highway network. *See* Congestion
   patterns, mapping
Urban Transportation Planning Package,
   Census Bureau's, 7

V

Variable relationships, future uses of maps
   to depict, 165, 167
Vegetation, Geoecological Data Base and,
   112-13
VSPC system, 38

W

Wainer, H., 163
Wallace, J. B., 53
Wallace, L., 156
Water Quality Management Program, 15-28
   applications and examples of, 20-23

methodology of, 17-18
policy issue and institutional setting of,
   16
software for, 18-20
Wilderness areas, Geoecological Data Base
   and evaluation of, 113-15
Window (zoom) mapping, 63
Wingo, R., 204
Wolf, D. J., 218

Y

Yale School of Forestry and Environmental
   Studies. *See* Deer habitat utilization,
   cartographic analysis

Z

Zeidenberg, L. D., 154